BLUEJAY

Teach Yourself

HINDI

Kavita Kumar (born in 1936) obtained her Master's degree in Economics from University of Delhi in 1960. From 1960 to 1965, she taught at the Directorate of Correspondence Courses, in the same University, Lady Irwin College, Delhi, Janki Devi College, Delhi and Government Girls College, Gorakhpur. During 1980-81, she taught English to students and other learners in Nara (Japan). Since the 1980s, she has been giving freelance lessons in English and Hindi to learners from several countries, and lessons in German to Indian nationals. She has kept herself engaged in writing several bilingual books in English, Hindi, German and Spanish.

The author has developed her own Individual-based teaching approach. The teaching strategies are adapted and learning materials prepared to meet the specific needs and learning abilities of individuals. Efficient language skills are imparted in an informal, easy manner to help maximize interest and speed during the learning process, making language learning a pleasure, not a burden.

Other books by the author

Hindi-English

- Hindi For Non Hindi Speaking People , Grammar
- Hindi For Non Hindi Speaking People, WORK BOOK
- Speak Hindi from Day One
- English Hindi Phrasebook
- Mastering English from Day One

Hindi-German

- Namaste -Einfeuhrung in die Grammatik und den praktischen Gebrauch de Hindi (main book)
- Namaste -Einfeuhrung in die Grammatik und den praktischen Gebrauch de Hindi (Work Book)
- Hindi - German Phrasebook

Hindi-Spanish

- Manual de hindi para hispanohablantes
- Gramática de hindi

Hindi

- Vyakaran-Ek navin Dristikon

English

- Mira -The Emancipated Soul

BLUEJAY

Teach Yourself

HINDI

A self-study and practice book for elementary students

Kavita Kumar

BLUEJAY

Bluejay Books Pvt. Ltd.
A-8/76, Ist Floor
Sector 16, Rohini
Delhi 110 085
info@bluejaybooksindia.com

Published by
Bluejay Books Pvt. Ltd.

First impression 2013
Second impression 2014

Printed and bound in India.

I wish to thank :

— all my students over the years for their sustained interest and efforts to learn Hindi. Their questions prompted me to think and dwell upon the genuine problems of learners of Hindi as foreign language and come up with explanations and sufficient practice material.

— friends for their sustained encouragement and support.

— ***Bluejay Books Pvt Ltd*** for trusting me to write *Bluejay Teach Yourself Hindi* for them.

For learners:

The elementary students are advised to do the first nine chapters covering all the basic tenses thoroughly and in the order in which they are given. With this back ground, the student can use the book selectively and flexibly by referring to the detailed table of contents and the index at the end to find the relevant chapter or pages that deal with the point he/she is interested in.

CONTENTS

Appendix 2: Vocabulary:

Boxes:

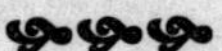

ABBREVIATIONS

adj.	adjective
adv.	adverb
comp. verb	compound verb
dir.	direct
E.	Example
Ex.	Exercise
f.	feminine
fml.	formal
fut.	future
G.	gender
imper.	imperative
indef.	indefinite
inf.	infinitive
infml.	informal
ipc	imperfective participial construction
m. /mas.	masculine
N.	number
obj.	object
obl.	oblique
pl.	plural
PN	proper noun
ppc.	perfective participial construction
ppn.	postposition
pres.	present
sg.	singular
subj.	subject
v.i.	verb intransitive
v.t.	verb transitive

G in transliteration stands for ग़ a borrowed sound Urdu.

1 Vowels (स्वर)

	Vowel	Symbol	Transliteration	Consonant + Vowel	Position	Pronunciation
1.	अ		a	क ka	inherent in C	shut, hut
2.	आ	ा	ā	का kā	follows C	bar, car
3.	इ	ि	i	कि ki	precedes C	hit ,sit
4.	ई	ी	ī	की kī	follows C	seat, meet
5.	उ	ु	u	कु ku	subscript	put, full
6.	ऊ	ू	ū	कू kū	subscript	fool, pool
7.	ऋ		ṛ	कृ kṛ	subscript	trip,grip
8.	ए	े	e	के ke	superscript	tape, hate
9.	ऐ	ै	ai	कै kai	superscript	tap, hat
10.	ओ	ो	o	को ko	follows C	coal, pole
11.	औ	ौ	au	कौ kau	follows C	caught hot

- The first vowel अ 'a' is inherent in all consonants for phonetic ease.

V= Vowel; S= Symbol; T= transliteration; C= consonant ;

- All other vowels have an alternative symbol representing the character.
- In writing, one vowel immediately following a consonant is affixed to it in symbol form. However if more than one vowel follow the consonant, the remaining vowel or vowels(if any) are written as characters.
- Hindi script has separate characters and their symbols for long and short vowels .
- The first vowel 'अ a' is inherent in all the consonants and has no symbol. When required to be used independent of consonant, the character 'अ' is used.
- The consonant without the inherent अ 'a', are written with a subscript stroke written left to right downwards e.g. क्

  The consonant क ka = क् k + अ a
- All Hindi vowels have their nasalized form. The symbol used is a crescent with a dot above it. Sometimes, to avoid crowding vowel symbols, only a dot is used.

  अं / अँ ṁ **कं /कँ kaṁ**
- 'Visarga transliterated as 'ḥ' occurs mostly in loan words from Sanskrit. It follows the consonant as two dots written one under the like (:).

  अः : ḥ कः kaḥ

- Devanāgrī script requires a horizontal bar on most letters of the alphabet. Always begin by making a horizontal bar; draw it just long enough for the letter that you plan to write. This is important, since some letters have an open top and do not require the horizontal bar.

Consonants

non-aspirate	aspirate	non-aspirate	aspirate	nasal
क	ख	ग	घ	ङ
ka	kha	ga	gha	ṅa (angaṁ)
च	छ	ज	झ	ञ
ca	cha	ja	jha	ña (añyām̐)
ट	ठ	ड	ढ	ण
ṭ	ṭha	ḍa	ḍha	ṇa
		ड़	ढ़	
		ṛa	ṛha	
त	थ	द	ध	न
ta	tha	da	dha	na
प	फ	ब	भ	म
pa	pha	ba	bha	ma
य	र	ल	व	semi vowels
ya	ra	la	va	
श	ष	स		sibilants
śa	ṣa	sa		
ह ha				glottal

क्ष kṣa (It is a combination of क् + ष) conjuncts

त्र tra (It is a combination of त् + र)

ज्ञ jña'/ gya (It is a combination of ज् + ञ . Sanskritarians pronounce it as 'jña' where as Hindi speakers pronounce it as 'gya')

Pronouns

Pronouns in the direct case

First Person:	maiṁ	मैं	(I)	ham	हम	(we)
Second Person:	tū	तू		tum	तुम	(you plural)
	(you sg,)			āp	आप	(you formal)
Third Person:	vah'	वह		yah	यह	'he', 'she', 'it'
	've'	वे		'ye'	ये	'they'

Simple postpositions

Postposition	English equivalent	Case
को (ko)	to	accusative (direct object) dative (indirect object)
से (se)	with, from, since, for	instrumental, ablative, time expressions
में (meṁ)	in	locative
पर (par)	on	locative
का, के, की (kā, ke, kī)	of	genitive(used in possessive case.)

Pronouns in the oblique case followed by any one of the above given postpositions को ko, से se, में meṁ, पर par.

direct			oblique + postposition			
maiṁ	मैं	⇨	mujh	मुझ	+	any pp_n **को ko, से se, में meṁ, पर par.**
ham	हम	⇨	ham	हम	+	any pp_n
tū	तू	⇨	tujh	तुझ	+	any pp_n
tum	तुम	⇨	tum	तुम	+	any pp_n
āp	आप	⇨	āp	आप	+	any pp_n
vah	वह	⇨	us	उस	+	any pp_n

pp_n = postposition; c = changes to

yah यह ⇨ is इस + any pp_n
ve वे ⇨ un उन + any pp_n
ve ये ⇨ in इन + any pp_n
kaun कौन ⇨ kis (sg.) किस + any pp_n
कौन ⇨ kin (pl.) किन + any pp_n

☞ **Oblique pronouns used as direct object or indirect object have two forms as shown below.**

mujhe / mujhko	मुझे / मुझको (to me)
hameṁ / hamko	हमें / हमको (to us)
tujhe / tujhko	तुझे / तुझको (to you intimate)
tumheṁ / tumko	तुम्हें / तुमको (to you informal)
āpko	आपको (to you formal)
use / usko	उसे / उसको (to him/her far)
ise / isko	इसे / इसको (to him/her near)
unheṁ / unko	उन्हें / उनको (to them far)
inheṁ / inko	इन्हें / इनको (to them near)
kise / kisko	किसे / किसको (to whom sg.)
kinheṁ / kinko	किन्हें / किनको (to whom pl.)
kisīko	किसीको to somebody (sg.)
kinhīṁko	किन्हींको to somebody (pl.)

- **Possessive pronouns (go to page 104)**

- **Relative pronouns:**

direct case jo जो (sg./ pl.) + any pp_n को ko, से se, में meṁ, पर par, का, के, की kā, ke, kī

oblique case jis जिस (sg.) + any pp_n को ko, से se, में meṁ, पर par, का, के, की kā, ke, kī

jin जिन (pl.) + any pp_n को ko, से se, में meṁ, पर par, का, के, की kā, ke, kī

Nouns

Masculine Nouns

- आ (ā)-ending masculine nouns :

case	masc. singular	masc. plural
direct case	आ ā	ए e
oblique case	ए e	ओं oṁ

Example:

direct case	kelā (banana)	केला	kele(bananas)	केले
oblique case	kele+pp_n	केले + pp_n	keloṁ + pp_n	केलों + pp_n

- **All other masculine nouns:**

case	masc. singular	masc.plural
direct case	–	–
oblique case	–	ओं oṁ or यों yoṁ

Examples: masculine nouns in direct and oblique case.

case	masc..singular		masc. plural	
direct case	ghar (house)	घर	ghar (houses)	घर
oblique case	ghar+ pp_n	घर + pp_n	ghar oṁ+pp_n	घरों + pp_n
direct case	mālī(gardener)	माली	mālī (gardener)	माली
oblique case	mālī+pp_n	माली + pp_n	māliyoṁ+pp_n	मालियों + pp_n
direct case	ālū (potato)	आलू	ālū (lemons)	आलू
oblique case	ālū + pp_n	आलू + pp_n	āluoṁ+ pp_n	आलुओं + pp_n
direct case	śiśu (baby)	शिशु	śiśu (babies)	शिशु
oblique case	śiśu + pp_n	शिशु+pp_n	śiśuoṁ+ pp_n	शिशुओं + pp_n

☞ **long ई ī and long ऊ ū are shortened before adding यों yoṁ or ओं oṁ in the oblique plural case .**

Feminine Nouns

case	fem.singular	fem. plural
direct case	**consonant, आ ā, उ u, ऊ ū-**	एँ **eṁ**
oblique case	–	ओं **oṁ**
direct case	इ i, ई ī	याँ **yāṁ**
oblique case	–	यों **yoṁ**

- **consonant ending fem. nouns:**

case	fem.singular		fem. plural	
direct case	aurat (woman)	औरत	aurteṁ (women)	औरतें
obli. case	aurat + pp_n	औरत +pp_n	aurtoṁ + pp_n	औरतों + pp_n

- **आ (ā) - ending fem. nouns**

direct case	chātrā (student)	छात्रा	chātrāeṁ (students)	छात्राएँ
oblique case	chātrā + pp_n	छात्रा + pp_n	chātrāoṁ + pp_n	छात्राओं + pp_n

- **ऊ ū or उ u -ending fem. nouns.**

We don't have many feminine nouns ending in long ū or short 'u'.)

direct case	vadhū (bride)	वधू	vadhueṁ(sons'wives)	वधुएँ
oblique case	vadhū+ pp_n	वधू+ pp_n	vadhuoṁ + pp_n	वधुओं + pp_n
direct case	vastu(thing)	वस्तु	vastueṁ(things)	वस्तुएँ
oblique case	vastu+ pp_n	वस्तु+ pp_n	vastuoṁ + pp_n	वस्तुओं+ pp_n

- **ī (ई) or i (इ)- ending feminine nouns:**

direct case	nadī(river)	नदी	nadiyāṁ (girls)	नदियाँ
oblique case	nadī+ pp_n	नदी + pp_n	nadiyoṁ + pp_n	नदियों + pp_n
direct case	ruci (interest)	रुचि	ruciyāṁ (interest)	रुचियाँ
oblique case	ruci + pp_n	रुचि + pp_n	ruciyoṁ + pp_n	रुचियों+ pp_n

Some basic rules of verb conjugation:

In Hindi all verbs in their infinitive form are ना nā - ending For example:–

जाना	jānā	to go	खाना	khānā	to eat
देखना	dekhnā	to look	कहना	kahnā	to say

☞ verb infinitive minus ना nā = verb root (v.r.)

v.r. + ता tā, ते te, ती tī = present participle

v.r. + आ ā, ए e, ई ī = past participle

☞ To make sentences in various tenses Hindi uses present or past participle + the auxiliary verb होना honā in the required tense.

For example:

- Present indefinite = v.r. + ता tā, ते te, ती tī (present participle) + present form of होना honā (हूँ hūṁ हो ho, है hai, हैं haiṁ)
- Past habitual = v.r. + ता tā, ते te, ती tī (present participle) + past form of होना honā, था thā, थे the, थी thī, थीं thīṁ.
- Past simple tense = v.r. + आ ā, ए e, ई ī (past participle)
- Present perfect tense = v.r. + आ ā, ए e, ई ī (past participle) + present form of होना honā
- Past perfect tense = v.r. + आ ā, ए e, ई ī (past participle) + past form of होना honā

☞ To make interrogative sentences put 'क्या kyā' at the beginning of a sentence.

☞ To make negative sentences put 'नहीं nahīṁ' before the main verb. In case of compound verbs, 'नहीं nahīṁ' can be placed between the main verb and the compounded part.

■ In Hindi the verb conjugation accords with the noun or pronoun in the direct case, that is not followed by any post postion .

☞ If the subject is followed by any post position such as 'ने ne', 'को ko' 'से se' etc, verb conjugation accords with the number and gender of the object.

☞ If both the subject and object are followed by any post position, the verb conjugation is always in masculine singular 'आ ā' form:

Impotant note:

Hindi has no translation for the English sentence starters 'It is', 'There is'. Hindi comes straight to the subject.

It is 4 o'clock. चार बजे हैं। cār baje haiṁ.

There is fog outside. बाहर धुंध है। bāhar dhundh hai.

Conjunctions

और	aur	and
व	va	"
अतः	ataḥ	"
एवम्	evam	"
यद्यपि / गोकि	yadyapi/goki	although
मानो	māno	as if
जैसे कि	jaise ki	as though (relative conjunct)
क्योंकि	kyoṁki	because
लेकिन	lekin	but
परन्तु	parantu	"
मगर	magar	"
पर	par	"
यदि / अगर	yadi/agar	if
तो	to	in that case
(तो has several uses. Ref. pg 225)		
तथापि	tathāpi	nevertheless
न ....न	na ......na.....	neither.. nor...
या ....या	yā .....yā	either.. or.....
बल्कि	balki	on the contrary
या / अथवा	yā /athvā	or
नहीं तो / वरना	nahīṁ to /varnā	or else
ताकि	tāki	so that
कि	ki	that
इसलिए	islie	therefore
यानी	yānī	that is
जो कि	jo ki	the one who, which

Compound Postpositions

के बाद	ke bād	after
के आगे	ke āge	ahead of
के कारण / की वजह से	ke kāraṇ /kī vajah se	because of
के मारे*	ke māre *	because of
के पहले	ke pahle	before

के मारे* **is used when the reason is intense causing discomfort and suffering.**

के पीछे	ke pīche	behind
के अतिरिक्त	ke atirikt	besides
के अलावा	ke alāvā	besides
के सिवा	ke sivā	except
के लिए	ke lie	for
के सामने	ke sāmne	in front of
की तरह / की भांति	kī tarah / kī bhāṁti	like
के पास *	ke pā s *	near
की ओर / की तरफ़	kī or/kī taraf	towards
की बजाय / की जगह	kī bajāy/kī jagah	instead of (Ref.pg.217
के ऊपर	ke ūpar	upon
के नीचे	ke nīce	under
के साथ	ke sāth	with
के बिना / के बग़ैर	ke binā / ke baGair	without
के बारे में	ke bāre meṁ	about
के चलते	ke calte	on account of X
के अनुसार	ke anusār	according to
के बावजूद	ke bāvjūd	despite
के बनिस्बत	ke banisbat	in comparison with

■ SENTENCE FORMATION

☞ The word order in Hindi: Subject + object /adjective + verb. The verb always comes at the end. (see chapter 3)

1. मैं अध्यापिका[f.] हूँ।	maiṁ adhyapikā[f.] hūṁ.	**I am a teacher.**
2. सड़क चौड़ी है।	saṛak cauṛī hai.	**The road is wide.**

Ex.1: Fill in the blanks with the appropriate form of the noun:

	m.sg.	m.pl.	Case
1.	लड़का laṛkā	a.......	Direct
	b.......	c.......	Oblique
	d.......	e.......	Vocative

*(See Box .pg.61)

2.	घर ghar	a.......	Direct
	b.......	c.......	Oblique
	d.......	e.......	Vocative
3.	कवि kavi	a.......	Direct
	b.......	c.......	Oblique
	d.......	e.......	Vocative
4.	निवासी nivāsī	a.......	Direct
	b.......	c.......	Oblique
	d.......	e.......	Vocative
5.	साधु sādhu	a.......	Direct
	b.......	c.......	Oblique
	d.......	e.......	Vocative
6.	आँसू āṁsū	a.......	Direct
	b.......	c.......	Oblique
	d.......	e.......	Vocative

Ex.2: Fill in the blanks with the appropriate form of the noun:

	f.sg.	**f.pl.**	**Case**
1.	औरत aurat	a.......	Direct
	b.......	c.......	Oblique
	d.......	e.......	Vocative
2.	माता mātā	a.......	Direct
	b.......	c.......	Oblique
	d.......	e.......	Vocative
3.	चूड़ी cūṛī	a.......	Direct
	b.......	c.......	Oblique
	d.......	e.......	Vocative

4. तिथि tithi	a.......	Direct
b.......	c.......	Oblique
d.......	e.......	Vocative
5. वस्तु vastu	a.......	Direct
b.......	c.......	Oblique
d.......	e.......	Vocative
6. वधू vadhū	a.......	Direct
b.......	c.......	Oblique
d.......	e.......	Vocative

Ex. 3: Fill in the blank spaces as shown :

1. इस देश में is deś meṁ	in this country	**इन देशों में** in deśoṁ meṁ	in these countries
2. इस थाली में is thālī meṁ	in this plate	....	in these plates
3. उस सड़क पर us saṛak par	in that street	....	in those streets
4. उस पलंग पर us palaṅg par	on that bed	....	on those beds
5. इस कमरे में is kamre meṁ	in this room	....	in those rooms
6. इस पुस्तक में is pustak meṁ	in this book	....	in those books
7. इस औरत ने is aurat ne	this woman	....	those women
8. इस पर्दे का is parde kā	of this curtain	....	of those curtains
9. इस बच्चे से is bacce se	from this child	....	from those children
10. इस प्याले को is pyāle ko	(to) this cup	....	(to) those cups

Ex. 4: Correct the sentences given below :

1. दो दरवाज़ा पर हरे पर्दे हैं।
2. कुछ सड़क पर आम के पेड़ हैं।
3. सब पौधा में सुन्दर फूल हैं।
4. कुछ गमलों में नए पौधा हैं।
5. चार बड़े बाग़ीचा में हरी–हरी घास है।
6. वे इन छात्र के काग़ज़ हैं।

1. do darvāzā par hare parde haiṁ.
2. kuch saṛak par ām ke peṛ haiṁ.
3. sab paudhā mem sundar phūl haiṁ.
4. kuch gamloṁ meṁ nae paudhā haiṁ.
5. cār baṛe bāGīcā meṁ harī-harī ghās hai.
6. ve in chātra ke kāGaz haiṁ.

Ex.5: Complete the following sentences :

1. यह नया घर है।

   इस नए घर में चार लोग हैं।

   इन ....

2. वह पुराना नल है।

   उस पुराने नल में हमेशा पानी रहता है।

   उन ....

3. यह बड़ा कमरा है।

   इस बड़े कमरे में मैं और मेरी बहन रहते हैं।

   इन ....

4. यह छोटा–सा रसोई उद्यान है।

   इस छोटे से रसोई उद्यान में हम सब्ज़ी उगाते हैं।

   इन ....

5. यह अच्छा कंगन है।

   इस अच्छे कंगन को पहन लो।

   इन ....

6. वह विद्वान साधू है।

उस विद्वान साधु से ज्ञान लो।

उन ....

1. yah nayā ghar hai.

is nae ghar meṁ cār log haiṁ.

in ....

2. vah purānā nal hai.

us purāne nal meṁ hameśā pānī rahtā hai.

un ....

3. yah baṛā kamrā hai.

is baṛe kamre meṁ maiṁ aur merī bahan rahte haiṁ.

in ....

4. yah choṭā-sā rasoī udyān hai.

is choṭe-se rasoī udyān meṁ ham sabzi ugāte haiṁ.

in ....

5. yah acchā kaṅgan hai.

is acche kaṅgan ko pahan lo.

in ....

6. vah vidvān sādhu hai.

us vidvān sādhu se gyan lo.

un ....

Key 1

a /b	c	d	e
1. लड़के / –	लड़कों	हे लड़के	हे लड़को
2. घर / –	घरों	हे घर	हे घरो
3. कवि / –	कवियों	हे कवि	हे कवियो
4. निवासी / –	निवासियों	हे निवासी	हे निवासियो
5. साधु / –	साधुओं	हे साधु	हे साधुओ
6. आँसू / –	आँसुओं	हे आँसू	हे आँसुओ

1. laṛke/-	laṛkoṁ	hey laṛke	hey laṛko
2. ghar /-	gharoṁ	hey ghar	hey gharo
3. kavi /-	kaviyoṁ	hey kavi	hey kaviyo
4. nivāsī/-	nivāsiyoṁ	hey nivāsī	hey nivāsiyo
5. sādhu/-	sādhuoṁ	hey sādhu	hey sādhuo
6. āṁsū/-	āṁsuoṁ	hey āṁsū	hey āṁsuo

Key 2

a/b	c	d	e
1. औरत / औरतें	औरतों	हे औरत	हे औरतो
2. माता / माताएँ	माताओं	हे माता	हे माताओ
3. चूड़ी / चूड़ियाँ	चूड़ियों	हे चूड़ी	हे चूड़ियो
4. तिथि / तिथियाँ	तिथियों	हे तिथि	हे तिथियो
5. वस्तु / वस्तुएँ	वस्तुओं	हे वस्तु	हे वस्तुओ
6. वधू / वधुएँ	वधुओं	हे वधू	हे वधुओ
1. aurat / aurteṁ	aurtoṁ	hey aurat	hey aurto
2. mātā / mātāeṁ	mātāoṁ	hey mātā	hey mātāo
3. cūṛī /cūṛīyāṁ	cūṛiyoṁ	he cūṛī	hey cūṛīyo
4. tithi /tithiyāṁ	tithiyoṁ	hey tithi	hey tithiyo
5. vastu / vastueṁ	vastuoṁ	he vastu	hey vastuo
6. vadhū /vadhueṁ	vadhuoṁ	he vadhū	hey vadhuo

Key 3

2. इन थालियों में	3. उन सड़कों पर	4. उन पलंगों पर
5. उन कमरों में	6. उन पुस्तकों में	6. उन औरतों ने
8. उन पर्दों का	9. उन बच्चों से	10. उन प्यालों को
2. in thāliyoṁ meṁ	3. un saṛkoṁ par	4- un palaṅgoṁ par
5. un kamroṁ meṁ	6. un pustakoṁ meṁ	7. un aurtoṁ ne
8. un pardoṁ par	9. un baccoṁ se	10. un pyaloṁ ko

Key 4

1. दरवाजों	2. सड़कों	3. पौधों
4. पौधे	5. बाग़ीचों	6. छात्रों
1. darvāzoṁ	2. saṛkoṁ	3. paudhoṁ
4. paudhe	5. bāGīcoṁ	6. chātroṁ

Key 5

1. इन नए घरों में ...।
2. उन पुराने नलों में ...।
3. इन बड़े कमरों में ...।
4. इन छोटे–से रसोई उद्यानों में ...।
5. इन अच्छे कंगनों को ...।
7. उन विद्वान साधुओं से ...।

1. in nae gharoṁ meṁ
2. un purāne naloṁ meṁ
3. in baṛe kamroṁ meṁ
4. in choṭe-se rasoī udyānoṁ meṁ
5. in acche kaṅgnoṁ ko
6. un vidvān sādhuoṁ se

Some time adverbs

आज	āj	today
कल	kal	tomorrow/ yesterday
परसों	parsoṁ	the day before yesterday / after tomorrow
नरसों	narsoṁ	two day s before yesterday / after tomorrow
कल सुबह	kal subah	tomorrow morning
पिछले हफ़्ते	pichle hafte	last week
अगले हफ़्ते	agle hafte	next week
सप्ताहान्त पर	saptāhānt par	on the weekend
सुबह	subah	in the morning
हर सुबह	har subah	every morning
शाम को	śām ko	in the evening
अब	ab	now
अभी	abhī	now(emphatic)
अभी–अभी	abhī-abhī	just now

2 Imperatives

- **Present Imperative**

तू tū (sg.) + verb root
तुम tum (sg. and plural) + verb root + o
आप āp (sg. and plural) + verb root + i + e / ye

Examples: verb जाना jānā to go

तू जा।	तुम जाओ।	आप जाइए।
tū jā.	tum jāo.	āp jāie.

☞ **Put मत 'mat' before the verb with तू 'tū' and तुम 'tum' and न 'na' before the verb in आप 'āp' form.**

For example:

1. तू मत जा।	tū mat jā.	Do not go!
2. तुम मत जाओ।	tum mat jāo.	Do not go!
3. आप न जाइए।	āp na jāie.	Please, do not go!

- **Irregular imperative :**

	तू **tū**	तुम **tum**	आप **āp**
करना karnā (to do)	कर kar	करो karo	कीजिए kījie
पीना pīnā(to drink)	पी pī	पिओ pio	पीजिए pījie
लेना lenā (to take)	ले le	लो lo	लीजिए lījie
देना denā (to give)	दे de	दो do	दीजिए dījie

- **Future Imperative**

Hindi uses this when the command or request is expected to be executed in the near or distant future.

तू / तुम tū / tum + infinitive

तू / तुम जाना	**tū / tum jānā**	**You go!**

आप āp + v.r. + iegā
☞ Regardless of ' āp' being masc. or fem., v.r. + iegā is used.

आप जाइएगा। **āp jāiegā.** **Please, you go.**

- **Subjunctive Imperative**

Hindi uses this very polite form ' v.r. + eṁ' with:		
• second person आप 'āp'. (m/f.)		
आप बैठें।	āp baiṭheṁ	Please, be seated.
आप अब सोएँ।	āp ab soeṁ	Please, sleep now
• Us imperative (= Let's us.....See subjunctive passive pg. 184)		
आइए, अन्दर बैठें।	āie, andar baiṭheṁ	Come, let's sit inside.
चलो, बाहर चलें।	calo, bāhar caleṁ	Let's go out.

Ex. 1: Translate into English:

1. छात्रा को बुलाओ। 2. कृपया यह किताब उनको दीजिए। 3. यह नया कुरता पहनो। 4. खाना पकाओ। 5. फल गाहक को बेचो। 6. दुकानदार से सामान ख़रीदो। 7. वहाँ बैठो। 8. फ़िल्म देखो। 9. हिन्दी बोलो 10. पंखा चलाओ। 11. नल बन्द करो। 12. बत्ती बुझाओ।

1. chātrā ko bulāo. 2. kṛpayā yah kitāb unko dījie. 3. yah nayā kurtā pahno. 4. khānā pakāo. 5. phal gāhak ko beco. 6. dukāndār se sāmān kharīdo 7. vahāṁ baiṭho. 8. film dekho. 9. hindī bolo 10. paṅkhā calāo. 11. nal band karo. 12. battī bujhāo.

Glossary:

छात्रा	*chātrā*	student	बुलाना	*bulānā*	to call
कृपया	*kṛpayā*	please	किताब	*kitāb*	book
उनको	*unko*	to them	देना	*denā*	to give
नया	*nayā*	new	कुरता	*kurtā*	shirt
पहनना	*pahnanā*	to wear	खाना	*khānā*	food
पकाना	*pakānā*	to cook	बेचना	*becnā*	to sell
फल	*phal*	fruit	गाहक	*gāhak*	customer
दुकानदार	*dukāndār*	shopkeeper	से	*se*	from

सामान	*sāmān*	goods	ख़रीदना	*kharīdnā*	to buy
वहाँ	*vahāṁ*	there	बैठना	*baiṭhnā*	to sit
देखना	*dekhnā*	to look	बोलना	*bolnā*	to speak
पंखा	paṅkhā	fan	लगाना	*lagānā*	here: to turn on
नल	*nal*	tap	बन्द	*band*	closed
करना	*karnā*	to do	बत्ती	*battī*	light
बुझाना	*bujhānā*	to turn off			

Ex. 2: Translate into English:

1. मुझको जल्दी पत्र भेजना। 2. यहीं ठहरना। 3. सबको मेरी नमस्ते कहना। 4. पौष्टिक भोजन खाना। 5. अच्छी तरह पढ़ना। 6. आप भारत में हिन्दी बोलिएगा। 7. आप सारनाथ अवश्य जाइएगा। 8. आप हम सब के लिए उपहार लाइएगा। 9. शराब न पीजिएगा। 10. दरवाज़े खिड़कियाँ ठीक से बन्द कीजिएगा।

1. mujh ko jaldī patra bhejnā. 2. yahīṁ ṭhaharnā. 3. sabko merī namaste kahnā. 4. pausṭik bhojan khānā . 5. acchī tarah paṛhnā . 6. āp bhārat meṁ hindī boliegā. 7. āp sārnāth avaśyă jāiegā. 8. āp ham sab ke lie uphār lāiegā. 9. śarāb na pījiegā. 10. darvāze khirkiyāṁ ṭhīk se band kijiegā.

Glossary:

जल्दी	*jaldī*	soon	पत्र	*patra*	letter
भेजना	*bhejnā*	send	यहीं	*yahīṁ*	here (emphatic)
ठहरना	*ṭhahrnā*	to stay	सबको	*sabko*	to everybody
कहना	*kahnā*	to say	पौष्टिक	*pausṭik*	nutritious
भोजन	*bhojan*	food	अच्छी तरह	*acchī tarah*	properly
पढ़ना	*paṛhnā*	to study	बोलना	*bolnā*	speak
अवश्य	*avaśyă*	certainly	उपहार	*uphār*	gifts
लाना	*lānā*	to bring	शराब	*śarāb*	alcohol
पीना	*pīnā*	to drink	दरवाज़े	*darvāze*	doors

Ex. 3: Rewrite these sentences in subjunctive imperative form:

1. आप यहां हिन्दी बोलिए 2. आप सारनाथ अवश्य जाइए। 3. आप हम सब के लिए उपहार लाइए। 4. शराब न पीजिए। 5. दरवाज़े खिड़कियाँ ठीक से बन्द कीजिए।

1. āp yahāṁ hindī bolie. 2. āp sārnāth avaśyă jāie. 3. āp ham sab ke lie uphār lāie. 4. śarāb na pījie. 5. darvāze khirkiyāṁ ṭhīk se band kījie.

Key 1

1. Call the student. 2. Please give this book to them. 3. Wear this new kurta. 4. Cook food. 5. Sell fruit to the customer. 6. Buy goods from the shopkeeper. 7. Sit there! 8. Watch the film. 9. Speak Hindi! !0. Turn on the fan. 11. Close the tap! 12. Turn the light off!

Key 2

1. Send me a letter soon. 2. Stay just here. 3. Say namaste from me to everybody. 4. Eat nutritious food. 5. Study well. 6. Please, speak Hindi in India. 7. Please certainly go to Sarnath. 8. Please bring gifts for us all. 9. Please don't drink alcohol. 10. Please shut the doors and windows properly.

Key 3

1. आप भारत में हिन्दी बोलें। 2. आप सारनाथ अवश्य जाएँ। 3. आप हम सब के लिए उपहार लाएँ। 4. शराब न पीएँ।5. दरवाज़े खिड़कियाँ ठीक से बन्द करें।

1. āp bhārat meṁ hindī boleṁ. 2. āp sārnāth avaśyă jāeṁ. 3. āp ham sab ke lie uphār lāeṁ. 4. śarāb na pīeṁ. 5. darvāze khirkiyāṁ ṭhīk se band kareṁ

Some Adjectives							
1. नाराज़	*nāraz*	annoyed		2. व्यस्त	*vyast*	busy
3. निराश	*nirāś*	disappointed		4. उदास	*udās*	sad
5. खिन्न	*khinn*	dejected		6. उबाउ	*ubāu*	boring
7. विस्मित	*vismit*	surprised-		8. प्रसन्न	*prasann*	happy
9. सन्तुष्ट	*santuṣṭ*	satisfied		10. हाज़िर जवाब	*hāzir javāb*	witty
11. उत्तेजित	*nāraz*	excited		12. चिन्तित	*cintit*	worried
13. झगड़ालू	*jhagṛālū*	quarrelsome		14. प्रतिभाशाली	*pratibhāśālī*	talented
15. लड़ाकू	*laṛākū*	belligerent		16. आशावादी	*āśāvādī*	optimistic
17. निराशावादी	*nirāśāvādī*	pessimistic		18. शर्मिन्दा	*śarmindā*	embarrased
19. औपचारिक	*aupcārik*	formal		16. अनौपचारिक	*anaupcārik*	informal

3 होना honā -- to be

Present forms of होना **honā:**

subject + noun/ adjective + 'हूँ', 'हो', 'है', 'हैं' hūṁ , ho, hai, haiṁ **to agree with N and G of the subj.**

Examples:

1. मैं साहसी हूँ। — I am courageous.
   maiṁ (m.sg.) sāhsī hūṁ.
2. वे (m.pl.) नेकदिल हैं। — They are goodhearted.
   ve (m.pl.) nekdil haiṁ.
3. तुम सावधान हो। — You are cautious.
   tum (m./f) sāvdhān ho.
4. वह (m.sg.) खिलाड़ी है। — He is an athlete.
   vah khilāṛī hai.

Ex. 1: Fill the suitable present forms of 'होना' honā i.e. हूँ hūṁ, है' hai, 'हो ho', 'हैं haiṁ, in t**he blank spaces.**

1. आज सोमवार (m.) है।
2. वे (m.pl.) **दयालु** ....
3. तुम होशियार .... ।
4. वह (m.sg.) चतुर ....
5. खिड़की (f.sg.) खुली................. ।.
6. मैं (m.sg.) चिंतित .... ।
7. बच्चा (m.sg.) भूखा .... ।
8. छात्र (m.sg.) प्रतिभावान...... ।
9. वह अल्पभाषी .... ।
10. रित्विक (m.sg.) बातूनी .... ।

1. āj somvār (m.) ....
2. ve (m.pl.) dayālu......................
3. tum hośiyār ....
4. vah (m.sg.) catur ....
5. khiṛkī (f.sg.)khulī........................
6. maiṁ (m.sg.) cintit ....
7. baccā (m.sg.) bhūkhā ....
8. chātra (m.sg.) pratibhāvān........
9. vah alpbhāṣī ....
10. ritvik (m.sg.)bātūnī............

Past forms of होना honā:

subject + **noun/ adjective**	+ था, थे, थी, थीं thā, the, thī, thīṁ to agree with N and G of the subj.

1. कल दशहरा* (m.sg.) था। Yesterday was Dashahra.
   kal daśahrā thā.
2. धोबिन (f.sg.) शिक्षित थी। The washer woman was educated.
   dhobin śikṣit thī.
3. मैं (m.) बीमार . था। I was sick.
   maiṁ bīmār thā.
4. बच्चे (m.pl) नटखट थे। The children were naughty.
   bacce naṭkhaṭ the.
5. फ़िल्म (f.) काफ़ी मनोरंजक थी। Film was quite entertaining.
   film kāfī manorañjak thī.

Ex. 2: Fill the suitable past forms of 'होना'... था, थे, थी, थीं in the blank spaces.

1. कल इतवार (m.) **था।** 2. शिक्षिका (f.sg.) निर्दयी .... ।
3. बच्चे (m.pl.) होशियार .... । 4. वे (f.) प्रसन्न .... ।
5. हम (m.) बहुत परेशान .... । 6. तुम (f.) चतुर .... ।
7. वे (m.) धनी .... । 8. दही (m.) खट्टा . ... ।
9. दूध (m.) सस्ता .... । 10. वस्त्र (m.) महँगा .... ।

1. kal itvār (m.sg.) thā. 2. śikṣikā (m.sg.) nirdayī ....
3. bacce hośiyār...................... 4. ve (f.) prasann ....
5. ham (m.pl.) bahut pareśān....... 6. tum (f.) catur ....
7. ve (m.pl.) dhanī .... 8. dahī (m.) khaṭṭā ....
9. dūdh (m.pl.) sastā................ 10. vastra (m.) mahṁgā..............

*A festival in India celebrating the victory of Ram over the demon Ravana.

Future forms of होना honā

subj.+ n./adj. + होऊँगा, होऊँगी, होगा, होगी, होगे, होगी, होंगे, होंगी
hoūṁgā, hoūṁgī, hogā, hogī, hoge, hogī, hoṁge, hoṁgī
to agree with N and G of the subj.

1. अध्यापक (m.pl.) ख़ुश होंगे। The teachers will be happy.
   adhyāpak khuś hoṁge.
2. पिता जी नाराज़ होंगे। Father will be annoyed.
   pitā jī nārāz hoṁge.
3. वहाँ भीड़ (f.) होगी। There will be crowd.
   vahāṁ bhīṛ hogī.
4. जनता (f.) निराश होगी। Public will be disappointed,
   jantā nirāś hogī.
5. फ़िल्म (f.) उबाऊ होगी। Film will be boring.
   film ubāū hogī.

Ex. 3: Fill suitable future forms of होना in the blank spaces.

1. कल दीक्षान्त समारोह (m.)होगा। 2. उसका विवाह (m.) कब ....?
3. परीक्षाएँ (f.pl.) कब ....? 4. मैं (m.) निराश .... ?
5. शाम को पाँच बजे मँत्री जी का का भाषण (m.).. .... । 6. परसों पाकिस्तान में चुनाव(m.) .... ।
7. पिता जी बहुत गुस्सा.................. । 8. जून में यहाँ बहुत गर्मी (f.) .... ।
9. अगले हफ़्ते पुस्तक मेला............ ।10. आप(m.) सफल........................ ।.

1. kal dīkṣānt samāroh hogā. 2. uskā vivāh (m.sg.) kab....?
3. parīkṣāeṁ kab ....? 4. maiṁ (m.) nirāś ....
5. śām ko pāṁc baje mantrī jī kā bhāṣaṇ(m.) .... 6. parsoṁ pākistān meṁ cunāv (m)..................
7. pitā jī bahut Gussā .... 8. jūn meṁ yahāṁ bahut garmī ....
9. agle hafte pustak melā (m.)........ 10. āp saphal ....

Glossary:

साहसी (adj.)	sāhsī	couragious.
नेकदिल (adj.)	nekdil	good hearted
सावधान (adj.)	sāvdhān	cautious
खिलाड़ी (adj.)	khilāṛī	athlete
प्रतिभावान (adj.)	pratibhāvān	talented
दयालु (adj.)	dayālu	kind
होशियार (adj.)	hośiyār	clever
चतुर (adj.)	catur	clever
गहरा, –रे, री (adj.)	gahrā, -e, -ī	deep
चिंतित (adj.)	cintit	worried
भूखा, भूखे, भूखी (adj.)	bhūkhā, -e, -ī	hungry
अल्पभाषी (adj.)	alpbhāṣī	reticent
बातूनी (adj.)	bātūnī	talkative
बूढ़ी (adj.)	būṛhī	old woman
दशहरा (m.)	daśharā	*Dashara
धोबिन (f.)	dhobin	waherwoman
शिक्षित (adj.)	śikṣiṭ	educated
बीमार (adj.)	bīmār	sick.
नटखट (adj.)	naṭkhaṭ	naughty
मनोरंजक (adj.)	manorañjak	entertaining
नादान (adj.)	nādān	innocent
शिक्षिका (f.sg.)	śikṣikā	teacher
निर्दयी (adj.)	nirdayī	cruel
प्रसन्न (adj.)	prasann	happy
परेशान (adj.)	pareśān	upset
धनी (adj.)	dhanī	rich
खट्टा, –टे,– टी (adj.)	khaṭṭā, -e, -ī	sour
सस्ता, –ते –ती (adj.)	sastā , -e, -ī	inexpensive
वस्त्र (m.)	vastra	clothing
महँगा, –गे –गी (adj.)	mahṁgā , -e, -ī	expensive
भीड़ (f.)	bhīṛ	crowd
दीक्षान्त समारोह (m.sg.)	dīkṣānt samāroh	convocation

परीक्षा (f.sg.)	parīkṣā	exam
विवाह (m.)	vivāh	marriage
मँत्री (m.sg.)	mantrī	minister
भाषण (m.)	bhāṣaṇ	speech

Key 1

1. है। 2. हैं। 3. हो। 4. है।
5. है। 6. हूँ। 7. है। 8. है ।
9. है। 10. है।

1. hai 2. haiṁ 3. ho 4. hai
5. hai 6. hūṁ 7. hai 8. hai
9. hai 10. hai.

Key 2

1. था। 2. थी। 3. थे। 4. थीं।
5. थे। 6. थीं। 7. थे। 8.. था।
9. था 10. था।

1. thā 2. thī. 3. the. 4. thīṁ.
5. the. 6. thīṁ. 7. the. 8. thā.
9. thā 10. thā.

Key 3

1.होगा। 2. होगा? 3. होंगी? 4. हूँगा।
5 होगा। 6. होंगे। 7. होंगे। 8. होगी ।
9. होगा। 10. होंगे।

1. hogā. 2. hogā. ? 3. hoṁgī? 4. hūṁgā.
5. hogā. 6. hoṁge 7. hoṁge 8. hogī
9. hogā 10. hoṁge.

Some Sentence Adverbs		
Fortunately	bhāgyă se	भाग्य से
By chance	saṁyog se	संयोग से
Actually	vāstav meṁ	वास्तव में
Probably	sambhavtā	सम्भवता

4 Present Indefinite

subj. + obj. + v.r. + tā ता m.sg + hūṁ, ho, hai, haiṁ
te ते m.pl. हूँ, हो, है, हैं
tī ती f.sg/pl
written together
agree with the N and G of the subj

☞ In the present indefinite negative sentences, the auxiliary verb hūṁ, ho, hai, haiṁ is usually dropped. In case the subject is fem.pl., the main verb has 'tīṁ'-ending . E. 4 below.

COMPREHENSION

1. मैंᶠ स्पेनी पढ़ाती हूँ।	I (f) teach Spanish.
maiṁ spenī paṛhātī hūṁ.	(paṛhānā पढ़ाना = to teach)
2. तुमᵐ भूगोल पढ़ते हो।	You (m.infml.) study geog-
tumᵐ bhūgolᵐ paṛhte ho.	raphy. (paṛhnā पढ़ना = to study)
3. वेᵐ तैरते हैं।	They (m.+f., far) swim.
veᵐ tairte haiṁ.	(tairnā तैरना= to swim)
4. वेᶠ· लौकी **नहीं खातीं।**	They(f.) don't eat bottlegourd.
veᶠ 'laukīᶠ **nahīṁ khātīṁ.**	(khānā खाना = to eat)
5. हमᵐ रेडियो **नहीं सुनते।**	We (m.) don't listen to the radio.
hamᵐ radio **nahīṁ sunte.**	(sunanā सुनना = to hear)

Ex.1: Translate into English:

1. पियूष अंग्रेज़ी पढा़ता है।
2. वह (f.) तीन भाषाएँ बोलती है।
3. माँ सुबह नाश्ता बनाती है।
4. हम सुबह नाश्ते में पराठा खाते हैं।
5. मैं रोज़ सुबह गरम पानी से नहाता हूँ।

6. अनिल रोज़ सुबह व्यायाम करता है।
7. पानी सौ अंश 'सैलसिअस' पर उबलता है।
8. क्या दुकानें शाम को आठ बजे बन्द होती हैं?
9. गाड़ी दो बजे छूटती है।
10. हम लहसुन और प्याज़ कभी नहीं खाते।

1. piyūṣ aṅgrezī paṛhātā hai.
2. vah (f.) tīn bhāṣāeṁ boltī hai.
3. māṁ subah nāśtā banātī hai.
4. ham subah nāśte meṁ prāṭhā khāte haiṁ.
5. maiṁ (m.) roz subah garam pānī se nahātā hūṁ.
6. anil roz subah vyāyām kartā hai.
7. pānī sau aṁś 'sailsias' par ubaltā hai.
8. kyā dukāneṁ śām ko āṭh baje band hotī haiṁ?
9. gāṛī do baje chūṭtī hai.
10. ham lahsun aur pyāz kabhī nahīṁ khāte.

Ex.2: Translate into English: Interrogative.

1. कौन अंग्रेज़ी पढ़ाता है?
2. वह कितनी भाषाएँ बोलती है?
3. माँ सुबह क्या बनाती है?
4. हम सुबह नाश्ते में क्या खातें हैं?
5. मैं सुबह कैसे पानी से नहाता हूँ?
6. अनिल रोज़ सुबह क्या करता है?
7. पानी कितने अंश सेलसिअस पर उबलता है?
8. दुकानें शाम को कितने बजे बन्द होती हैं?

1. kaun aṅgrezī paṛhātā hai?
2. vah (f.) kitnī bhāṣāeṁ boltī hai?
3. māṁ subah kyā banātī hai?
4. ham subah nāśte meṁ kyā khāte haiṁ?
5. maiṁ (m.) subah kaise pānī se nahātā hūṁ?
6. anil roz subah kyā kartā hai?
7. pāni kitne aṁś 'sailsias' par ubaltā hai?
8. dukāneṁ śām ko kitne baje band hotī haiṁ?

Glossary:

बोलना (v.i.)	bolnā	speak
भाषा (f.)	bhāṣā	language

तैयार करना (v.t.)	taiyār karnā	prepare
नाश्ता (m.)	nāśtā	breakfast
नहाना (v.i.)	nahānā	to take a bath
गरम (adj.)	garam	hot
व्यायाम करना (v.t.)	vyāyām karnā	to exercise
अंश (m.)	aṃś	degrees
उबलना (v.i.)	ubalnā	to boil
सुबह (nf./ adv.)	subah	in the morning
रोज़ सुबह (adv.)	roz subah	every morning
शाम को (adv.)	śām ko	in the evening
छूटना (v.i.)	chūṭnā	here: to depart
लहसुन (m.)	lahsun	garlic
प्याज़ (m.)	pyāz	onion

Ex. 3: Complete the sentences in the present simple tense using the verbs in parentheses and the appropriate form of 'होना' as shown in the example :

1. माँ (f.sg.) हमारे लिए खाना पकाती है। (पकाना)
2. दादी जी (f.sg.) हमको रोज़ कहानी ....(सुनाना)
3. नौकर (m.sg.) घर का सब काम..................................(करना)
4. डॉक्टर (m.sg.) मरीज़ों को दवाई..................................(देना)
5. नाई (m.sg.) लोगों के बाल...(काटना)
6. मोची (m.sg.) जूता ....(बनाना)
7. दुकानदार (m.sg.) गाहकों को सामान............................(बेचना)
8. गाहक (m.sg.).दुकानदार से सामान...............................(ख़रीदना)
9. धोबी (m.sg) कपड़े..(धोना)
10. मरीज़ (m.sg.) डॉक्टर से दवाई...................................(लेना)

1. māṁ(f.sg.) hamāre lie khānā pakātī hai. (pakānā)
2. dādī jī (f.sg.) hamko roz kahānī..................................(sunānā)
3. naukar (m.sg.) ghar kā sab kām..................................(karnā)
4. ḍaukṭar (m.sg.) marīzoṁ ko davāī.............................(denā)
5. nāī (m.sg.) logoṁ ke bāl. ....(kāṭnā)
6. mocī (m.sg.) jūtā...(banānā)

7. dukāndār (m.sg.)gāhakoṁ ko sāmān...................... (becnā)
8. gāhak (m.sg.) dukāndār se sāmān ....(kharīdnā)
9. dhobī (m.sg) kapṛe...(dhonā)
10. marīz (m.sg.) ḍaukṭar se davāī................................ (lenā)

Glossary

दादी जी (f.sg)	dādī jī	grandmother
कहानी (f.sg)	kahānī	story
सुनाना (v.t.)	sunānā	to narrate
नौकर (m.)	naukar	servant
काम (m.)	kām	work
नाई (m.)	nāī	barbar
बाल (m.)	bāl	hair
काटना (v.t.)	kāṭnā	to cut
मोची (m.)	mocī	cobler
जूता (m.sg)	jūtā	shoe
बनाना (v.t.)	banānā	to make
दुकानदार (m.)	dukāndār	shopkeeper
सामान (m.)	sāmān	goods
बेचना (v.t.)	becnā	to sell
गाहक (m.)	gāhak	customer
ख़रीदना (v.t.)	kharīdnā	to buy
धोबी (m.)	dhobī	washerman
कपड़े (m.pl)	kapṛe	clothes
धोना (v.t.)	dhonā	to wash
मरीज़ (m.)	marīz	patient
दवाई (f.sg)	davāī	medicine
लेना (v.t.)	lenā	to take

Key 1

1. Piush teaches English.
2. She speaks three languages.
3. Mother prepares breakfast in the morning.
4. We all have 'prāṭhā' for breakfast.
5. I take a bath with hot water every morning.
6. Anil exercises every morning.

7 Water boils at 100^0 Celcius.
8. Do the shops close at 8 o'clock in the evening?
9. The train leaves at 2 o'clock.
10. We never eat garlic and onion.

Key 2

1. Who teaches English?
2. How many languages does she speak?
3. What does mother prepare in the morning?
4. What do we eat for breakfast in the morning?
5. With what kind of water do I have bath in the morning?
6. What does Anil do every morning?
7 At what degree celcius does the water boil?
8. At what time do the shops close in the evening?

Key 3

1. पकाती है। 2. सुनाती हैं। 3. करता है।
4. देता है। 5. काटता है। 6. बनाता है।
7. बेचता है। 8. ख़रीदता है। 9. धोता है।
10. लेता है।

1. pakātī hai 2. sunātī haiṁ. 3. kartā hai.
4. detā hai. 5. kāṭtā hai. 6. banātā hai.
7. bectā hai 8. <u>kh</u>arīdtā hai 9. dhotā hai
10. letā hai.

Emphatics: ही hī / ई ī		
यह yah + ही hī = यही yahī	(pron.)	this very;
वह vah + ही hī = वही vahī	(pron.)	that very
यहाँ yahāṁ + hī ही = यहीं yahīṁ	(adv.)	right here
वहाँ vahāṁ + hī ही = वहीं vahīṁ =	(adv.)	right there
हम यहीं बैठेंगे।	ham yahīṁ baiṭheṁge.	We will sit right here.
मैं यही लूँगा।	maiṁ yahī lūṁgā.	I will take this one!

5 Past Habitual

■ The past habitual tense is used for activities that we did in the past but don't do anymore.

subj. + obj. + verbroot + tā ता (m.sg.) + thā, the, thī, thīṁ
te ते (m.pl.) था, थे, थी, थीं
tī ती (f. sg. and pl.)
written together
agree with the Number

☞ था, थे, थी, थीं thā, the, thī, thīṁ is usually dropped while narrating a group of activities that one did habitually, intermittently in the past, but does not do any more. E. 6 given below:

1. नौकर^{m} खाना पकाता था।
naukar^{m} khānā pakātā thā.
The servant (m) used to cook food.

2. बच्चे$^{m.pl}$ फल^{m} खाते थे।
bacce$^{m.pl}$ phal khāte the.
Children used to eat fruit.

3. वे$^{f.hon}$ कहानियाँ लिखती थीं।
ve^{f} kahāniyāṁ likhtī thīṁ.
She(honorific) used to write stories.

4. वे$^{m.pl.}$ क्रिकेट खेलते थे।
ve$^{m.pl.}$ kriket̤ khelte the.
They (m.) used to play cricket .

5. हम$^{m.pl.}$ टी.वी. देखते थे।
ham$^{m.pl.}$ t̤ī.vī. dekhte the.
We (m) used to watch T.V.

6. बचपन में हम दिन भर खाते–खेलते। रोज़ रात को दादी हमें कोई कहानी सुनातीं।

bacpan meṁ ham$^{m.pl.}$ din-bhar khāte-khelte. roz rāt ko dādī hameṁ koī kahānī sunātīṁ.

During childhood we would eat and play all day . Every day at night grandmother would narrate story.

Ex. 1: Translate into English:

1. मेरा भाई एक 'बैंक' में काम करता था । 2. मैं 'कनाडा' में रहता था। 3. मैं अंग्रेज़ी सीखता था। 4. इस सड़क पर एक जूतों की दुकान होती थी । 5. मेरी दादी हर वक्त फ़िल्में देखती थीं। 6. जब हम छोटे थे, हम दिन भर दौड़ते–कूदते थे। 7. हम प्रतिदिन गंगा में नहाते थे । 8. मैं प्रत्येक शाम को अपनी प्रेमिका से मिलता था । 9. मेरे पिता जी प्रायः सप्ताहान्त पर दूरदर्शन देखते थे। 10. हम हर गर्मी में समुद्रतट पर जाते थे ।

1. merā bhāī ek baiṁk meṁ kām kartā thā.
2. maiṁ 'kanādā' meṁ rahtā thā.
3. maiṁ aṅgrezī sīkhtā thā.
4. is saṛak par ek jūtoṁ kī dukān hotī thī.
5. merī dādī har vaqt filmeṁ dekhtī thīṁ .
6. jab ham choṭe the, ham din bhar dauṛte-kūdte the.
7. ham pratidin gaṅgā meṁ nahāte the.
8. maiṁ pratyek śām ko apnī premikā se miltā thā.
9. mere pitā jī prāyaḥ saptāhānt par dūrdarśan dekhte the.
10. ham har garmī meṁ samudrataṭ par jāte the.

Glossary:

रहना (v.i.)	rahnā	to live
दौड़ना–कूदना (v.i.)	dauṛnā-kūdnā	to run and jump
प्रतिदिन (adv.)	pratidin	every day
प्रत्येक (adj.)	pratyek	every
प्रायः (adv.)	prāyaḥ	usually
प्रेमिका (f.)	premikā	beloved
समुद्रतट (m.)	samudrataṭ	beach

Ex. 2: Translate into Hindi: Use past habitual and present simple tense as required:

1. I used to play the guitar. Now I play the sitar.
2. We used to live in a big house. Now we live in a small house.
3. I used to go to work by car. These days I go on foot.
4. We used to live in Delhi. Now we live in Chandigarh.
5. Didn't they use to live in your neighborhood?
6. Didn't you use to wear glasses when you were a student?
7. Which languages did you use to speak when you were abroad?
8. Did you use to have long hair when you were a little girl?
9. I didn't use to like coffee at all; I drink it a lot these days.
10. I used to sleep very late. Now I go to bed very early.

Glossary:

to play (an instrument)	वाद्य बजाना (v.t.)	vādyă bajānā
by car	कार से (adv.)	kār se
on foot	पैदल (adv.)	paidal
neighborhood	पड़ोस (m.)	paṛos
to wear	पहनना (v.t.)	pahnanā
glasses	ऐनक (f.)	ainak
abroad	विदेश (m.)	videś
long hair	लम्बे बाल (adj.+ m.)	lambe bāl
late	देर से (adv.)	der se
early	जल्दी (adv.)	jaldī

Ex.3: Complete the sentences in the 'past habitual tense' using the verbs in parentheses and the appropriate past form of 'होना':

1. मैं (f.) रोज़ आठ घण्टे हिन्दी पढ़ती थी। (पढ़ना)
2. पक्षी (f.pl.) प्रातःकाल सामने पेड़ पर............................ (चहचहाना)
3. जनवरी में यहाँ प्रायः रोज़ बर्फ़ (f.) ....(पड़ना)
4. अध्यापक (m.) छात्रों को मिठाई .... (बाँटना)
5. इस सभागार में अकसर लोग भाषण (m.) ....(देना)
6. बच्चे (m.pl.) हर वक़्त शोर ....(मचाना)
7. प्रधानाचार्य हमें अकारण नहीं.......................................(डाँटना)
8. वह औरत (f.) बहुत तेज़ .... (भागना)
9. मैं (f.) चित्रकारी (f.) .... (सीखना)
10. वह (m.) बहुत अच्छा सितार.. (बजाना)

1. maiṁ (f.) roz āṭh ghaṇṭe hindī paṛhtī thī. (paṛhnā)
2. pakṣī (f.) prātaḥkāl sāmne peṛ par............................(cahcahānā)
3. janvarī meṁ yahāṁ prāyaḥ roz barf (f.) ....(paṛnā)
4. adhyāpak (m.pl.) chātroṁ ko miṭhāī ....(bāṁṭnā)
5. is sabhāgār meṁ aksar log bhāṣaṇ ....(denā)
6. bacce (m.pl.) har vaqt śor ....(macānā)
7. pradhānācāryă (m.hon.) hameṁ akāraṇ nahīṁ.....(ḍāṁṭnā)
8. vah aurat (f.) bahut tez .... (bhāgnā)
9. maiṁ (f.) citrakārī ....(sīkhnā)
10. vah (m.) bahut acchā *sitār* .... (bajānā)

Glossary:

पक्षी (m.pl.)	pakṣī	birds
प्रातःकाल (m/adv)	prātaḥkāl	early morning
चहचहाना (v.i)	cahcahānā	to chirp
बाँटना (v.t)	bāṁṭnā	to distribute
सभागार	sabhāgār	hall
भाषण (m.)	bhāṣaṇ	speech
प्रधानाचार्य	pradhānācāryă	principal
अकारण	akāraṇ	without reason
डाँटना (v.t)	ḍāṁṭnā	to scold
चित्रकारी (f.)	citrakārī	painting

Key 1

1. My brother used to work in a bank.
2. I used to live in Canada.
3. I used to learn English.
4. There used to be a shoe shop in this street.
5. My grand mother used to watch films all the time.
6. When we were younger, we used to run and jump all day.
7. We used to bathe in the Ganges every day.
8. I used to meet my beloved every evening.
9. My father used to watch television at the weakend.
10. Every summer we used to go to the beach.

Key 2

1. मैं (m.) पहले गिटार बजाती थी। अब मैं सितार बजाती हूँ।
2. पहले हम बड़े घर में रहते थे। अब हम छोटे घर में रहते हैं।
3. मैं (m.) कार से दफ़्तर जाता था। आजकल मैं पैदल जाता हूँ।
4. पहले हम दिल्ली में रहते थे। अब हम चंडीगढ़ में रहते हैं।
5. क्या वे तुम्हारे पड़ोस में नहीं रहते थे?
6. जब तुम (m.) छात्र थे, क्या तुम ऐनक नहीं पहनते थे?
7. जब तुम (f.) विदेश में थे, तुम कौन–कौन सी भाषाएँ बोलते थे?
8. जब तुम छोटी लड़की थीं, क्या तुम्हारे बाल (m.) लम्बे होते थे?
9. मैं (m.) कॉफ़ी बिलकुल पसन्द नहीं करता था। आजकल मैं बहुत पीता हूँ।
10. मैं (m.) बहुत देर से सोता था। अब मैं बहुत जल्दी सोता हूँ।

1. maiṁ (f.) pahle giṭār bajātī thī. ab maiṁ sitār bajātī hūṁ.
2. pahle ham baṛe ghar meṁ rahte the. ab ham choṭe ghar meṁ rahte haiṁ.

3. maiṁ (m.) 'kār' se daftar jātā thā. ājkal maiṁ paidal jātā hūṁ.
4. pahle ham dilli meṁ rahte the. ab ham candīgarh meṁ rahte haiṁ.
5. kyā ve (m.pl.) tumhāre paṛos meṁ nahīṁ rahte the?
6. jab tum (m.) chātra the, kyā tum ainak nahīṁ pahnte the?
7. jab tum (m.) videś meṁ the, tum kaun-kaun-sī bhāṣāeṁ bolte the?
8. jab tum choṭī laṛkī thīṁ, kyā tumhāre bāl (m.) lambe hote the?
9. maiṁ (m.) 'kaufī' bilkul pasand nahīṁ kartā thā; ājkal maiṁ bahut pītā hūṁ.
10. maiṁ bahut der se sotā thā. ab maiṁ bahut jaldī sotā hūṁ.

Key 3

2. चहचहाते थे।	3. पड़ती थी।	4. बाँटते थे।
5. देते थे।	6. मचाते थे।	7. डाँटते थे।
8. भागती थी।	9. सीखती थी।	10. बजाता था।
2. cahcahāte the.	3. paṛtī thī.	4. bāṁṭte the.
5. dete the.	6. macāte the	7. ḍāṁṭte the
8. bhāgtī thī	9. sīkhtī thī.	10. bajātā thā.

Colors रंग raṅg

white	सफ़ेद	safed
black	काला	kālā
yellow	पीला	pīlā
blue	नीला	nīlā
green	हरा	harā
brown	भूरा	bhūrā
red	लाल	lāl
maroon	लाल–भूरा	lāl-bhūrā
purple	बैंजनी	baiṁjnī
pink	गुलाबी	gulābī
grey	स्लेटी	saleṭī

To convey 'lighter' or 'darker' shade, use हल्का halkā or गाढ़ा / गहरा gāṛhā /gahrā before the color. For example

light blue	हल्का नीला	halkā nīlā
dark blue	गाढ़ा / गहरा नीला	gāṛhā /gahrā nīlā

6 Past SimpleTense

Present simple Tense : Intransitive Verb

subj. + v.r. +	ā / yā $^{m.sg}$,	e $^{m.pl.}$,	ī $^{f.sg/pl}$,
	आ / या $^{m.sg}$,	ए $^{m.pl}$,	ई $^{f.sg/pl}$,
	agree with N & G of the subj.		

1. बच्चा$^{m.sg.}$ सोया । — The child slept
   baccā soyā.
2. गाड़ी$^{f.sg..}$ नहीं आई । — The train did not come.
   gaṛī nahīṁ āī .

Past Simple Tense : Transitive Activity

subj. + obj. + v.r. +	ā / yā $^{m.sg}$,	e $^{m.pl.}$,	ī $^{f.sg/pl}$,
+ ने	आ / या $^{m.sg}$,	ए $^{m.pl}$,	ई $^{f.sg/pl}$,
	agree with N & G of the object		

1. उसने चावल$^{f.sg.}$ खाया — He/She ate rice.
   usne cāval khāyā.
2. हमने एक फ़िल्म देखी। — We watched a movie.
   hamne ek film dekhī .

☞ **In case of transitive verb, but object not explicitly stated, use m.sg past form of the form.**

1. हमने सुना। — hamne sunā. — We heard.
2. उन्होंने बताया। — unhoṁne batāyā . — They told.

(pronoun + ने 'ne') are written together .

मैंने	maiṁne	हमने	hamne
तूने	tūne	तुमने	tumne
		तुम लोगों ने	tum logoṁ ne
आपने	āpne	आप लोगों ने	āp logoṁ ne

उसने	usne	उन्होंने	unhoṁne
इसने	isne	इन्होंने	inhoṁne
किसने	kisne	किन्होंने	kinhoṁne

(noun + ने 'ne') are written separately:

आदमी ने ādmi ne, कमल ने kamal ne,

Irregular verbs in the Past simple, Present and Past Perfect tenses:				
जाना 'jānā'	गया gayā	गए gae	गई gaī	गई gaīṁ
होना 'honā'	हुआ huā	हुए hue	हुई huī	हुई huīṁ
करना karnā	किया kiyā	किए kie	की kī	कीं kīṁ
लेना (lenā)	लिया liyā	लिए lie	ली lī	लीं līṁ
देना (denā)	दिया diyā	दिए die	दी dī	दीं dīṁ

Ex. 1: Translate into English.

1. बाढ़ में कई लोग बेघर हो गए ।
2. उसकी टाँग टूट गई ।
3. हमने कल एक अच्छी फ़िल्म देखी ।
4. मैंने उसे सब सच्चाई बताई।
5. क्या तुमने पत्र डाल दिया?
6. मैंने फूल घर में रख दिए।
7. मुझे चोट लग गई ।
8. उसकी किताब फट गई ।
9. आज मैं डाकघर नहीं गई ।
10. अनिल की गाड़ी छूट गई।

1. bāṛh meṁ kaī log beghar ho gae .
2. uskī tāṁg ṭūṭ gaī.
3. hamne kal ek acchī film dekhī.
4. maiṁne use sab saccāī batāī.
5. kyā tumne patra ḍāl diyā?
6. maiṁne phūl ghar meṁ rakh die.
7. mujhe coṭ lag gaī.
8. uskī kitāb phaṭ gaī.
9. āj maiṁ ḍākghar nahīṁ gaī.
10. anil kī gāṛī chūṭ gaī.

Glossary

बाढ़ (f.)	bāṛh	flood
कई (adj.)	kaī	several
बेघर (adj.)	beghar	homeless

टाँग (f.)	tāṁg	leg
टूटना (v.i.)	ṭūṭnā	to break
सच्चाई (f.)	saccāī	truth
बताना (v.t.)	batānā	to tell
रखना (v.t.)	rakhnā	to put
पत्र डालना (v.t.)	patra ḍālnā	to post a letter
फूल (m.)	phūl	flower
सारा (adj.)	sārā	entire
चोट लगना (v.i.)	coṭ lagnā	to get injured
फटना (v.i.)	phaṭnā	to tear
फट जाना (comp. v.i.)	phaṭ jānā	to tear
डाकघर (m.)	ḍākghar	post office
गाड़ी छूट जाना (v.i.)	gāṛī chūṭ jānā	to miss the train

Ex. 2: Translate into Hindi:

1. He collided with somebody. ....
2. Who did he collide with? ....
3. Something fell off the wall. ....
4. What fell off the wall? ....
5. She whispered something in my ear ....
6. What did she whisper in your ear? ....
7. Somebody hit me in the head with a stick..
8. Who hit you in the head with a stick? ....

Glossary:

to collided with	के साथ भिड़ना (v.i.)	ke sāth bhiṛnā
somebody	कोई (indef. pron.)	koī
with somebody	किसीके साथ	kisī ke sāth
something	कुछ, कोई चीज़	kuch, koī cīz
ear	कान	kān
fall	गिरना (v.i.)	girnā
whisper	फुसफुसाना (v.i.)	phusphusānā
to hit	मारना (v.t.)	mārnā
stick	लाठी (f.)	lāṭhī
head	सिर (m.)	sir

comp. verb = compound verb see pg. 197

Ex.3: Complete the sentences given below in simple past tense using the intransitive verbs given in parentheses :

1. निर्मला दस बजे **सोई** । . (सोना)।
2. हम (m.) जल्दी .... (सोना)।
3. पिता जी कैसे .... (आना)?
4. विनिल कल अपराह्न में .... (लौटना)।
5. आज मूसलाधार बारिश .. .. (होना)।
6. भीड़ (f.) इधर–उधर .... (दौड़ना)।
7. उड़ान (f.) समय से नहीं .... (पहुँचना)।
8. आप लोग (m.pl.) कितने बजे .... (उठना) ?
9. वह (f.) सपरिवार दावत में .... (आना) ।
10. वह (f.) कुछ नहीं .... (बोलना)।

1. nirmala das baje **soī.** .... (sonā)
2. ham (m.) jaldī .... (sonā).
3. pitā jī kaise .... (ānā)?
4. vinil kal aprāhn meṁ .... (lauṭnā).
5. āj mūslādhār bāriś (f.).. ...... (honā).
6. bhīṛ (f.) idhar-udhar.. ...... (dauṛnā).
7. uṛān (f.) samay se nahīṁ. .... (pahuṁcnā).
8. āp log (m.pl.) kitne baje.. (uṭhnā)?
9. vah (f.) saparivār dāvat meṁ .... (ānā)
10. vah (f.) kuch nahīṁ... .... (bolnā).

Glossary:

सोना (v.i.)	sonā	to sleep
दस बजे (adv.)	das baje	at ten o'clock
भीड़ (f.)	bhīṛ	crowd
इधर–उधर (adv.)	idhar-udhar	here and there
समय से (adv.)	samay se	in time
कितने बजे (adv.)	kitne baje	at what time
सपरिवार (adj.)	saparivār	with family
दावत (f.)	dāvat	party
कुछ नहीं (neg. indef. pron.)	kuch nahīṁ	nothing
बोलना (v.i./v.t.)	bolnā	to speak
लौटना (v.i)	lauṭnā	to return

Ex.4: Complete the sentences given below in simple past tense using the transitive verbs given in parentheses :

1. मैंने पिता जी को पत्र (m.) **लिखा**। (लिखना) ।
2. तुमने आज का समाचार–पत्र (m.) .... (पढना) ?
3. मैंने आज एक घड़ी (f.)...................................(खरीदना) ।
4. उन्होंने हाल में अपनी पुरानी 'कार' (f.)..............(बेचना) ।
5. उसने नया वस्त्र (m.).... .... (पहनना) ।
6. चाचा ने मुझको नई पोशाक (f.)...........................(दिलाना) ।
7. किसने आपको.. (बुलाना)।
8. आपने जलपान (m.) ....(करना)?
9. बच्चे ने दवाई (f.) नहीं...(खाना)।
10. हमने पेड़ से आम (m.pl.) ....(तोड़ना)।

1. maiṁne pitā jī ko patra (m.) likhā. (likhnā).
2. tumne āj kā samācār patra (m.)...................... (paṛhnā)?
3. maiṁne āj ek ghaṛī (f.)....................................(kharīdnā).
4. unhoṁne hāl meṁ apnī purānī 'kār' (f.)..........(becnā).
5. usne nayā vastra (m.)..(pahananā).
6. cācā ne mujhko naī pośāk (f.)..........................(dilānā) .
7. kisne āpko...(bulānā).
8. āpne jalpān (m.) ....(karnā)?
9. bacce ne davāī (f.) nahīṁ................................ (khānā) .
10. hamne peṛ se ām (m.pl.) .... (toṛnā).

Glossary

समाचार पत्र (m.)	samācār patra	newspaper
हाल में (adv.)	hāl meṁ	recently
पुराना, –ए, –ई (adj.)	puranā, -e, -ī	old
नया,–ए, –ई (adj.)	nayā, -e, -i	new
वस्त्र (m.)	vastra	piece of clothing
पोशाक (f.).	pośāk	dress
चाचा (m.).	bhaiyā	brother
जलपान (m.)	jalpān	snacks
तोड़ना (v.t.)	toṛnā	to pluck/pick

Key 1

1. Many people became homeless in the floods.
2. He broke his leg.
3. We watched a good movie yesterday.
4. I told him the entire truth.
5. Did you mail the letter?
6. I kept the flowers in the house.
7. I got injured.
8. Her book got torn.
9. I did not go to the post office today.
10. Anil missed the train.

Key 2

1.	वह किसी के साथ भिड़ गया।	2.	वह किसके साथ भिड़ गया?
3.	कोई चीज़ दीवाऱ से नीचे गिरी।	4.	दीवाऱ से क्या गिरा?
5.	उसने मेरे कान मे कुछ फुसफुसाया।	6.	उसने आपके कान मे क्या फुसफुसाया।?
7.	किसीने मेरे सिर पर लाठी मारी।	8.	किसने आपके सिर पर लाठी मारी?
1.	vah kisī ke sāth bhiṛ gayā.	2.	vah kiske sāth bhiṛ gayā?
3.	koī cīz dīvār se nīce girī.	4.	dīvār se kyā girā ?
5.	usne mere kān meṁ kuch phusphusāyā .	6.	usne āpke kān meṁ kyā phusphusāyā ?
7.	kisīne mere sir par lāṭhī mārī.	8.	kisne āpke sir par lāṭhī mārī?

Key 3

2. ... सोए।	3. ... आए।	4. ... लौटा।
5. .... हुई।	6. ... दौड़ी।	7. ...पहुँची।
8. ... उठे?	9. .... आई।	10. ... बोली।
2. ... soe	3. āe	4. lauṭā
5. ... huī	6. dauṛī	7. pahuṁcī
8. ... uṭhe?	9. āī	10. bolī

Key 4

2. पढ़ा।	3. खरीदी।	4. बेची।
5. पहना।	6. दिलाई।	7. बुलाया।

8. किया? 9. खाई। 10. तोड़े।

2. paṛhā. 3. kharīdī. 4. becī.
5. pahnā. 6. dilāī. 7. bulāyā
8. kiyā? 9. khāī. 10. toṛe.

Use of question words in Hindi

कौन	kaun	who	क्यों	kyoṁ	why
कब	kab	when	कैसे	kaise	how
क्या	kyā	what	कहाँ	kahāṁ	where.

☞ In **Hindi normally the question words do not come at the begin ning of th e sentence. For example:**

वहाँ कौन है?	vahāṁ kaun hai?	Who is there?
वह कब आएगा?	vah kab āegā?	When will he come?
यह कैसे होगा?	yah kaise hogā?	How will this happen?

Exception क्या kyā :

☞ It comes at the beginning of the sentence if the answer to the question is 'yes 'or 'no'.

क्या यह सेब है? kyā yah seb hai? Is this an apple?

☞ **It comes later in the sentence if the answer to the question is some object.**

यह क्या है? yah kyā hai? What is this?

7 Present and Past Perfect Tenses

Present Perfect Tense* : Intransitive Verb*

subj. + v.r. + ā / yā m.sg, e m.pl., ī f.sg/pl, + hūṁ, ho, hai, haiṁ
आ / या m.sg, ए m.pl, ई f.sg/pl, + हूँ, हो, है, हैं
agree with N & G of the subj.

*** Past perfect tense sentence construction are the same as Present Perfect Tens . Insted of** हूँ, हो, है, हैं hūṁ, ho, hai, haiṁ **use** था, थे, थी, थीं thā, the, thī, thīṁ

1. बच्चा m.sg. बहुत सोया है। — The child has slept a lot.
   baccā bahut soyā hai.
2. धोबी m.sg.. अभी–अभी आया है । — The washertman has come just now.
   dhobī abhī-abhī āyā hai.
3. औरत m.sg. क्यों रोई थी? — Why had the woman cried?
   aurat kyoṁ roī thī?
4. आप दिल्ली से क्या लाए# थे? — What had you brought from Delhi?
   āp dillī se kyā lāe the.

Present Perfect Tense* : Transitive Activity

subj. + obj. + v.r. + ā / yā m.sg, e m.pl., ī f.sg/pl, + hai, haiṁ
\+ ने आ / या m.sg, ए m.pl, ई f.sg/pl, + है, हैं
agree with N & G of the object

1. उसने चावल f.sg. खाया है। — He/She has eaten rice.
   usne cāval khāyā hai.
2. हमने एक फ़िल्म देखी है। — We have watched a movie.
   hamne ek film dekhī hai.

#लाना v.t.is used intransitively in the past simple and perfective tenses.

3. उसने हमें मिठाई f.sg दी थी। He/She had given us sweets.
usne hameṁ miṭhāī dī thī.

4. हमने किताबें f.pl. खरीदी थीं। We had bought books.
hamne kitābeṁ kharīdī thīṁ.

☞ **In case of transitive verb, but object not explicitly stated, use m.sg. past form of the verb.**

1. हमने सुना है। hamne sunā hai. We have heard.
2. उन्होंने कहा है। unhoṁne kahā hai. They have said.
3. हमने सुना था। hamne sunā thā. We had heard.
4. उन्होंने कहा था। unhoṁne kahā thā. They had said.

Ex. 1: Translate into English:

1. तुम लोगों ने ठीक सुना है।
2. उसने सब काम ठीक से किया है।
3. क्या आपने उनको सच बताया है?
4. आज आपने हमारे लिए क्या पकाया है?
5. मैंने ये पुस्तकें पुस्तकालय से ली हैं।
6. उसने सारी रात यह उपन्यास पढ़ा था।
7. उन्होंने कई साल भारतीय संगीत सीखा था।
8. मैंने पैसे अलमारी में रखे थे।
9. वे अमरीका आने से पहले दस साल भारत में रहे थे।
10. खिड़कियाँ किसने खोली थीं?

1. tum logoṁ ne ṭhīk sunā hai.
2. usne sab kām ṭhīk se kiyā hai.
3. kyā āpne unko sac batāyā hai?
4. āj āpne hamāre lie kyā pakāyā hai?
5. maiṁne ye pustakeṁ putakālay se lī haiṁ.
6. usne sārī rāt yah upanyās paṛhā thā.
7. unhoṁne kaī sāl bhārtīyă saṅgīt sīkhā thā.
8. maiṁne paise almārī meṁ rakhe the.
9. ve amrīkā āne se pahle das sāl bhārat meṁ rahe the.
10. khiṛkiyāṁ kisne kholī thīṁ?

Glossary

ठीक (adj.)	ṭhīk	correct
ठीक से (adv.)	ṭhīk se	properly
सच (m.)	sac	truth
बताना (v.t.)	batānā	to tell
पुस्तकालय (m.)	pustakālay	library
उपन्यास (m.)	upanyās	novel
भारतीय (adj.)	bhārtīyă	Indian
संगीत (m.)	saṅgīt	music
कई साल (adj. + m.)	kaī sāl	many years
सीखना (v.t.)	sīkhnā	to learn

Ex. 2: Translate into Hindi:

1. The film has just started.
2. I have just mailed the letter.
3. They have just paid the rent.
4. The thief had fled before the police arrived.
5. They soon realised that they had made a big mistake.
6. The city had changed a lot in my absence.
7. The concert had begun long before they arrived.
8. Someone had broken into their house at midnight.

Glossary:

just	अभी–अभी (adv.)	abhī-abhī
to start	शुरू होना (v.i.)	śurū honā
mail a letter	पत्र डालना (v.t.)	patra ḍālnā
rent	किराया (m.)	kirāyā
pay rent	किराया देना (v.t.)	kirāyā denā
flee	भाग जाना (v.i.)	bhāg jānā
realise	एहसास होना (v.i.)	ehsās honā
mistake	ग़लती (f.)	Galtī
city	शहर (m.)	śahar
change	बदलना (v.t.)	badalnā
absence	अनुपस्थिति (f.)	anupasthiti
break into	जबरन घुसना (v.i.)	jabran ghusna
midnight	आधी रात (f.)	ādhī rāt

Ex.3: Complete the sentences given below using the verbs in parentheses in the present /past perfect tense :

1. मौसम (m.) बदल **गया है।** .... (जाना)
2. डाकिया (m.) ....(आना)
3. दही (m.)...(जमना)
4. बिजली (f.).. (चला जाना)
5. रोगी (m.) ठीक.. (होना)
6. मैंने पिछले साल धनुर्विद्या (f.) सीखी थी।..............................(सीखना)।
7. श्री कपूर परसों सुबह हमारे यहाँ .... (आना)।
8. उन्होंने थोड़ी देर पहले यह ख़बर (f.) .... (भेजना)।
9. पेशी से पहले अपराधी (m.) हिरासत से ....(भागना)।
10. हम (m.) सन् १९८०(उन्नीस सौ अस्सी) में जापान .... (जाना)।

1. mausam badal gayā hai. (jānā)
2. ḍākiyā (m.)-- (ānā)
3. dahī (m.)---(jamnā)
4. bijlī (f.)-- (calā jānā)
5. rogī (m.) ṭhīk---(honā)
6. maiṁne pichle sāl (f.) dhanurvidyā **sīkhī thī.**...............(sīkhnā)
7. śrī kapūr parsoṁ subah hamāre yahāṁ............................(ānā)
8. unhoṁne thoṛī der pahle yah <u>kh</u>abar (f.) .... (bhejnā)
9. peśī se pahle aprādhī (m.) hirāsat se............................. (bhāgnā)
10. ham (m.pl.) san 1980 (unnies sau assī) meṁ 'jāpān'..... (jānā)

Glossary:

बदलना (v.i.)	badalnā	to change
दही जमना (v.i.)	dahī jamnā	yogurt to set
बिजली (f.)	bijlī	electricity
चला जाना (v.i.)	calā jānā	to go away
रोगी (m.)	rogī	patient
थोड़ी देर पहले (adv.)	thoṛī der pahle	a short while ago
धनुर्विद्या (f.)	dhanurvidyā	archery

ख़बर (f.)	<u>kh</u>abar	news
पेशी (f.)	peśī	appearance in the court
अपराधी (f.)	aprādhī	criminal
हिरासत (f.)	hirāsat	custody

Key 1

1. You have heard correct.
2. He / She has done everything properly.
3. Have you told them the truth?
4. What have you cooked for us today?
5. I have taken these books from the library.
6. He/ She had read this novel all night.
7. They had learnt Indian music for several years.
8. I had kept the money in the cupboard.
9. They had lived in India for ten years before coming to America.
10. Who had opened the windows?

Key 2

1. फ़िल्म अभी–अभी शुरू हुई है।
2. मैंने अभी–अभी पत्र डाला है।
3. उन्होंने अभी–अभी किराया दिया है।
4. पुलिस के पहुँचने से पहले चोर भाग गया था।
5. उन्हें जल्दी एहसास हो गया कि उन्होंने बहुत बड़ी ग़लती की थी।
6. मेरी अनुपस्थिति में शहर बहुत बदल गया था।
7. उनके पहुँचने से बहुत पहले गोष्ठी शुरू हो चुकी थी।
8. कोई उनके घर में आधी रात को जबरन घुस गया था।

1. film abhī-abhī śurū huī hai.
2. maiṁne abhī-abhī patra ḍālā hai.
3. unhoṁne abhī-abhī kirāyā diyā hai .
4. pulis ke pahuṁcne se pahle cor bhāg gayā thā.
5. unheṁ jaldī ehsās ho gayā ki unhoṁne bahut baṛī Galatī kī thī.
6. merī anupasthiti meṁ śahar bahut badal gayā thā.
7. unke pahuṁcne se bahut pahle goṣṭhī śurū ho cukī thī.
8. koī unke ghar meṁ ādhī rāt ko jabran ghus gayā thā.

In perfective tenses, hindi uses compound verbs for some special nuance such as completion of action, change of state, rashness or suddenness of an activity etc
Ref. Compound Verbs pg. 197

Key 3

2. आ गया है।
3. जम गया है।
4. चली गई है।
5. हो गया है।
7. आए थे।
8. भेजी थी।
9. भाग गया था।
10. गए थे।

2. ā gayā hai.
3. jam gayā hai.
4. calī gaī hai.
5. ho gayā hai.
7. āe the.
8. bhejī thī.
9. bhāg gayā thā.
10. gae the.

किसी + --- (Indefinite pronoun); किस + --- (Interrogative)

1. मैं किसी चीज़ को देख रही हूँ।
2. आप किस चीज़ को देख रही हैं?
3. वे किसी चीज़ के बारे में बात कर रहे थे।
4. वे किसी चीज़ के बारे में बात कर रहे थे?
5. मैंने विश्वा को किन्हीं लोगों के साथ जाते हुए देखा।
6. आपने विश्वा को किन लोगों के साथ जाते हुए देखा?
7. हमने उनको किसीसे बात करते हुए सुना।
8. आपने किनको किससे बात करते हुए सुना?

1. maiṁ kisī cīz ko dekh rahī huṁ.
2. āp kis cīz ko dekh rahī haiṁ?
3. ve kisī cīz ke bāre meṁ bāt kar rahe the.
4. ve kis cīz ke bāre meṁ bāt kar rahe the?
5. maiṁne viśvā ko kinhīṁ logoṁ ke sāth jāte hue dekhā.
6. āpne viśvā ko kin logoṁ ke sāth jāte hue dekhā?
7. hamne unko kisīse bāt karte hue sunā.
8. āpne kinko kisse bāt karte hue sunā?

1. I am looking at something.
2. What are you looking at?
3. They were talking about something.
4. What were they talking about?
5. I saw Vishva going with some people.
6. With whom (pl.) did you see Vishva going?
7. We heard them talking with somebody.
8. Whom (pl.) did you hear talking with whom?

8 Present and Past simple progressive tenses

Present simple progressive*

subj. + obj. + v.r.+ rahā $^{m.sg.}$, rahe $^{m.pl.}$, rahī $^{f.sg/pl}$ + hūṁ, ho, hai, haiṁ
रहा $^{m.sg}$, रहे $^{m.pl}$, रही $^{f.sg/pl}$, + हूँ, हो, है, हैं
to agree with N & G of the subj.

☞ Past simple progressive sentence construction is exactly like the Present simple progressive. Use था, थे थी, थीं thā, the, thī, thīṁ.instead of हूँ, हो, है, हैं hūṁ, ho, hai, haiṁ

☞ In Hindi present /past simple as well as perfect progressive sentence construction is exactly the same. Whether it is period of time or point of time, the time clause is followed by 'से se'.

1. करीना किताब **ख़रीद रही** है।
karīnā kitāb kharīd rahī hai.
Karina is buying a book.

2. बच्चे (m.pl.) घर के सामने मैदान में खेल रहे हैं।
bacce (mpl.) ghar ke sāmne maidān meṁ khel rahe haiṁ.
The children are playing in the field in front of the house.

3. अध्यापक (m.sg.) छात्रों को पाठ पढ़ा रहा था।
adhyāpak chātroṁ ko pāṭh paṛhā rahā thā.
The teacher was teaching the lesson to the students.

4. छात्र (m.pl.) अध्यापक से प्रश्न पूछ रहे थे।
chātra adhyāpak se praśna pūch rahe the.
The students were asking the teacher questions

Ex. 1: Translate into English

1. ताज एक्सप्रैस प्लेटफ़ारम की ओर आ रही है। 2. बहुत–से यात्री प्लेटफ़ारम पर खड़े हैं। 3. वे वहाँ गाड़ी पर चढ़ने का इन्तज़ार कर रहे हैं। 4. उनमें से अधिकांश भारतीय है, परन्तु कुछ विदेशी हैं। 5. गाड़ी स्टेशन पर पहुँच गई है। 6. विदेशी यात्री गाड़ी पर चढ़ रहे हैं। 7. भारतीय यात्री कुलियों को बुला रहे हैं। 8. वे उनसे मोलभाव कर रहे हैं।

1. tāj eksprais pleṭfāram kī or ā rahī hai. 2. bahut se yātrī pleṭfāram par khaṛe haiṁ. 3. ve vahāṁ gāṛī par caṛhne kā intzār kar rahe haiṁ. 4. un meṁ se adhikāṁś bhārtīyă haiṁ, parantu kuch videśī bhī haiṁ. 5. gāṛī sṭeśan par pahuṁc gaī hai. 6. videśī yātrī gāṛī par caṛh rahe haiṁ. 7. bhārtīyă yātrī kuliyoṁ ko bulā rahe haiṁ. 8. ve unse molbhāv kar rahe haiṁ.

Glossary:

ताज ऐक्सप्रैस (PN.)	tāj eksprais	Taj Express
प्लेटफ़ारम (m.)	pleṭfāram	platform
बुलाना (v.t.)	bulānā	to call
मोलभाव (m.)	molbhāv	bargaining
मोलभाव करना (v.t.)	molbhāv karnā	to bargain
यात्री (m.)	yātrī	passenger
खड़ा होना (v.i.)	khaṛā honā	to stand
गाड़ी पर चढ़ना (v.i.)	gāṛī par caṛhnā	to get on the train
X का इन्तज़ार करना (v.t.)	X kā intzār karnā	to wait for X
अधिकांश (adj./adv.)	adhikāṃś	mostly, larger part
भारतीय (n./adj.)	bhārtīyă	Indian(s)
परन्तु (conj.)	parantu	but
कुछ (adj.)	kuch	some
विदेशी (n./adj.)	videśī	foreigners

Ex. 2: Complete the sentences given below using the verbs in parentheses in the present/past simple continuous form :

1. शत्रुघन (PN m.) समाचारपत्र पढ़ रहा है। (पढ़ना)
2. बच्चा (m.sg.) अध्यापक को ध्यान से.................................(सुनना)

3. अनन्या (f.) कुछ ....(लिखना)
4. छात्र (m.pl.) गर्मी की छुट्टियों में कहाँ...............................?(जाना)
5. आज हमारे घर के पास संगीत गोष्ठी (f.) ....(होना)
6. रात भर शिमला में बहुत बर्फ़ (f.) पड़ रही थी। (पड़ना)
7. पिछले हफ़्ते हमारे शहर में बहुत बारिश (f.) ....(होना)
8. क्या आप की घड़ी (f.) ठीक..................................... ? (चलना)
9. पक्षी (m.pl.) आकाश में.. ....(उड़ना)
10. कल रात को गरज चमक के साथ आँधी (f.) ....(आना)

1. śatrughan (m.) samācār patra **paṛh rahā hai.** (paṛhnā).
2. baccā (m.sg.) adhyāpak ko dhyān se...................... (sunanā).
3. ananyā kuch.. (likhnā).
4. chātra (m.pl) garmī kī chuṭṭiyoṁ meṁ kahāṁ.... ....(jānā).
5. āj hamāre ghar ke pās sangīt goṣṭhī (f.)..........................(honā).
6. rāt bhar śimlā meṁ bahut barf (f.)**paṛ rahī thī.** ....(paṛnā).
7. pichle hafte hamāre śahar meṁ bahut bāriś..................(honā).
8. kyā āp kī ghaṛī (f.) ṭhīk...?(calnā).
9. pakṣī ākaś meṁ...(uṛnā).
10. kal rāt ko garaj camak ke sāth āṁdhī .(f.).......................(ānā).

Ex. 3: Translate into Hindi: Present simple continuous :

1. What are they doing ?
2. Where are they going?
3. Why are you guys laughing ?
4. What are they looking at?
5. Who are they calling ?
6. Where were those boys going ?
7. Was it snowing ?
8. Was it raining ?
9. Was the maid turning the lights off?
10. Who was ringing the doorbell?

Key 1

1. The Taj Express is moving towards the platform.
2. Many passengers are standing on the platform.
3. They are waiting there to board the train.
4. Most of them are Indians but some of them are foreigners.
5. The train has arrived at the platform.
6. Foreign travelers are getting on the train.
7. Indian travelers are calling the porters.
8. They are bargaining with them.

Key 2

2. सुन रहा है। 3. लिख रही है। 4. जा रहे हैं?
5. हो रही है। 7. हो रही थी। 8. चल रही थी?
9. उड़ रहे थे। 10. आ रही थी।

2. sun rahā hai. 3. likh rahī hai. 4. jā rahe haiṁ?
5. ho rahī hai. 7. ho rahī thī. 8. cal rahī thī?
9. uṛ rahe the. 10. ā rahī thī.

Key 3

1. वे क्या कर रहे/रही हैं?
2. वे कहाँ जा रहे/रही हैं?
3. आप लोग क्यों हँस रहे/रही हैं?
4. वे किस चीज को देख रहे/रही हैं?
5. वे किसको बुला रहे/रही हैं?
6. वे लड़के कहाँ जा रहे थे?
7. क्या बर्फ़ पड़ रही थी?
8. क्या बारिश पड़ रही थी?
9. क्या नौकरानी बत्तियाँ बुझा रही थी?
10. कौन द्वार पर घण्टी बजा रहा था?

1. ve kyā kar rahe/rahī haiṁ?
2. ve kahāṁ jā rahe/rahī haiṁ?
3. āp log kyoṁ haṁs rahe/rahī haiṁ?
4. ve kis cīz ko dekh rahe/rahī haiṁ?
5. ve kis ko bulā rahe/rahī haiṁ?
6. ve laṛke kahāṁ jā rahe the?
7. kyā barf paṛ rahī thī?
8. kyā bāriś paṛ rahī thī?
9. kyā naukrānī battiyāṁ bujhā rahī thī?
10. kaun dvār par ghaṇṭī bajā rahā thā?

9 Future Tense

Future Simple

subject +	obj. +	(v.r. + future endings)
मैं maiṁ		ऊँगा m.sg, ऊँगी f.sg/pl, ūṁgā m.sg, ūṁg ī m.pl
तुम tum	....	ओगे m.pl ओगी f.pl, oge, og ī,
वह, यह vah, yah		ऐगा m.sg. एगी f.sg., egā, eg ī,
वे, ये हम, आप ve, ye,ham ap		एंगे m.pl ऐंगी f.pl, eṁge m.pl, eṁgī f.sg/
		agree with N & G of the subj.

1. मैं अगले साल बीस साल का हूँगा/होऊँगा
   maiṁ[m] agle sāl bīs sāl kā hūṁgā/hoūṁgā .
   I will be twenty next year.
2. कल से दुकानें सुबह सात बजे खुलेंगी।
   kal se dukāneṁ[f.pl] subah sāt baje khuleṁgī
   From tomorrow the shops will open at 7 a.m.
3. मैं सन्दीप को अगले हफ़्ते मिलूँगी।
   maiṁ[m] sandīp ko agle hafte milūṁgī.
   I will meet Sandip next week.
4. हम कल अपने देश लौटेंगे।
   ham[m] kal apne deś lauṭeṁge.
   We shall return to our country tomorrow.

Ex.1: Translate into English:

1. लगता है इस साल वर्षा बिलकुल नहीं होगी। 2. इस बार होली कौन–से महीने में होगी? 3. क्या तुम बड़े होकर विदेश यात्रा करोगे? 4. मैं अभावग्रस्त औरतों के लिए एक आश्रम बनाऊँगा। 5. आज हम सब बाहर घूमने जाएँगे। 6. मैं सोचता हूँ कल से मैं सुबह जल्दी उठूँगा। 7. हम बैंक से कर्ज़ लेंगे। 8. वह जुआ खेलना कभी नहीं छोड़ेगा। 9. मेरा भाई अगले साल अवश्य शादी करेगा। 10. आप क्या लेंगे, चाय या कॉफ़ी?

1. lagtā hai is sāl varṣā[f.sg] bilkul nahīṁ hogī 2. is bār holī kaun se mahīne meṁ hogī? 3. kyā tum[m] baṛe hokar videś yātrā karoge? 4. maiṁ[m] abhāvgrast aurtoṁ ke lie ek āśram banāūṁgā. 5. āj ham sab bāhar ghūmne jāeṁge. 6. maiṁ soctā hūṁ kal se maiṁ[m] subah jaldī uṭhūṁgā. 7. ham[m/m+f] 'baiṅk' se karz leṁge. 8. vah[m] juā khelnā kabhī nahīṁ choṛegā? 9. merā bhāī[m] agle sāl avaśyă śādī karegā. 10. āp[m] kyā leṁge, cāy yā kaufī?

Glossary:

अगला,–ले,–ली (adj.)	aglā, -e, -ī	next
साल (m.)	sāl	year
इस साल	is sāl	this year
वर्षा (f.)	varṣā[f.sg]	rains
बिलकुल नहीं	bilkul nahīṁ	absolutely not
होली (f..)	holi	Holi*
सात बजे	sāt baje	at 7 o'clock
खुलना (v.i.)	khulnā	to open
कौन–से महीने में	kaun se mahīne meṁ	in which month
बड़ा होकर	baṛā hokar	here: when one grows up
विदेश (m.)	videś	foreign country
यात्रा करना (v.tj.)	yātrā karnā	to travel
अभावग्रस्त (adj.)	abhāvgrast	needy
आश्रम (m.)	āśram	hermitage
घूमने जाना (v.i.)	ghūmne jānā	go leisure wandering

* Holi=Hindu festival held on full moon of the 12th month of the Hindu calendar called Phalgun

मैं सोचता हूँ	maiṁ socta hūṁ	in my opinion
जुआ खेलना (v.t.)	juā khelnā	to gamble
छोड़ना (v.t.)	choṛnā	to stop
कर्ज़ (m.)	karz	debt
अवश्य (adv.)	avaśyă	certainly
शादी (f.)	śādī	marriage

Ex. 2: Translate into Hindi

1. They[m/m+f] will come next week.
2. I[m] will always help you.
3. Where will they[m.formal] go during winter?
4. My sister will be angry with me.
5. I[f.] will shop all day today.
6. From now on, I[m] will exercise every day.
7. She will study in India for three years.
8. Next year she will live in the students' hostel.
9. Vehan will always work hard.
10. Will you become a doctor?

Ex.3: Complete the sentences given below usingthe verbs given in parentheses in the simple future tense:

1. मैं (f.) परसों नौका विहार **करूँगी।** (करना)
2. संगोष्ठी (f.) अगले हफ़्ते .... । (होना)
3. विवाह में कौन–कौन .... ? (आना)
4. क्या वे (f.) कल यहाँ .... ? (होना)
5. श्री तरोष जापान से कब .... ? (लौटना)
6. गौरी और नीना अगले साल महाविद्यालय में .... । (पढ़ना)
7. धोबी (m.) परसों कपड़े .... । (लाना)
8. आप (f.) शाम को कौन–सी फ़िल्म ....? (देखना)
9. क्या वे लोग (m) पैदल ....? (आना)
10. जी नहीं, वे (m) बस से .... । (आना)

1. maiṁ (f.) parsoṁ naukā vihār **karūṁgī.** (karnā).

2. saṅgoṣṭhī (f.) agle hafte .... (honā).
3. vivāh meṁ kaun- kaun............................ (ānā)?
4. kyā ve kal yahāṁ .... (honā)?
5. śrī taroṣ jāpān se kab .... (lauṭnā)?
6. gaurī aur n**ī**nā agle sāl mahāvidyālay meṁ......... (paṛhnā)
7. dhobī parsoṁ kapṛe .... (lānā)
8. āp (f.) śām ko kaun sī film .... (dekhnā)?
9. kyā ve log (m.) paidal .... (ānā)?
10. jī nahīṁ, ve (m.) 'bas' se .... (ānā)

Ex. 4: Write answers as shown in the given example :

> क्या तुम हमारे साथ भारत चलोगी?
> ⇨ जी हाँ, मैं चलूँगी। /
> ⇨ जी नहीं, मैं नहीं चलूँगी।

1. क्या तुम (f.) मुझे पत्र लिखोगी? ....
2. क्या आप (m.) ये वाले जूते खरीदेंगे? ....
3. क्या आप (f.) आज शाम को मेरे घर आएँगी? ....
....
4. क्या तुम (m.) मेरे साथ शतरंज खेलोगे? ....
5. क्या आप लोग कचौरी–जलेबी खाने चलेंगे? ....

> kyā tum(f.) hamāre sāth bhārat calogī?
> ⇨ jī hāṁ, maiṁ āpke sāth bhārat calūṁgī.
> ⇨ jī nahīṁ, maiṁ āpke sāth bhārat nahīṁ calūṁgī.

1. kyā tum (f.) mujhe patra likhogī?
2. kyā āp(m.) ye vāle jūte kharīdeṁge?
3. kyā āp (f.) āj śām ko mere ghar āeṁgī?
4. kyā tum (m.) mere sāth śatrañj khel**oge**?
5. kyā āp log kacaurī-jalebī khāne caleṁge?

kacaurī = a snack; jalebī= a syrupy sweet

Planned future

subj. +	obj. +	(v.r. + ne ने) +	kī soc की सोच	+ rahā रहा rahe रहे rahī रही	+	hona होना
* also possible :		(v.r. + ne ने) +	kī yojnā banā की योजना बना	+ rahā रहा rahe रहे rahī रही	+	hona होना

1. मैं अगले महीने मुम्बई जाने की सोच (/योजना बना) रही हूँ।
   maiṁ agle mahīne mumbaī jāne kī soc (/yojnā banā) rahī hūṁ.
   I am thinking of going/ planning to go to Mumbai next week.
2. पिता जी नया घर ख़रीदने की सोच (/योजना बना) रहे हैं।
   pitā jī nayā ghar <u>kh</u>arīdne kī soc (/yojnā banā) rahe haiṁ.
   Father is thinking of buying / planning to buy a new house.

Progressive future

future time clause	+ subj. +	obj. +	v.r. +	रहा rahā रहे rahe / रही rahī)* agree with the N & G of the subj.	+	future form of होना honā

1. कल इस समय हम 'फुटबॉल 'खेल रहे होंगे।
   kal is samay ham 'fuṭbaul 'khel rahe hoṁge.
   Tomorrow at this time we will be playing football.
2. परसों इस समय आप यात्रा कर रहे होंगे।
   parsoṁ is samay āp yātrā kar rahe hoṁge.
   The day after tomorrow, you will be traveling at this time.

Future perfect

subj. + obj. + (v.r. +आ ā / ए e/ ई ī)* + future form of होना honā

* In case of compound verb, use (root of the main verb) + (root of final verb + आ ā / ए e/ ई ī) + future form of होना honā
* In case verb intransitive, it agrees with the N and G of the subject.
* In case verb transitive, it agrees with the N and G of the object.

1. माँ कल १० बजे तक दिल्ली पहुँच चुकी होंगी।
   māṁ kal das baje tak dillī pahuṁc cukī hoṁgī.
   Mother will have arrived in Delhi by 10 o'clock tomorrow.
2. जब तक आप न्यूयार्क आएँगे, बर्फ़ (f.) पड़नी बन्द हो चुकी होगी।
   jab tak āp 'new york' āeṁge, barf (f.)paṛnī band ho cukī hogī.
   By the time you come to New York, it will have stopped snowing.

Future perfect continuous:

time clause + subj. को ko + obj. + (v.r. +ते te हुए hue) + .time period + हो ho + fut. form of जाना jānā (to agree with N & G of the time period

1. अगले साल उसे हिन्दी सीखते हुए एक वर्ष (sg.) हो जाएगा।
   agle sāl use hindī sīkhte hue ek sāl (sg.)ho jāegā.
   She will have been learning Hindi for one year by next year.
2. मई के अन्त तक इस 'थिएटर' को बनते हुए पाँच वर्ष (pl.) हो जाएँगे।
   maī ke ant tak is 'thieṭar' ko bante hue pāṁc varṣ (pl.) ho jāeṁge.
   This theatre will have been under construction for five years by the end of May.

Ex.5: Translate into English:

1. मेरी बहन अपनी रिहाइश (f.) बदलने की सोच रही है।
2. आप गर्मी की छुट्टियों में क्या करने की योजना बना रहे हैं?
3. आप नया 'रेफ़िजरेटर' किस कमरे में रखने की सोच रहे हैं?
4. अगले रविवार को सुबह छः बजे से शाम को छः बजे तक हम आगरा में ताजमहल देख रहे होंगे।

5. भारत जाने से पहले मैंने हिन्दी (f.) बोलनी सीख ली होगी।
6. अगले महीने तक उसने नया काम (m.) ढूँढ़ लिया होगा।
7. बैठक (f.) शाम को चार बजे तक ख़तम हो चुकी होगी।
8. मैं (m.) नौ बजे तक नाश्ता कर चुका होऊँगा।

1. merī bahan apnā rihaiīś (f.) badalne kī soc rahī hai.
2. āp garmī kī chuṭṭiyoṁ meṁ kyā karne kī yojnā banā rahe haiṁ ?
3. āp nayā 'refrigerator' kis kamre meṁ rakhne kī soc rahe haiṁ?
4. agle ravivār ko subah chaḥ baje se śām ko chaḥ baje tak ham āgrā meṁ tājmahal dekh rahe hoṁge.
5. bhārat jāne se pahle maiṁne hindī bolnī sīkh lī hogī.
6. agle mahīne tak usne nayā kām (m.) ḍhūṁḍh liyā hogā.
7. baiṭhak (f.) śām ko cār baje tak khatam ho cukī hogī.
6. maiṁ nau baje tak naśtā kar cukā hoūṁgā.

Key1

1. It seems there will be absolutely no rains this year. 2. In which month will Holi be this year? 3. Will you travel to foreign countries when you grow up? 4. I will make an 'ashram' for destitute women. 5. Today we will all go out for leisure wandering. 6. I think I will get up early from tomorrow morning.7. We will take loan from the bank. 8. He will never stop gambling.? 9. My brother will certainy get married next year. 10. What will you have, tea or coffee?

Key 2

1. वे अगले हफ़्ते आएँगे। 2. मैं सदैव आपकी मदद करूँगा। 3. वे सर्दी में कहाँ जाएँगे? 4. मेरी बहन मुझसे नाराज़ होगी। 5. आज मैं सारा दिन ख़रीदारी करूँगी। 6. अबसे मैं रोज़ व्यायाम करूँगा। 7. वह तीन साल भारत में पढ़ेगी। 8. अगले साल वह छात्रावास में रहेगी। 9. वेहान सदैव मेहनत करेगा। 10.क्या तुम डॉक्टर बनोगे / बनोगी?

1. ve agle hafte āeṁge. 2. maiṁ sadaiv āpkī madad karūṁgā. 3. ve sardī meṁ kahāṁ jāeṁge. 4. merī bahan mujh se nārāz hogī. 5. āj maiṁ sārā din kharīdārī karūṁgī. .6. ab se maiṁ roz vyāyām karūṁgā. 7. vah tīn sāl bhārat meṁ paṛhegī . 8. agle sāl vah chātrāvās meṁ rahegī. 9. vehān sadaiv mehnat karegā. 10. kyā tum ḍaukṭar banoge/-gī?

Key 3

2. होगी। 3. आएगा। 4. होंगी। 5. लौटेंगे।
6. पढ़ेंगी 7. लाएगा। 8. देखेंगी। 9. आएँगे।
10. आएँगे।

2. hogī 3. āegā 4. hoṁgī 5. lauṭeṁge
6. paṛheṁgī 7. lāegā 8. dekheṁgī 9. āeṁge
10. āeṁge

Key 4

1. जी हाँ, मैं पत्र लिखूँगी। / जी नहीं, मैं पत्र नहीं लिखूँगी।
2. जी हाँ, मैं येवाले जूते ख़रीदूँगा। / जी नहीं, मैं ये वाले जूते नहीं ख़रीदूँगा।
3. जी हाँ, मैं आज शामको आपके घर आऊँगी। / जी नहीं, मैं आज शामको आपके घर नहीं आऊँगी।
4. जी हाँ, मैं आपके साथ शतरंज खेलूँगा। / जी नहीं, मैं आपके साथ शतरंज नहीं खेलूँगा।
5. जी हाँ, हम लोग कचौरी–जलेबी खाने चलेंगे। / जी नहीं, हम लोग कचौरी–जलेबी खाने नहीं चलेंगे।

1. jī hāṁ, maiṁ patra likhūṁgī.
   jī nahīṁ, maiṁ patra nahīṁ likhūṁgī.
2. jī hāṁ, maiṁ ye vāle jūte kharīdūṁgā.
   jī nahīṁ, maiṁ yevāle jūte nahīṁ kharīdūṁgā.
3. jī hāṁ, maiṁ āj śām ko āpke ghar āūṁgī.
   jī nahīṁ, maiṁ āj śām ko āpke ghar nahīṁ āūṁgī.
4. jī hāṁ, maiṁ āpke sāth śatrañj khelūṁgā?
   jī nahīṁ, maiṁ āp ke sāth śatrañj nahīṁ khelūṁgā?
5. jī hāṁ, ham log kacaurī-jalebī khāne caleṁge?
   jī nahīṁ, ham log kacaurī-jalebī khāne nahīṁ caleṁge?

Key 5

1. My sister is thinking of changing her residence.
2. What are you planning to do during the summer holidays ?
3. In which room are you thinking of putting the new refrigerator ?
4. Next Sunday from 6 o'clock in the morning to 6 o'clock in the evening, we will be seeing TajMahal in Agra

5. Before going to India I will have learnt how to speak Hindi.
6. By next month he will have found a new job.
7. The meeting will have finished by 4 o'clock in the evening.
8. I will have had breakfast by 9 o'clock

***

• **to have an object** = **के पास होना ke pās honā**	
1. आज मेरे पास पैसे बिलकुल नहीं है। I don't have any money today. āj mere pās paise bilkul nahīṁ haiṁ. 2. रोमा के पास कई उपयोगी सुझाव है। Rani has several useful ideas. romā ke pās kaī upyogī sujhāv haiṁ. 3. मेरे पास कहने को कुछ नहीं। I have nothing to say. mere pās kahne ko kuch nahīṁ.	
• **to have kith and kin, limbs of** the body and landed property:	= X का, के, की + ...
1. **उसके दो बेटे और एक बेटी है।** He has two sons and a daughter. uske do beṭe aur ek beṭī hai. 2. **मेरे दो हाथ हैं।** I have two hands. mere do hāth haiṁ. 3. **मेरा कोई भाई नहीं।** I don't have a brother. mera koī bhāī nahiṁ . 3. उनकी बहुत जमीन–जायदाद है। They have much landed property. unkī bahut zamīn jāyădād hai.	
• **to have servants who are neither an object of possession nor kith and kin, normally one would say: =** X के यहाँ,	
1. मेरे यहाँ दो नौकर हैं। I have two servants. mere yahāṁ do naukar haiṁ. 2. उनके यहाँ कोई नौकर नहीं। They don't have any servant. . unke yahāṁ koī naukar nahīṁ.	

10 Presumption

■ **Presumptive language structures are used when the speaker is almost (but not 100%) sure of some event or activity.**

Present Presumptive: Presumption about 'being' or 'non being' of something:

subj. + ... + future form of होना honā to agree with the subject

1. वे इसी शहर में होंगे। — They must be in this city
ve isī śahar meṁ hoṁge.
2. इसका दाम ज़्यादा–से–ज़्यादा सौ रुपए होगा। — It's maximum price must be be a hundred rupees.
iskā dām zyādā-se-zyādā sau rupae hogā.

Presumption about a habitual activity:

(subj. + ...+ (v.r. + tā, te, tī , ता,ते, ती) + future form of होना honā agree with the subject

1. वह रोज़ तैरती होगी। — She must be swimming every day.
vah roz tairtī hogī.
2 वे लोग अक्सर गंगा स्नान करते होंगे। — They must be having a bath in the Ganges often.
ve log aksar gaṅgā snān karte hoṁge.

☞ **आता ātā / आते āte / आती ātī + future form of होना honā**
= **the subject is on the way expected to arrive any moment.**

3. महमान आते होंगे। — Guests must be coming.
mahmān āte hoṁge.

Progressive Presumptive : Presumption about some action in progress at a certain time:

subj. +	obj. +	(v.r. + रहा, रहे, रही)	+ fut. form of होना
	if any	rahā, -e, -ī	honā
			agree with the subject

1. छात्राएँ पढ़ रही होंगी। — The sudents must be studying.
   chātrāeṁ paṛh rahī hoṁgī.

2. मेरे ख़याल में वे इस समय नौका विहार कर रहे होंगे। — I think they must be having a boat ride at this time.
   mere khayāl meṁ ve is samay naukā vihār kar rahe hoṁge.

Past Presumptive

subj. + obj. + (v.r. + आ ā ,ए e, ई ī)* + fut. form of होना honā*
if any

*** (a) to agree with the subject when verb intransitive. (E. 1)**
(b) to agree with the object when v.t. Also subject + ने ne is used.(E. 2)
(b) when it is transitive verb without mentioning the object, use only masc. singular third person i.e. -आ ā–form. (E. 3)

- **Alternatively (v.r. + चुकना cuknā) + future form of होना honā in present or past presumptive.:(E. 4, 5)**

☞ **चुकना cuknā and होना honā always agree with the subject.**

1. वह[m.] अब तक चला गया होगा। — He must have left by now.
   vah[m.] ab tak calā gayā hogā.

2. किसीने उसे ख़बर दी होगी। — Some one must have given him the news.
   kisīne use khabar dī hogī.

3. कल सभा में क्या हुआ होगा? — What could have happened in the meeting yesterday?
   kal sabhā meṁ kyā huā hogā?

4. वे (m.pl.) शाम को छः बजे तक सब काम कर चुकते होंगे। — They must be finished with all their work by 6 p.m.

	ve śām ko chaḥ baje tak sab kām kar cukte hoṁge.	(habitual presumptive)
5.	वह (m.sg.) स्कूल से लौट चुका होगा।	He must have already returned from school.
	vah skūl se lauṭ cukā hogā.	(past presumtive)

Ex. 1: Translate into English.

1. सपना ने परीक्षा बहुत अच्छे अंको से उत्तीर्ण की। अवश्य ही उसके परिवार को उस पर गर्व होगा।
2. वह सदैव बहुत महँगे कपड़े पहनती है। वह अवश्य बहुत अमीर होगी।
3. "मुझे मेरा बटुआ नहीं मिल रहा।"
   "तुम अवश्य मैटरो में छोड़ आई होगी।"
4. "मुझे अपना एक कानों का नहीं मिल रहा।"
   'तुम ने कहीं गिरा दिया होगा।"
5. वे बहुत जल्दी पहुँच गए। अवश्य टेक्सी से आए होंगे।
6. मेरी मित्र ने, जैसा उसके अधिकारी ने बताया था, ठीक उस का उलटा किया । अवश्य ही उसने हिदायतें ठीक से नहीं समझी होंगी।
7. वे हाल में यहाँ रहने आए हैं। वे बहुत लोगों को नहीं जानते होंगे।
8. उसने अभी–अभी भारी भरकम भोजन किया है। उसे इतनी जल्दी भूख नहीं लगी होगी।

1. sapnā ne parīkṣā bahut acche aṅkoṁ se uttīrṇ kī. avaśyă hī uske parivār ko us par garv hogā.
2. vah sadaiv bahut mahṁge kapṛe pahantī hai. vah avaśyă bahut amīr hogī.
3. "mujhe merā baṭuā nahīṁ mil rahā."
   "tum avaśyă 'maiṭro' meṁ choṛ āī hogī."
4. "mujhe apnā ek kānoṁ kā nahīṁ mil rahā."
   "tumne kahīṁ girā diyā hogā."
5. ve bahut jaldī pahuṁc gae. avaśyă 'ṭaiksī' se āe hoṁge.
6. merī mitra ne, jaisā uske adhikārī ne batāyā thā, ṭhīk uskā ulṭā kiyā. avaśyă hī usne hidāyateṁ ṭhīk se samjhī nahīṁ hoṁgī.
7. ve hāl meṁ yahāṁ rahne āe haiṁ. ve bahut logoṁ ko nahīṁ jānte hoṁge.
8. usne abhī-abhī bhārī bharkam bhojan kiyā hai. use itnī jaldī bhūkh nahīṁ lagī hogī.

Glossary:

परीक्षा (f.)	parīkṣā	exam
अंक (m.)	aṅk	marks
उत्तीर्ण करना (v.t.)	uttīrṇ karnā	to pass
परिवार (m.)	parivār	family
अमीर (adj.)	amīr	rich
बटुआ (m.)	baṭuā	wallet
कानों का (m.)	kānoṁ kā	ear-ring
ठीक (adj.)	ṭhīk	here: exactly
उलटा (m/adj.)	ulṭā	opposite
हिदायत (f.)	hidāyat	instruction
भारी–भरकम (adj.)	bhārī bharkam	heavy
भूख लगना (v.i.)	bhūkh lagnā	to feel hungry

Ex. 2: Translate into Hindi.

1. He could not have cheated during the exam.
2. He could not have abused his power.
3. Her husband could not have been cruel to her.
4. He must have become happy.
5. The baby must have cried for a long time.
6. They must have visited the temples of Varanasi.
7. He must have been driving fast.
8. She must have been working hard.
9. The children must have been playing in the field.

Glossary:

to cheat	नकल करना (v.t.)	nakal karnā
to abuse	दुष्प्रयोग करना (v.t.)	duṣprayog karnā
cruel	निर्दयी (adj.)	nirdayī
happy	ख़ुश (adj.)	<u>kh</u>uś
to follow	पीछा करना (v.t.)	pīchā karnā
pretty	सुन्दर (adj.)	sundar
religious	धार्मिक (adj.)	dhārmik
to drive	वाहन चलाना (v.t.)	vāhan calānā
to work hard	परिश्रम करना (v.t.)	pariśram karnā
field	मैदान (m.)	maidān

Key 1

1. Sapna passed the exam with really good grades. Her family must be proud of her.
2. She always wears very expensive clothes. She must be very rich.
3. "I can't find my bag." "You must have left it on the metro."
4. "I can't find one of my ear rings." " You must have dropped it somewhere."
5. They arrived very soon. They must have come by taxi.
6. My friend did exactly the opposite of what her boss told her to do. She can't have understood the instructions.
7. They came to live here recently. They can't know many people.
8. He/She just had a big meal. He/She can't be hungry again so soon.

Key 2

1. उसने परीक्षा में नकल नहीं की होगी।
2. उसने अपनी ताकत का दुष्प्रयोग नहीं किया होगा।
3. उसका पति उसके साथ निर्दयी नहीं हुआ होगा।
4. वह अवश्य खुश हुआ होगा।
5. बच्चा काफ़ी देर तक रोया होगा।
6. उन्होंने बनारस के मंदिर देखे होंगे।
7. वह अवश्य वाहन तेज़ चला रहा होगा।
8. वह अवश्य परिश्रम कर रही होगी।
9. बच्चे मैदान में खेल रहे होंगे।

1. usne parīkṣa meṁ nakal nahīṁ kī hogī.
2. usne apnī tākat kā duṣprayog nahīṁ kiyā hogā.
3. uskā pati uske sāth nirdayī nahīṁ huā hogā.
4. vah avaśyă khuś huā hogā.
5. baccā kāfi der tak royā hogā.
6. unhoṁne banāras ke mandir dekhe hoṁge.
7. vah avaśyă vāhan tez calā rahā hogā.
8. vah avaśyă pariśram kar rahī hogī.
9. bacce maidān meṁ khel rahe hoṁge.

11 Subjunctive

■ **Subjunctive in Hindi is used to express possibility, probability apprehension, wishes, permission, passive, imperative and conditional.**

Present subjunctive

subj.	+ obj.	+ (v.r. + ता, ते, ती)	+ होऊँ, हो, होओ, हों
	(if any)	tā, te, tī	hoūṁ, ho, ho'o, hoṁ

agree with the number and gender of the subject

☞ **This language structure can be used both for transitive and intransitive verbs.**

Past subjunctive : Intransitive verb

subject	+ (v.r.	+ आ/या, ए, ई)	+ होऊँ, हो, होओ, हों
		ā/yā, e, ī	hoūṁ, ho, ho'o, hoṁ

agree with the number and gender of the subject

Past subjunctive : Transitive Verb

(subj. + ने)	+ obj.	+ (v.r. + आ/या, ए, ई)	+ हो, हों
	(if any)	ā/yā, e, ī	ho, hoṁ

agree with the number and gender of the object

Future subjunctive

subj.	+ obj.	+ (v.r	+ ऊँ, ए, ओ, एँ)
	(if any)		ūṁ, e, o, eṁ

agree with the number of the subject

☞ **Future subjunctive does not discriminate between masculine and feminine; it relates only to number and person.**

12 Probability

शायद' (perhaps), संभवता (probably) हो सकता है' (it is likely)

Present probability

probability expression	+ subj. nom. case	+ obj. (if any)	+ v.r. +	ता, ते, ती tā, te, tī	+ होउँ, हो, होओ, हों hoūṁ, ho, ho'o,hoṁ agree with the subject

1. शायद वह **(m.)** हिन्दी जानता हो।
   śāyad vah **(m.)** hindī jāntā ho.

   Perhaps he knows Hindi.

2. हो सकता है वह **(f.)** अभी भी तैरती हो।
   ho saktā hai vah **(f.)** abhī bhī tairtī ho

   Its likely that she still swims.

Past probability v.i.

probability expression	+ subj. nom. case	+ (v.r +	आ, ए, ई) ā, e, ī	+ होउँ, हो, होओ हों hoūṁ, ho, ho'o, hoṁ agree with the subject

1. हो सकता है वे **(m.pl.)** कल चल गए हों।
   ho saktā hai ve kal cale gae hoṁ.

   Its likely they already left yesterday.

2. शायद वह **(f.)** अब तक खाना बना चुकी हो।
   śāyad vah **(f.)** ab tak khānā banā cukī ho.

   Perhaps she has already cooked food by now.

Past Probability v.t.

probability expression	+ (subj. + ने) +	obj.	+ v.r +	आ, ए, ई ā, e, ī	+	हो, हों, ho, hoṁ agree with the object

1. हो सकता है नौकर ने खाना (m.) बना दिया हो।
ho saktā hai naukar ne khānā banā diyā ho.
The servant might have already cooked the meal.

2. हो सकता है उसने बड़ा मकान ख़रीद लिया हो।
ho saktā hai usne baṛā makān <u>kh</u>arīd liyā ho.
It is likely he has already bought a big house.

Future probability

probability expression	+	subj. nom. case	+	obj. (if any)	+ v.r +	उँ, ए, ओ, एँ ūṁ, e, o, eṁ agree with the subject

1. शायद मैं अगले साल शादी करूँ।
śāyad maiṁ agle sāl śādī karūṁ.
Perhaps I will marry next year.

2. हो सकता है आज शाम तक गरज–चमक के साथ आँधी आए।
ho saktā hai āj śām tak garaj-camak ke sāth āṁdhī āe.
There might be a storm with thunder and lightening by evening today.

Ex.1: Translate into English:

1. शायद वह ठण्डी कॉफ़ी ज़्यादा पसन्द करती हो।
2. शायद वह स्कूल में अध्यापक हो।
3. हो सकता है वह झूठ बोल रही हो।
4. हो सकता है वे इस वक़्त दूरदर्शन देख रहे हों।
5. हो सकता है माँ देर से सोई हों।
6. हो सकता है वह अपने परिवार से मिलने गई हो।

7. हो सकता है अनिल रत्न शास्त्र सीख़ने लास एंजलीस जाय।
8. हो सकता है वे खेल में जीत जाएँ।
9. हो सकता है हम आज शाम को बाहर खाएँ।

1. śāyad vah ṭhaṇḍī kaufi zyādā pasand kartī ho.
2. śāyad vah skūl meṁ adhyāpak ho.
3. ho saktā hai vah jhūṭh bol rahī ho.
4. ho saktā hai ve is vaqt dūrdarśan dekh rahe hoṁ.
5. ho saktā hai māṁ der se soī hoṁ.
6. ho saktā hai vah apne parivār se milne gaī ho.
7. ho saktā hai anil ratan śāstra sīkhne ke lie Los Angeles jāe.
8. ho saktā hai ve khel meṁ jīt jāeṁ.
9. ho saktā hai ham āj śām ko bāhar khāeṁ.

Ex.2: Translate into Hindi:

1. She (hon.) might know about it.
2. Mother might be in the kitchen.
3. Children might be playing in the play ground.
4. She might be having a bath.
5. She might have seen a miracle.
6. They might have gone to the movies.
7. They might not have invited Vedant to the party.
8. We might meet at the concert tonight.
9. She might marry one of her colleagues.

Key 1

1. She might be preferring cold coffee.
2. He might be a school teacher.
3. She might be telling a lie.
4. They might be watching TV at this time.
5. Mother might have gone to bed late.
6. She might have gone to visit her family.
7. Anil might go to Los Angeles to study gemology.
8. They might win the game.
9. We might eat out tonight.

Key 2

1. शायद वे इसके बारे में जानती हों।
2. शायद माँ रसोईघर में हों।

3. हो सकता है बच्चे खेल के मैदान में खेल रहे हों।
4. हो सकता है वे स्नान कर रहे हों।
5. हो सकता है उसने कोई चमत्कार देखा हो।
6. हो सकता है वे फ़िल्म देखने गए हों।
7. हो सकता है उन्हों ने वेदान्त को दावत में न बुलाया हो।
8. हो सकता है हम आज शाम को गोष्ठी में मिलें।
9. हो सकता है वह अपने एक सहकर्मी से शादी करे।

1. śāyad ve is ke bāre meṁ jāntī hoṁ.
2. śāyad māṁ rasoīghar meṁ hoṁ.
3. ho saktā hai bacce khel ke maidān meṁ khel rahe hoṁ .
4. ho saktā hai ve snān kar rahe hoṁ.
5. ho saktā hai usne koī camatkār dekhā ho.
6. ho saktā hai ve film dekhne gae hoṁ.
7. ho saktā hai unhoṁne vedānt ko dāvat meṁ na bulāyā ho.
8. ho saktā hai ham āj śām ko gosṭhī meṁ mileṁ.
9. ho saktā hai vah apne ek sahkarmī se śādī kare.

Days Of the Week

सोमवार[m]	somvār	Monday	मंगलवार[m]	maṅgalvār	Tuesday
बुधवार[m]	budhvār	Wednesday	गुरुवार[m]	guruvār	Thursday
शुक्रवार[m]	śukravār	Friday;	शनिवार[m]	śanivār	Saturday
रविवार[m]	ravivār	Sunday.			

- **All days of the week are masculine.**

on Monday	सोमवार को	somvār ko
on Tuesday	मंगलवार को	maṅgalvār ko

Times of the Day

प्रभात / सुबह	prabhāt /subah	early morning/morning
पूर्वाह्न	pūrvāhn	forenoon
दोपहर	dopahar	noon
अपराह्न	aprāhn	afternoon
शाम / सन्ध्या	śām /sandhyā	evening
रात / आधी रात	rāt / ādhi rāt	night/mid night

13 Apprehensions

ऐसा न हो कि
aisā na ho ki **subjunctive clause = lest, in case**
कहीं ऐसा न हो कि
kahīṁ aisā na ho ki

Future simple	**Apprehension**
• गाड़ी छूट जाएगी।	**ऐसा न हो कि गाड़ी** छूट जाए।
gāṛī chūṭ jāegī.	aisā na ho ki gāṛī chūṭ jāe
The train will depart!	Lest the train departs!
• उसे नौकरी नहीं मिलेगी।	**कहीं ऐसा न हो कि** उसे नौकरी न मिले।
use naukrī nahīṁ milegī.	kahīṁ aisā na ho ki use naukrī na mile.
He will not get the job.	In case he doesn't get the job!

Ex.: Rewrite the simple future tense sentences in apprehension structure as shown in the examples given above.

1. वे हमारा घर ढूँढ़ न पाएँगे। ....
2. हम शादी में न जा सकेंगे। ....
3. उसे छुट्टी न मिलेगी। ....
4. आपको व्यापार में घाटा होगा। ....
5. वह परीक्षा में उत्तीर्ण न होगा। ....

1. ve hamārā ghar ḍhūṁḍh na pāeṁge. ....
2. ham śādī meṁ na jā sakeṁge...
3. use chuṭṭī na milegī. ....
4. āpko vyāpār meṁ ghāṭā hogā. ....
5. vah parīkṣā meṁ uttṛīṇ na hogā. ....

Key

1. कहीं ऐसा न हो कि वे हमारा घर ढूँढ़ न पाएँ।
2. कहीं ऐसा न हो कि हम शादी में न जा सकें।
3. कहीं ऐसा न हो कि उसे छुट्टी न मिले।

4. कहीं ऐसा न हो कि आपको व्यापार में घाटा हो।
5. कहीं ऐसा न हो कि वह परीक्षा में उत्तीर्ण न हो।

1. kahīṁ aisā na ho ki ve hamārā ghar ḍhūṁḍh na pāeṁ.
2. kahīṁ aisā na ho ki ham śādī meṁ na jā sakeṁ.
3. kahīṁ aisā na ho ki use chuṭṭī na mile.
4. kahīṁ aisā na ho ki āpko vyāpār meṁ ghāṭā ho.
5. kahīṁ aisā na ho ki vah parīkṣā meṁ uttīrṇ na ho.

Telling Time

■ **Talking about complete hour : nh + bajā hai/baje haiṁ:**

कितने बजे हैं?	kitne baje haiṁ	What time is it?
एक बजा है।	ek bajā hai.	It is one o'clock.
दो बजे हैं।	do baje haiṁ	It is two o'clock.

■ **a quarter past — savā + nh + bajā hai[sg.]/baje haiṁ:**

सवा (एक) बजा है।	savā (ek) bajā hai.	It is a quarter past one.
सवा दो बजे हैं।	savā do baje haiṁ	It is a quarter past two.

■ **a quarter to —- paun/paune + nh + bajā hai/baje haiṁ**

पौन बजा है।	paun bajā hai.	It is a quarter to one.
पौने दो बजे हैं।	paune do baje haiṁ	It is a quarter to two.

■ **half past the hour**

डेढ़ बजा है।	ḍeṛh bajā hai.	It is half past one.
ढ़ाई बजे हैं।	ḍhāi baje haiṁ	It is half past two.
साढ़े चार बजे हैं।	sāṛhe cār baje haiṁ	It is half past four.

■ **minutes past the hour = nh + bajkar + nm**

दो बजकर पाँच मिनट	do bajkar pāṁc minaṭ	five past two
दस बजकर बीस मिनट	das bajkar bīs minaṭ	twenty past ten

■ **minutes before the hour = nh + bajne meṁ + nm**

दो बजने में पाँच मिनट	do bajne meṁ pāṁc minaṭ	five to two
दस बजने में बीस मिनट	das bajne meṁ bīs minaṭ	twenty to ten

nh = number of hours; nm= number of minutes

14 Inceptive compound

(verb root + ने ne) + lagnā

to begin to do something

subj. **nom. case**	**+ object** **if any**	**+ (v.r. + ने) + लगना ***

*** (v.r. + ने) is invariable; लगना lagnā agree with N and G of the subject in the required tense.**

1. मैं सुबह–सुबह पढ़ने लगता / लगती हूँ। **(present simple)**
   maiṁ subah-subah paṛhne lagtā / lagtī hūṁ.
   I begin to study early morning.
2. मैं सुबह–सुबह पढ़ने लगता था / लगती थी। **(past habitual)**
   maiṁ subah-subah paṛhne lagtā thā / lagtī thī.
   I used to begin to study early morning.
3. मैं सुबह–सुबह पढ़ने लगा /लगी। **(past simple)**
   maiṁ subah-subah paṛhne lagā / lagī .
   I began to study early morning.
4. मैं सुबह–सुबह पढ़ने लगा/ लगी हूँ। **(present perfect simple)**
   maiṁ subah-subah paṛhne lagā / lagī hūṁ.
   I have begun to study early morning.
5. मैं उसके आने से पहले पढ़ने लगा था/लगी थी। **(past perfect)**
   maiṁ uske āne se pahle paṛhne lagā thā. / lagī thī.
   I had already begun to study before he /she came.
6. मैं सुबह–सुबह पढ़ने लगूँगा / लगूँगी। **(future simple)**
   maiṁ subah-subah paṛhne lagūṁgā / lagūṁgī.
   I will begin to study early morning.
7. मैं सूर्योदय से पहले पढ़ने लगा हूँगा।/ लगी हूँगी। **(future perfect)**
   maiṁ sūryoday se pahle paṛhne lagā hūṁgā / lagī hūṁgī.
   I will have begun to study before the sunrise.

8. हो सकता है मैं सूर्योदय से पहले पढ़ने लगूँ। **(subjunctive)**
ho saktā hai maiṁ sūryoday se pahle paṛhne lagūṁ.
I may begin to study before the sunrise.

Ex.1: Translate into English:

1. मंदिरों में प्रायः सुबह सुबह भजन–कीर्तन होने लगता हैं।
2. त्योहारों पर कई दिन पहले से बाज़ारों में रौनक़ दिखाई देने लगती है।
3. हमारा कुत्ता डाकिये को देखते ही भौंकने लगता था।
4. विद्यार्थी और अभिभावक वर्तमान शिक्षा प्रणाली पर सवाल उठाने लगे हैं।
5. मैं सेवा निवृत्ति के पश्चात ध्यान–अभ्यास करना शुरू करूँगा।
6. हो सकता है वह एक–दो सालों में आप को अपना गुरु मानने लगे।

1. mandiroṁ meṁ prāyaḥ subah-subah bhajan-kīrtan hone lagtā hai.
2. tyohāroṁ par kaī din pahle se bāzāroṁ meṁ raunaq dikhāī dene lagtī hai.
3. hamārā kuttā ḍākiye ko dekhte hī bhauṁkne lagtā thā.
4. vidyārthī aur abhibhāvak vartmān śikṣā praṇālī par savāl uṭhāne lage haiṁ.
5. maiṁ sevā nivṛtti ke paścāt dhyān abhyās karne lagūṁgā.
6. ho saktā hai vah ek-do sāloṁ meṁ āpko apnā guru mānane lage.

Glossary:

भजन–कीर्तन (m.)	bhajan-kīrtan	singing the glory of God
त्योहार (m.)	tyohār	festivals
रौनक़ (m.)	raunaq	excitement
शिक्षा (f.)	śikṣā	education
विद्यार्थी (m.)	vidyārthī	student(s)
अभिभावक (m.)	abhibhāvak	guardian
वर्तमान (adj.)	vartmān	present
शिक्षा प्रणाली (f.)	śikṣā praṇālī	education system
मानना (v.t.)	mānanā	accept, believe
सवाल उठाना (v.t.)	savāl uṭhānā	to question
सेवा निवृत्ति (f.)	sevā nivṛtti	retirement
के पश्चात (postposition.)	ke paścāt	after
गुरु (m.)	guru	mentor

Ex.2: Translate into English:

1. He (hon.) often begins to scold for no reason.
2. The athletes come to this field in the evening and begin to play.
3. It was very cold. I began to freeze.
4. Why did you begin to tremble on seeing him / her?
5. It seems it will soon begin to rain.

Glossary:

for no reason	अकारण (adj./adv.)	akāraṇ
to scold	डाँटना (v.t.)	ḍāṁṭnā
athletes	खिलाड़ी (m.)	khilāṛī
field	मैदान (m.)	maidān
to freeze(feel very cold)	ठिठुरना (v.i.)	ṭhiṭhurnā
to tremble	काँपना (v.i.)	kāṁpnā
rain	वर्षा (f.).	varṣā

Key 1

1. Usually 'bhajan-kirtan' begins in the temples very early in the morning.
2. Several days before festivals, excitement is visible in the markets.
3. Our dog used to begin to bark as soon as it saw the doctor.
4. The students and the guardians have begun to question the present education system.
5. I will begin to practise meditation after my retirement.
6. A couple of years from now, he might begin to accept you as his mentor.

Key 2

1. वे अक्सर अकारण डाँटने लगते हैं।
2. खिलाड़ी शाम को इस मैदान में आकर खेलने लगते हैं।
3. ठण्ड बहुत थी। मैं ठिठुरने लगा।
4. तुम उसको देखकर काँपने क्यों लगे?
5. ऐसा लग रहा है कि जल्दी ही वर्षा होने लगेगी।

1. ve (m.hon.) aksar akāraṇ ḍāṁṭne lagte haiṁ.
2. khilāṛī śām ko is maidān meṁ ā kar khelne lagte haiṁ.
3. ṭhaṇḍ bahut thī. maiṁ ṭhiṭhurne lagā.
4. tum usko dekhkar kāṁpne kyoṁ lage?
5. aisā lag rahā hai ki jaldī hī varṣā hone lagegī.

15 Permissive Compound

verb root + ने ne) + denā

to let someone do something

subj. + (indirect obj. को ko) + **direct obj. + (v. r. +** ने ne)* + denā*[1]

* (v.r. + ने ne) is invariable.

*[1] 'देना denā' agrees with the subject or object in the required tense.

1. आप मुझे जाने दीजिए।
   āp mujhe jāne dījie.
   Please (you formal)let me go.
   (imperative present)
2. आप उसको जाने दीजिएगा।
   āp usko jāne dījiegā.
   Please (you formal)let him go.
   (imperative future)
3. वे मुझको जाने देते हैं।
   ve mujhko jāne dete haiṁ.
   They let me go
   (present simple)
4. वे मुझको जाने देते थे।
   ve mujhko jāne dete the.
   They used to let me go.
   (past habitual)
5. उन्होंने मुझको जाने दिया।
   unhoṁne mujhko jāne diyā.
   They let me go.
   (past simple)
6. उन्होंने मुझको जाने दिया था।
   unhoṁne mujhko jāne diyā thā.
   They had let me go.
   (past perfect)
7. उन्होंने मुझको जाने दिया है।
   unhoṁne mujhko jāne diyā hai.
   They have let me go.
   (present perfect)
8. वे मुझको जाने देंगे।
   ve mujhko jāne deṁge.
   They will let me go.
   (future simple)
9. हो सकता है वे मुझको जाने दें।
   ho saktā hai ve mujhko jāne deṁ
   They may let me go.
   (probability)
10. उनको मुझे जाने देना पड़ेगा।
   unko mujhe jāne denā paṛegā.
   They will have to let me go.
   (compulsion)

10\. उनको मुझे जाने देना चाहिए।
   unko mujhe jāne denā cāhie.
   They ought to let me go.
   (advice)

Ref. पड़ना paṛnā pg.175 **Ref.** चाहिए cāhie pg. 149

Ex. 1: Translate into Hindi:

1. Please (you formal)let him rest. (imperative present)
2. Please (you formal)let him sleep. (imperative future)
3. They let him study. (present simple)
4. They used to let me play in their house. (past habitual)
5. I let her play chess. (past simple)
6. We had let them watch the dance. (past perfect)
7. She has let me cook food by myself. (present perfect)
8. Will they let me stay at their place? (future simple)
9. They may not let me go to India. (probability)

Ex.2: Translate into English:

1. मेरे दादा–दादी हमें घर में अंग्रेज़ी नहीं बोलने देते ।
2. माँ मुझे बचपन में कोई वाहन नहीं चलाने देती थीं।
3. पिता जी हमें रात को अकेले फ़िल्म देखने नहीं जाने देते थे।
4. मेरी अध्यापिका ने मुझे बहस में भाग नहीं लेने दिया।
5. मेरे भाई ने मुझे अपना कैमरा प्रयोग नहीं करने दिया।
6. दादी हमें नवरात्र* में मांसाहारी भोजन नहीं खाने देंगी।
7. शायद मेरे पति मुझे संगीत प्रतियोगिता में भाग न लेने दें।
8. हो सकता है कि मेरे ससुरालवाले मुझे बच्चा गोद लेने दें।

1. mere dādā-dādī hameṁ ghar meṁ aṅgrezī nahīṁ bolne dete.
2. māṁ mujhe bacpan meṁ koī vāhan nahīṁ calāne detī thīṁ.
3. pitāji hameṁ rāt ko akele film dekhne nahīṁ jāne dete the.
4. merī adhyāpikā ne mujhe bahas meṁ bhāg nahīṁ lene diyā.
5. mere bhāī ne mujhe apnā 'kaimrā' prayog nahīṁ karne diyā.
6. dādī hameṁ navrātra meṁ māṃsāhārī bhojan nahīṁ khāne deṁgī.
7. śāyad mere pati mujhe saṅgīt pratiyogitā meṁ bhāg na lene deṁ.
8. ho saktā hai ki mere sasurālvāle mujhe baccā god lene deṁ.

Glossary:

बचपन (m.)	bacpan	childhood
वाहन (m.)	vāhan	vehicle
अध्यापिका (f.)	adhyāpikā	teacher
बहस (f.)	bahas	argument

* नवरात्र (m.) navrātra: first 9 days of the light half of the month Cait and Ashvin (1th and 7st month respectively of the Hindu calendar)during which the Goddess Durga is worshipped

भाग लेना (v.t.)	bhāg lenā.	to take part in
अपना (adj.)	apnā	one's own
प्रयोग (m.)	prayog	use
नवरात्र	navrātra	Navratra
मांसाहारी (adj.)	māṃsāhārī	nonvegetarian
संगीत (m.)	saṅgīt	music
प्रतियोगिता (f.)	pratiyogitā	competition
ससुरालवाले (m.)	sasurālvāle	in-laws
बच्चा गोद लेना (v.t.)	baccā god lenā	to adopt a child

Ex. 3: Translate into Hindi: Use v.r. + ने + *देना* (=to let someone do something):

1. Raman lets his wife wear what she likes.
2. Prachi let her husband donate for flood relief fund.
3. Will you let me go trekking in the mountains?
4. They may not let us eat out.
5. Father will probably never let me go out with my friends at night.
6. My parents always let me do what I like.
7. Dad doesn't normally let any one touch his computer.
8. Grandmother never lets anybody sit on her bed.
9. Please let me listen to music.
10. Let him/her come in.

Glossary:

what she likes	जो वह चाहे (rel. clausej.)	jo vah cāhe
donate	दान देना (v.t.)	dān denā
to let wear	पहनने देना (v.t.)	pahnane denā
mountains	पहाड़ (m.)	pahāṛ
trekking	पदयात्रा (f.)	padyātrā
it is likely	हो सकता है	ho saktā hai
week	सप्ताह (m.)	saptāh
eat out	बाहर खाना (inf.)	bāhar khānā
probably	संभवता (adv.)	sambhavtā
always	हमेशा (adv.)	hameśā
what I like	जो मैं चाहूँ	jo maiṁ cāhūṁ
parents	माता–पिता (m.pl.)	mātā-pitā
to use	इस्तेमाल करना (v.t.)	istemāl karnā

usually	सामान्यता (adv)	sāmānyătā
bed	पलंग (m.)	palaṅg
please	कृपया (adv.)	kṛpayā
music	संगीत (m.)	saṅgīt

Key 1

1. कृपया उसे आराम करने दीजिए। (imperative present)
2. कृपया उसे सोने दीजिएगा। (imperative future)
3. वे उसे पढ़ने देते हैं। (present simple)
4. वे मुझे अपने घर में खेलने देते थे। (past habitual)
5. मैंने उसे शतरंज खेलने दिया। (past simple)
6. हमने उन्हें नृत्य देखने दिया था। (past perfect)
7. उसने मुझे भोजन स्वयं पकाने दिया है। (present perfect)
8. क्या वे मुझे अपने यहाँ रहने देंगे? (future simple)
9. हो सकता है वे मुझे भारत न जाने दें। (probability)

1. kṛpayā use ārām karne dījie. (imperative present)
2. kṛpayā use sone dījiegā. (imperative future)
3. ve use paṛhne dete haiṁ. (present simple)
4. ve muje apne ghar meṁ khelne dete the .(past habitual)
5. maiṁne use śatrañj khelne diyā. (past simple)
6. hamne unheṁ nṛtyă dekhne diyā thā. (past perfect)
7. usne mujhe bhojan svayaṁ pakāne diyā hai (present perfect)
8. kyā ve mujhe apne yahāṁ rahne deṁge? (future simple)
9. ho saktā hai ve mujhe bhārat na jāne deṁ. (probability)

Key 2

1. My grandparents do not let us speak at home in English .
2. Mother did not use to let me drive any vehicle in my childhood.
3. Father did not use to let us go alone at night to watch a film.
4. My teacher did not allow me to take part in the debate.
5. My brother did not let me use his camera.
6. Grandmother will not let us eat nonvegetarian food during the Navratra.
7. My husband might not let me take part in the music competition.
8. It is likely that my in-laws will let me adopt a child.

Key 3

1. रमन अपनी पत्नी को जो वह चाहे पहनने देता है।
2. प्राची ने अपने पति को बाढ़ पीड़ितों के लिए एक महीने का वेतन दान देने दिया।
3. क्या तुम मुझे पहाड़ों में पदयात्रा करने जाने दोगे?
4. हो सकता है वे हमें बाहर न खाने दें।
5. संभवता पिता जी मुझे मेरे मित्रों के साथ रात को अकेले बाहर कभी नहीं जाने देंगे।

8. मेरे माता पिता हमेशा मुझे, जो मैं चाहूँ, करने देते हैं।
7. पिता जी सामान्यता किसीको भी अपना कम्प्यूटर नहीं छूने देते।
8. दादी जी कभी भी किसीको अपने पलंग पर नहीं बैठने देतीं।
9. कृपया मुझे संगीत सुनने दीजिए।
10. उसको अन्दर आने दो।

1. raman apnī patnī ko jo vah cāhe pahnane detā hai.
2. prācī ne apne pati ko bāṛh pīṛitoṁ ke lie ek mahīne kā vetan dān dene diyā.
3. kyā tum mujhe pahāṛoṁ meṁ padyātrā karne jāne doge?
4. ho saktā hai ve hameṁ bāhar na khāne deṁ.
5. sambhavtā pitā jī mujhe mere mitroṁ ke sāth rāt ko akele bāhar kabhī nahīṁ jāne deṁge.
6. mere mātā pitā hameśā mujhe jo maiṁ cāhūṁ karne dete haiṁ.
7. pitā jī sāmānyătā kisīko bhī apnā kampyūṭar nahīṁ chūne dete.
8. dādī jī kabhī bhī kisīko apne palaṅg par nahīṁ baiṭhne detīṁ.
9. kṛpayā mujhe saṅgīt sunane dījie.
10. use andar āne do

Seasons ऋतुएँ		ṛtueṁ
spring	बसन्त ऋतु	basant ṛtu
summer	ग्रीष्म ऋतु	grīṣm ṛtu
rainy season	वर्षा ऋतु	varṣā ṛtu
autumn	शरदऋतु	śarad ṛtu
early winter	हेमन्त ऋतु	hemant ṛtu
late winter	शिशिर ऋतु	śiśir ṛtu

16 Habit Structure

subj. + obj. + का, के, की kā /ke/ kī + आदी होना ādī honā in the required tense

* का, के, की, **kā /ke/ kī depends on the number and gender of the subject:**

1. मैं (f.) सुबह जल्दी उठने **की आदी हूँ।** (present indefinite)
   maiṁ (f.) subah jaldī uṭhne kī ādī hūṁ.

   I am used to getting up early in the morning.
2. सब छात्र (m.pl.) परिश्रम करने **के आदी थे।** (past habitual)
   sab chātra (m.pl.) pariśram karne ke ādī the.

   All the students were used to working hard.
3. वह (m.) रात को देर तक जागने **का आदी हो गया।** (past simple)
   vah (m.) rāt ko der tak jāgne kā ādī ho gayā.

   He got used to keeping awake late at night.
4. मैं (f.) भारतीय भोजन खाने **की आदी हो गई हूँ।** (present perfect)
   maiṁ (f.) bhārtīyă bhojan khāne kī ādī ho gaī hūṁ.
   I have gotten used to eating Indian food.
5. आप (f.) छोटे घर में रहने की **आदी हो जाएँगी।** (future simple)
   āp(f.) choṭe ghar meṁ rahne kī ādī ho jāeṁgī.

   You will get used to living in a small house.

subject को ko + object + की आदत kī ādat + होना honā

* **की आदत kī ādat is invariable.**

1. मुझको सुबह जल्दी उठने **की आदत** है।
   mujhko subah jaldī uṭhne kī ādat hai.

   I am used to getting up early in the morning.

2. सब छात्रों को परिश्रम करने **की आदत थी।**
   sab chātroṁ ko pariśram karne kī ādat thī.
   All the students were used to working hard.
3. उसको रात को देर तक जागने **की आदत हो गई।**
   usko rāt ko der tak jāgne kī ādat ho gaī.
   He got used to keeping awake late at night.
4. मुझको भारतीय भोजन खाने **की आदत हो गई है।**
   mujhko bhārtīyă bhojan khāne kī ādat ho gaī hai.
   I have gotten used to eating Indian food.
5. आपको (f.) छोटे घर में रहने की **आदत हो जाएगी।**
   āpko choṭe ghar meṁ rahne kī ādat ho jāegī.
   You will get used to living in a small house.

Ex. 1: Fill in the blanks with का, के, की kā /ke/ kī ādī honā

1. मैं (m.) सुबह व्यायाम करने .... **आदी हूँ।**
2. क्या तुम (m.) सुबह व्यायाम करने............................**आदी हो?**
3. क्या आप (m.) मरुस्थल में रहने ....**आदी हैं ?**
4. मैं (f.) जवाब–तलब करने ....**आदी नहीं।**
5. वे (f.) सुबह–सुबह स्नान करने ....**आदी थीं।**
6. ये सब औरतें घर का काम करने ....**आदी थीं।**
7. माता जी सुबह सपरिवार पूजा करने ....**आदी थीं।**
8. वे (m.pl./hon.) गर्म मुल्क में रहने .... **आदी हो गए ।**
9. भारत में कर्मचारी (m.pl.)बार–बार हड़ताल करने ....**आदी हो गए हैं।**
10. वे (m.) मेरे घर में अपना काम स्वयं करने .... **आदी हो जाएँगे।**

1. maiṁ (m) subah vyāyām karne .... ādī hūṁ.
2. kyā tum (m) subah vyāyām karne .... ādī ho?
3. kyā āp (m.) marusthal meṁ rahne .... ādī haiṁ?
4. maiṁ (f.) javāb talab karne .... ādī nahīṁ.
5. ve (f.) subah-subah snān karne.................................ādī thīṁ.
6. ye sab aurteṁ ghar kā kām karne .... ādī thīṁ.
7. mātā jī subah saparivā r pūjā karne .... ādī thīṁ.
8. ve (m.pl./hon.) garm mulk meṁ rahne .... ādī ho gae haiṁ.
9. bhārat mem karmcārī (m.pl.) bār-bār haṛtāl karne ....
   ādī ho gae haiṁ.
10. ve (m.) mere ghar meṁ apnā kām svayaṁ karne ...ādī ho jāeṁge.

Glossary:

मरुस्थल (m.)	marusthal	desert
जवाब–तलब (f.)	javāb-talab	interrogation
सुबह–सुबह (adv)	subah-subah	early morning
सपरिवार (adj.)	saparivār	with family
गर्म मुल्क (m.)	garm mulk	hot country
कर्मचारी (m.)	karmcārī	employee
हड़ताल (f.)	haṛtāl	strike
स्वयम् (adj.)	svayaṁ	oneself

Ex. 2: Change as per example : Change का, के, की आदी होना kā /ke/ kī ādī honā **to** की आदत होना kī **ādat** honā **.**

> मैं (f.) सुबह जल्दी उठने की आदी हूँ।
> ➯ मुझे सुबह जल्दी उठने की आदत है।

1. वे (m.) ठण्डे देश में रहने के आदी हैं।

   ....

2. हम (f.pl./hon.) सुबह–सुबह चाय पीने की आदी नहीं हैं।

   ....

3. वह f.) बहुत शारीरिक मेहनत करने की आदी नहीं थी।

   ....

4. मैं (m.) बाईं ओर वाहन चलाने का आदी नहीं था।

   ....

5. वह (m.) सुबह जल्दी जागने का आदी हो गया है।

   ....

6. वे (m.pl./hon.) देहात में रहने के आदी हो गए थे।

   ....

7. वह (m.) छात्रावास में जाकर अपना काम स्वयं करने का आदी हो जाएगा। ....

> maiṁ (f.) subah jaldī uṭhne kī ādī hūṁ.
> ➯ muje subah jaldī uṭhne kī ādat hai.

1. ve (m.hon.) ṭhaṇḍe deś meṁ rahne ke ādī haiṁ.
2. ham (f.) subah-subah cāy pīne kī ādī nahīṁ haiṁ.
3. vah (f.) bahut śārīrik mehnat karne kī ādī nahīṁ thī.
4. maiṁ (m.)bāīṁ or vāhan calāne kā ādī nahīṁ thā.
5. vah (m.)subah jaldī jāgne kā ādī ho gayā hai.
6. ve (m.pl.) dehāt meṁ rahne ke ādī ho gae the.
7. vah (m.) chātrāvās meṁ jā kar apnā kām svayaṁ karne kā ādī ho jāegā.

Glossary:

शारीरिक मेहनत (f.)	śārīrik mehnat	physical work
बाईं ओर (adj. + f.)	bāīṁ or	the left side
वाहन (m.)	vāhan	vehicle
देहात (m.)	dehāt	countryside
छात्रावास (m.)	chātrāvās	students' hostel

Ex. 3: Translate into Hindi: Use 'की आदत होना kī ādat honā in sentences 1-3, and का, के, की आदी होना kā, ke, kī ādī honā' in sentences 4-6.

1. We are not used to living in the plains.
2. I am not used to much noise.
3. I am not used to climbing the stairs.
4. I (m) am used to drinking boiled water.
5. She has gotten used to Indian food.
6. You (m.) will soon get used to customs and traditions here.

Glossary:

plains	मैदान	maidān
noise	हल्ला–गुल्ला	hallā-gullā
stairs	सीढ़ियाँ	sīṛhiyāṁ
customs and traditions	रीति–रिवाज़	rīti-rivāz

Key 1

1	का	kā ;	2,3,8 ,9, 10	के	ke
4,5, 6, 7	की	kī			

Key 2

1. उनको (m.) ठण्डे देश में रहने की आदत हैं।
2. हमें सुबह–सुबह चाय पीने की आदत नहीं हैं।
3. उसको बहुत शारीरिक मेहनत करने की आदत नहीं थी।
4. मुझको बाईं ओर वाहन चलाने की आदत नहीं थी।
5. उसको सुबह जल्दी जागने की आदत हो गई है।
6. उनको देहात में रहने की आदत हो गई थी।
7. वह छात्रावास में जाकर अपना काम स्वयं करने का आदी हो जाएगा।

1. unko ṭhaṇḍe deś meṁ rahne kī ādat hai.
2. ham eṁ subah-subah cāy pīne kī ādat nahī ṁ hai.
3. usko bahut śārīrik mehnat karne kī ādat nahīṁ thī.
4. mujhko bāīṁ or vāhan calāne kī ādat nahīṁ thī .
5. usko subah jaldī jāgne kī ādat ho gaī hai.
6. unko dehāt meṁ rahne kī ādat ho gaī thī.
7. usko chātrāvās meṁ jā kar apnā kām svayaṁ karne kī ādat ho jāegī.

Key 3

1. हमें मैदानों में रहने की आदत नहीं है।
2. मुझे बहुत हल्ले–गुल्ले की आदत नहीं।
3. मुझको सीढ़ियाँ चढ़ने की आदत नहीं है।
4. मैं (m.) उबला पानी पीने का आदी हूँ।
5. वह (f.) भारतीय भोजन की आदी हो गई है।
6. तुम (m.) जल्दी ही यहाँ के रीति–रिवाज़ों के आदी हो जाओगे।

1. hameṁ maidānoṁ meṁ rahne kī ādat nahīṁ hai.
2. mujhe bahut halle-gulle kī ādat nahīṁ.
3. mujhko sīṛhiyāṁ caṛhne kī ādat nahīṁ hai.
4. maiṁ (m.) ublā pānī pīne kā ādī hūṁ.
5. vah (f.) bhārtīyă bhojan kī ādī ho gaī hai.
6. tum (m.) jaldī hī yahāṁ ke rīti-rivāzoṁ ke ādī ho jāoge.

17 Continuative Compound

(v.r.+ ता ta/ ते te/ ती tī) + रहना rahnā

In case of action verbs :

subj. + obj. + v.r.+ ता ta / ते te / ती tī + रहना rahnā + होना honā
agree with N & G of the subject in required tense

1. तुम काम करते रहो। You keep on working.
   tum kām karte raho.
2. तुम मेरे घर आते रहना। You keep coming to my house.
   tum mere ghar āte rahnā.
3. आप मेरे साथ काम करते रहें। You keep working with me.
   āp mere sāth kām karte raheṁ.
4. रमोला दिन भर बोलती रहती है। Ramola keeps talking all day.
   ramolā din bhar boltī rahtī hai.
5. कुत्ता दिन रात भौंकता रहता था। The dog used to keep barking day and night.
   kuttā din-rāt bhauṁktā rahtā thā.
6. वे व्यायाम करते रहे। The kept exercising.
   ve vyāyām karte rahe.
7. माँ दिन भर भोजन बनाती रही थीं। Mother had kept cooking all day.
   māṁ din bhar bhojan banātī rahī thīṁ.
8. मैं इस विषय पर काफ़ी सोचती रही हूँ। I have kept thinking much on this matter.
   maiṁ is viṣay par kāfī soctī rahī hūṁ.
9. मैं आजीवन हिन्दी पढ़ाती रहूँगी। I will keep teaching Hindi all my life.
   maiṁ ājīvan hindī paṛhātī rahūṁgī.

Verbs describing continuing state :

subj. + v.r.+ आ ā / ए e / ई ī + रहना rahnā + होना honā
agree with N & G of the subject in required tense

1. आप लेटे रहिए। — Keep lying down.
   āp leṭe rahie.
2. आप बैठे रहें। — Keep sitting
   āp baiṭhe raheṁ
3. सोमा दिन भर सोई रहती है। — Soma keeps sleeping all day.
   somā din bhar soī rahtī hai.
4. मेरा शब्दकोश सदैव इस मेज़ पर पड़ा रहता है। — My dictionary always keeps lying on this table.
   merā śabdkoś sadaiv is mez par paṛā rahtā hai.

Ex.1: Translate into English:

1. वह सबकी आलोचना करता रहता है।
2. वह बार-बार एक ही ग़लती करती रहती है।
3. माँ मुझे हमेशा बड़ों के प्रति मेरे फ़र्ज़ याद दिलाती रहती थीं।
4. मुझे लगता है, आज रात भर बारिश होती रहेगी।
5. आपको निरन्तर प्रयास करते रहना चाहिए।*
6. आप सब को शरणार्थियों की मदद करते रहना चाहिए था।*
7. हमें मध्य रात्रि तक जागते रहना पड़ा।
8. आपको लम्बे समय तक अभ्यास करते रहना पड़ेगा।

1. vah sabkī ālocnā kartā rahtā hai.
2. vah bār-bār ek hī Galtī kartī rahtī hai.
3. māṁ mujhe hameśā baṛoṁ ke prati mere farz yād dilātī rahtī thīṁ.
4. mujhe lagtā hai āj rāt bhar bāriś hotī rahegī.
5. āpko nirantar prayās karte rahnā cāhie.*

Ref. चाहिए cāhie pg. 149 **Ref.** पड़ना paṛnā pg.174

6. āp sab ko śaraṇārthiyoṁ kī madad karte rahnā cāhie thā.*
7. hameṁ madhyă rātri tak jāgte rahnā paṛā.
8. āpko lambe samay tak abhyās karte rahnā paṛegā.

Glossary:

आलोचना (f.)	ālocnā	criticism
एक ही (adj.)	ek hī	the same
बार-बार (adv.)	bār-bār	again and again
ग़लती (f.)	Galtī	mistake
बड़े (m.)	baṛe	elders
के प्रति (ppn.)	ke prati	towards
फ़र्ज़ (m.)	farz	duty
याद दिलाना (v.t.)	yād dilānā	to remind
निरन्तर (adv.)	nirantar	non stop
प्रयास (m.)	prayās	effort
शरणार्थी (m.)	śaraṇārthī	refugee
मध्य रात्रि (f.)	madhya rātri	mid night
जागना (v.i.)	jāgnā	be awake
अभ्यास (m.)	abhyās	practice

Ex.2: Translate into Hindi: Continuative compound :

1. He keeps humming all the time.
2. We keep visiting them.
3. The dog kept whimpering all day.
4. All of us kept on laughing like crazy.
5. You guys keep on having fun.
6. Please all of you keep on doing your work.
7. Mother had to keep doing house chores.
8. You will have to keep on trying.
9. They should keep on helping the earthquake victims.
10. You should have kept on supporting your leader.

Glossary:

hum	गुनगुनाना (v.t.)	gungunānā
visiting s.o	के यहाँ जाना (v.i.)	ke yahāṁ jānā
to whimper	कराहना (v.i.)	karāhnā

to have fun	मौज–मस्ती करना (v.t.)	mauj-mastī karnā
to help	सहायता करना (v.t.)	sahāyatā karnā
to make effort	प्रयास करना (v.t.)	pryās karnā
earthquake victims	भूकम्प पीड़ित (m.)	bhūkamp pīṛit
to support	समर्थन देना (v.t.)	samarthan denā

Ex.3: Rewrite the sentences using the continuative compound in the required tense. :

1. आप अपना काम कीजिए। ....
2. तुम उसको समझाओ। ....
3. आप रोज़ सुबह सैर कीजिएगा। ....
4. तुम सदैव मन लगाकर पढ़ना। ....
5. आप स्वस्थ रहने के लिए सदैव पौष्टिक आहार लें। ....
6. वे अकसर हमें अपने यहाँ बुलाते हैं। ....
7. बच्चे इसवाले मैदान में खेलते थे। ....
8. प्रताप बैठा। ....
9. हम दोनों रात भर बतियाए थे। ....
10. उसने परीक्षा के लिए बहुत पढ़ा है। ....
11. दिन–प्रति–दिन महँगाई बढ़ेगी। ....

1. āp apnā kām kījie. ....
2. tum usko samjhāo. ....
3. āp roz subah sair kījiegā. ....
4. tum sadaiv man lagākar paṛhnā. ....
5. āp svasth rahne ke lie sadaiv pauṣṭik āhār leṁ.
6. ve aksar hameṁ apne yahāṁ bulāte haiṁ..
7. bacce isvāle maidān meṁ khelte the. ....
8. pratāp baiṭhā.
9. ham donoṁ rāt bhar batiyāe the ....
10. usne parīkṣā ke lie bahut paṛhā hai. ....
11. din-prati-din mahṁgāī baṛhegī. ....

Glossary

मन लगाना (v.t.)	man lagānā	to concentrate
स्वस्थ (m.)	svasth	healthy
पौष्टिक आहार (m.)	pauṣṭik āhār	nutritious diet
बतियाना (f.)	batiyānā	to talk
परीक्षा (f.)	parīkṣā	exam
दिन–प्रति–दिन (f.)	din-prati-din	day by day
महँगाई (f.)	mahṁgāī	inflation

Key 1

1. He keeps criticising everybody.
2. She keeps making the same mistake again and again.
3. Mother used to keep reminding me of my duties towards elders.
4. I think, it will keep raining all night.
5. You should keep on trying.
6. All of you should have kept helping the refugees.
7. We had to keep awake until midnight.
8. You will have to keep pracitising for a long time.

Key 2

1. वह हर वक़्त गुनगुनाता रहता है।
2. हम उनके यहाँ अकसर जाते रहते है।
3. कुत्ता सारा दिन कराहता रहा।
4. हम सब पागलों की तरह हँसते रहे।
5. तुम लोग मौज–मस्ती करते रहो।
6. कृपया आप सब अपना–अपना काम करते रहें।
7. माँ को घर के काम करते रहना पड़ा।
8. आप को प्रयास करते रहना पड़ेगा।
9. उनको भूकम्प पीड़ितों की मदद करते रहना चाहिए।
10. आपको अपने नेता को समर्थन देते रहना चाहिए था।

1. vah har vaqt gungunātā rahtā hai.
2. ham unke yahāṁ aksar jāte rahte haiṁ.
3. kuttā sārā din karāhtā rahā.
4. ham sab pāgloṁ kī tarah haṁste rahe.
5. tum log mauj-mastī karte raho.
6. kṛpayā āp sab apnā-apnā kām karte raheṁ.
7. māṁ ko ghar ke kām karte rahnā paṛā.
8. āpko prayās karte rahnā paṛegā.
9. unko bhūkamp pīṛitoṁ kī madad karte rahnā cā hie.
10. āpko apne netā ko smarthan dete rahnā cāhie thā.

Key 3

1. आप अपना काम करते रहिए।
2. तुम उसको समझाते रहो।
3. आप रोज़ सुबह सैर करते रहिएगा।
4. तुम सदैव मन लगाकर पढ़ते रहना।
5. आप स्वस्थ रहने के लिए सदैव पौष्टिक आहार लेते रहें।
6. वे अक्सर हमें अपने यहाँ बुलाते रहते हैं।
7. बच्चे इसवाले मैदान में खेलते रहते थे।
8. प्रताप बैठा रहा।
9. हम दोनों रात भर बतियाते रहे थे।
10. वह परीक्षा के लिए बहुत पढ़ती रही है।
11. दिन–प्रति–दिन महँगाई बढ़ती रहेगी।

1. āp apnā kām karte rahie.
2. tum usko samjhāte raho.
3. āp roz subah sair karte rahiegā.
4. tum sadaiv man lagākar paṛhte rahnā.
5. āp svasth rahne ke lie sadaiv pauṣṭik āhār lete raheṁ.
6. ve aksar hameṁ apne yahāṁ bulāte rahte haiṁ.
7. bacce isvāle maidān meṁ khelte rahte the.
8. pratāp baiṭhā rahā.
9. ham donoṁ rāt bhar batiāte rahe the.
10. vah parīkṣā ke lie bahut paṛhtī rahī hai.
11. din-prati-din mahṁgāī baṛhtī rahegī.

macro time periods		
present	वर्तमान	vartmān
past	अतीत	atīt
future	भविष्य	bhaviṣyă

18 Progressive Compound

(v.r.+ ता ta/ ते te/ ती tī) + जाना jānā

subj. + obj. + (v.r.+ ता ta/ ते te/ ती tī) + जाना jānā + होना honā

agree with N & G of the subject

in required tense

Uses :

(1) negative connotation,disapproval of the activity. Examles 1-2

(2) gradual change . Examples 3-4

Examples:

1. वह खाता जाता है।
   vah khātā jatā hai.
   He goes on eating.

2. वह एक बार बोलने लगता था,
   तो बोलता ही जाता था।
   vah ek bār bolne lagtā thā, to
   boltā hī jātā thā.
   Once he started speaking, he would just go on speaking.

3. इस इलाक़े में दिन–प्रति–दिन
   अपराध बढ़ते जा रहे हैं।
   is ilāqe meṁ din-prati-din
   aprādh baṛhte jā rahe haiṁ.
   Day by day crimes in this area are increasing.

4. लगातार बारिशों के कारण नदी में
   पानी का स्तर बढ़ता जा रहा है।
   lagātār bāriśoṁ ke kāraṇ nadī
   meṁ pānī kā star baṛhtā jā rahā hai.
   Because of non-stop rains, the level of water in the river is gradually increasing

Ex.: **Change as per example using the progressive compound :**

शिक्षण संस्थानों में अनुशासनहीनता फैल रही है।
⇨ शिक्षण संस्थानों में अनुशासनहीनता फैलती जा रही है।

1. विश्व में प्रदूषण बढ़ रहा है। ....
2. सरकार मज़दूरों की ग़ैरज़रूरी माँगें मान रही है। ....
3. नवयुवक असंस्कारी हो रहे हैं। ....
4. भष्टाचार फैल रहा है। ....
5. बेरोज़गारी बढ़ रही है। ....
6. सब नदियों में जल प्रदूषित हो रहा है। ....

śikṣaṇ saṃsthānoṁ meṁ anuśāsanhīntā phail rahī hai.
⇨ śikṣaṇ saṃsthānoṁ meṁ anuśāsanhīntā phailtī jā rahī hai.

1. viśva meṁ pradūṣaṇ baṛh rahā hai. ....
2. sarkār mazdūroṁ kī Gairzarūrī māṁgeṁ mān rahī hai.
   ....
3. navyuvak asaṃskārī ho rahe haiṁ. ....
4. bhraṣṭācār phail rahā hai. ....
5. berozgārī baṛh rahī hai. ....
6. sab nadiyoṁ meṁ jal pradūṣit ho rahā hai.
   ....

Glossary:

शिक्षण संस्थान (m.)	śikṣaṇ saṃsthān	educational institution(s)
अनुशासनहीनता (f.)	anuśāsanhīntā	indescipline
फैलना (v.i.)	phailnā	to spread
प्रदूषण (m.)	pradūṣaṇ	pollution
सरकार (f.)	sarkār	government
मज़दूर (m.)	mazdūr	laborer
ग़ैरज़रूरी adj.)	Gairzarūrī	unnecessary
नवयुवक (m.)	navyuvak	young man
असंस्कारी (adj.)	asaṃskārī	unculturd
भष्टाचार (m.)	bhraṣṭācār	corruption
बेरोज़गारी (f.)	berozgārī	unemployment
बढ़ना (v.i.)	baṛhnā	to grow

Key

1. विश्व में प्रदूषण बढ़ता जा रहा है।
2. सरकार मज़दूरों की ग़ैरज़रूरी माँगें मानती जा रही है।
3. नवयुवक असंस्कारी होते जा रहे हैं।
4. भष्टाचार फैलता जा रहा है।
5. बेरोज़गारी बढ़ती जा रही है।
6. सब नदियों में जल प्रदूषित हो्ता जा रहा है।

1. viśva meṁ pradūṣaṇ baṛhtā jā rahā hai
2. sarkār mazdūroṁ kī Gairzarūrī māṁge māntī jā rahī hai.
3. navyuvak asaṃskārī hote jā rahe haiṁ.
4. bhraṣṭācār phailtā jā rahā hai.
5. berozgārī-baṛhtī jā rahī haiṁ.
6. sab nadiyoṁ meṁ jal pradūṣit hotā jā rahā hai.

(v.r. + ne) + 'के योग्य / के लायक (न) होना'

be/ not be worth v...ing

1. यह घर खरीदने काबिल नहीं। yah ghar kharīdne kābil nahīṁ.	This house is not worth buying.
2. यह समस्या चिन्ता करने लायक नहीं। yah samasyā cintā karne lāyak nahīṁ	This problem is not worth worrying.
3. कुशीनगर देखने लायक स्थान है। kuśīnagar dekhne lāyak sthān hai.	Kushinagar is a place worth visiting.

19 Adjectives

In Hindi adjectives in their base form are classified into two groups.

- आ - ending adjectives such as

बड़ा baṛā (big), छोटा choṭā (small)

बूढ़ा būṛhā = old (person), पुराना purānā = old (thing) etc.

- adjectives with endings other than आ ā such as

जवान **javān =young** ; बासी bāsī = **stale,**

लड़ाकू laṛākū = **quarrelous etc**

☞ The आ ā-ending adjectives change to ए e, ई ī-ending to accord with the number and gender of the noun or pronoun they qualify in the required case, direct or oblique as shown below.

mas.singular	**mas.plural**	**case**
big room, बड़ा कमरा baṛā kamrā	big rooms, बड़े कमरे baṛe kamre	direct
in big room, बड़े कमरे में baṛe kamre meṁ	in big rooms बड़े कमरों में baṛe kamroṁ meṁ	oblique.
fem.singular	**fem. .plural**	**case**
big road बड़ी सड़क baṛī saṛak	big roads बड़ी सड़कें baṛī saṛkeṁ	direct
on big road बड़ी सड़क पर baṛī saṛak par	on big road बड़ी सड़कों पर baṛī saṛkoṁ par	oblique

- **All other adjectives with any other ending always remain the same regardless of the number, gender and the case of the noun they qualify. For example :**

singular	plural	case
beautiful child सुन्दर बच्चा (m.) sundar baccā	beautiful children सुन्दर बच्चे sundar bacce	direct
to beautiful child सुन्दर बच्चे को sundar bacce ko	to beautiful children सुन्दर बच्चों को sundar baccoṁ ko	oblique
beautiful woman सुन्दर औरत (f.) sundar aurat	beautiful women sundar aurteṁ sundar aurteṁ	direct
to beautiful woman सुन्दर औरत को sundar aurat ko	to beautiful women सुन्दर औरतों को sundar aurtoṁ ko	oblique

ADJECTIVES: COMPARATIVES AND SUPERLATIVES :

- **comparative = X + से + base form of adjective**

☞ से अधिक, से कहीं अधिक, से कम, से कहीं कम, की तुलना में, की बनिस्बत

se adhik, se kahīṁ adhik, se kam, se kahīṁ kam, kī tulnā meṁ, ki banisbat

X से अच्छा	X se acchā	better than X
X से सस्ता	X se sastā	less expensive than X
X से भारी	X se bhārī	heavier than X
X से झगड़ालू	X se jhagṛālū	more quarrelsome than X

1. उनका घर हमारे घर से बड़ा है। unkā ghar hamāre ghar se baṛā hai — Their house is bigger than our house.
2. आज कल से ज़्यादा ठण्डा है। āj kal se zyādā ṭhaṇḍā hai. — Today is colder than yesterday.

- **Superlative = सब से + base form of the verb.**

सबसे अच्छा	sab se acchā	the best
सबसे महँगा	sab se mahṁgā	the most expensive
सबसे छोटा	sab se choṭā	the smallest
सबसे सुन्दर	sab se sundar	the most beautiful
सबसे दयालु	sab se dayālu	the kindest

1. यह सबसे अच्छा है। yah sab se acchā hai. — This is the best.
2. वह कक्षा में सबसे छोटा है। vah kakṣā mem sab se choṭā hai. — He is the smallest in class.

- **More superlative expression are: ' adjective + se + adjective'**

सुन्दर–से–सुन्दर	sundar-se-sundarthe	the most beautiful
अमीर–से–अमीर	amīr-se-amīr	the poorest
परमप्रिय	parampriyă	most dear

Ex.1: Translate into English:

1. समीर सुष्मा से छोटा है।
2. पूर्वी ओवी से ज़्यादा बुद्धिमान है।
3. पूर्वी दोनों में से अधिक परिश्रमी भी है।
4. मेरी पुत्री मुझसे कहीं अमीर है।
5. पुन्नी तेजु से कम होशियार है।
6. ग्रामीण जीवन शहरी जीवन की तुलना में शान्त होता है।
7. हमारा गाँव दस वर्ष पहले की तुलना में अधिक जनसंकुल है।
8. मैं पैसे की तुलना में सेहत को कहीं अधिक मूल्यवान मानता हूँ।
9. मुझे बड़े शहरों में रहने की बनिस्बत छोटे कस्बों में रहना ज़्यादा अच्छा लगता है।

1. samīr suśmā se choṭā hai.
2. pūrvī ovī se zyādā buddhimān hai.
3. pūrvī donoṁ meṁ se adhik pariśramī bhī hai.
4. merī putrī mujh se kahīṁ amīr hai.
5. punnī tejū se kam hośiyār hai.
6. grāmīṇ jīvan śahrī jīvan kī tulnā meṁ śānt hotā hai.
7. hamārā gāṁv das varṣ pahle kī tulnā meṁ adhik jan-saṅkul hai.
8. maiṁ paise kī tulnā meṁ sehat ko kahīṁ adhik mūlyăvān māntā hūṁ
9. mujhe baṛe śahroṁ meṁ rahne kī banisbat choṭe kasboṁ meṁ rahnā zyādā acchā lagtā hai.

Glossary:

परिश्रमी (adj.)	pariśramī	hardworking
से कहीं (comparative.)	se kahīṁ	much more
ग्रामीण (adj.)	grāmīṇ	village(adjectival use)
ग्रामीण जीवन (adj.+ m.)	grāmīṇ jīvan	village life
शहरी जीवन (adj.+ m)	śahrī jīvan	city life
की तुलना में (comparative)	kī tulnā meṁ	compared to
शान्त (adj.)	śānt	peaceful
जनसंकुल (adj.)	jan-saṅkul	crowded
मूल्यवान (adj.)	mūlyăvān	valuable
मानना (v.t.)	mānanā	to believe
की बनिस्बत (ppn)	kī banisbat	in comparison with
कस्बा (m.)	kasbā	district (a small town)

Ex.2: Translate into Hindi:

1. She sings much better than her friend.
2. Our dog is much more ferocious than our neighbour's dog.
3. That house is bigger than this one.
4. This house is not as big as that one.
5. Ritvik's Hindi is getting better and better every day.

Glossary:

ferocious	खूंखार (adj.)	khūṁkhār
neighbour	पड़ोसी (m.)	pṛosī
to improve	सुधरना (v.i.)	sudharnā

Ex. 3: Translate into Hindi:

1. Mutual hatred is the worst thing.
2. The sunset at Kanyakumari is the most beautiful one.
3. Smoking is the most harmful thing for one's health.
4. He is the tallest man in the world.

Glossary:

mutual	आपसी (adj.)	āpsī
hatred	घृणा (f.)	ghṛṇā
compared to	की तुलना में	kī tulnā meṁ
sunset	सूर्यास्त (m.)	sūryāst
smoking	धूम्रपान (m.)	dhūmrapān
health	स्वास्थ्य (m.)	svāsthyă
harmful	हानिकर (adj.)	hānikar

Ex. 4: Superlatives:

1. मेले में सुन्दर–से–सुन्दर औरतें थीं।
2. होली–दीवाली पर ग़रीब–से–ग़रीब भी नए कपड़े पहनते हैं।
3. स्वयम्वर* में एक–से–एक सूरमाओं ने भाग लिया।
4. हमारे स्कूल में एक–से–एक प्रतिभाशाली विद्यार्थी पढ़ते हैं।
5. सुजाता मेरी परम प्रिय दोस्त है।

1. mele meṁ sundar-se-sundar aurteṁ thīṁ.
2. holī dīwalī par Garīb-se-Garīb bhī nae kapṛe pahnte haiṁ.
3. svayaṁvar* meṁ ek-se-ek sūrmāoṁ ne bhāg liyā.
4. hamāre skūl meṁ ek-se-ek pratibhāśālī vidyārthī paṛhte haiṁ.
5. sujātā merī parampriyă dost hai.

.Glossary:

सुन्दर–से–सुन्दर	sundar-se-sundar	the most beautiful
ग़रीब–से–ग़रीब	Garīb-se-Garīb	poorest of the poor
एक–से–एक	ek-se-ek	one better than the other
स्वयम्वर(m)	svayaṁvar	wedding*
सूरमा (n./adj)	sūrmā(n/adj.)	brave
प्रतिभाशाली (adj.)	pratibhāśālī	talented
परमप्रिय(adj.)	parampriyă	most dear

*An ancient tradition in India. The eligible grooms were invited all at one time and the bride had the freedom to choose her husband to be.

Key1

1. Samir is younger than Sushma.
2. Poorvi is more intelligent than Ovi.
3. Also, Poorvi is more hardworking of the two.
4. My daughter is much richer than me.
5. Punni is less clever than Teju.
6. Village life is peaceful in comparison with city life.
7. Our village is more crowded compared to (what it was) ten years ago.
8. I believe health to be much more valuable compared to money.
9. I prefer to live in small districts compared to living in the big cities.

Key2

1. वह अपनी मित्र से कहीं अच्छा गाती है।
2. हमारा कुत्ता हमारे पड़ोसियों के कुत्ते से कहीं ज्यादा खूंखार है।
3. वह घर इसवाले से बड़ा है।
4. यह घर उतना बड़ा नहीं जितना वहवाला।
5. रितविक की हिन्दी दिन–पर–दिन सुधर रही है।

1. vah apnī mitra se kahīṁ acchā gātī hai.
2. hamārā kuttā hamāre pṛosiyoṁ ke kutte se kahīṁ zyādā khūṁkhār hai.
3. vah ghar is vāle se baṛā hai.
4. yah ghar utnā baṛā nahīṁ jitnā vahvālā.
5. ritvik kī hindī din-par-din sudhar rahī hai.

Key 3

1. आपसी घृणा सब से बुरी चीज़ है।
2. कन्याकुमारी का सूर्यास्त सब से सुन्दर होता है।
3. धूम्रपान स्वास्थ्य के लिए सब से ज़्यादा हानिकर होता है।
4. वह विश्व में सब से लम्बा आदमी है।

1. apsī ghṛṇā sab se burī cīz hai.
2. kanyākumārī kā sūryāst sab se sundar hotā hai.
3. dhūmrapān svāsthyă ke lie sab se zyādā hānikar hotā hai.
4. vah viśva meṁ sab se lambā ādmī hai.

Key 4

1. There were most beautiful women in the fare. (one more beautiful than the other)
2. The poorest of the poor also wear new clothes at Holi and Divali.

3. The bravest of the brave (one more brave than the other) had come to the 'svayaṁvar'*
4. The most talented students study in our school.
5. Sujata is my dearest friend.

न...न......na.....na.... neither...nor

1. न सुधीर का दोष था, न अनिल का। na sudhir kā doṣ thā, na anil kā.	**Neither Sudhir nor Anil was to blame.**
2. न हम सोए, न हमने काम ही किया। na ham soe, na ham ne kām hī kiyā.	We neither slept nor worked.

या...या...yā .....yā .... either...or

1. या तो तुम खुद करो, या मुझे करने दो।
   yā to tum khud karo, yā mujhe karne do.
   Either do it yourself or let me do it.
2. या तो अपनी ईमानदारी साबित करो, या दण्ड चुकाओ।
2. yā to apnī imāndārī sābit karo, ya daṇḍ cukāo.
   Either prove your honesty or pay the fine.

दोष	doṣ	fault
ईमानदारी	īmāndārī	honesty
साबित करना	sābit karnā	to prove
दण्ड	daṇḍ	fine
चुकाना	cukānā	to pay

20 Possessive Case

In Hindi the genitive case endings का kā, के ke, की kī. accord with the N and G of the object possessed and not that of the possesser as shown in the table given below.

☞ **In the oblique case even when the postposition is implied and not explicitly used, , if the object possessed is a masculine noun of any ending, का kā changes to के ke .**
However के 'ke' preceding mas.pl. noun, and ' की 'kī' preceding fem. sg. or plural noun remains unchanged in the obl. case.

☞ **Their English equivalent is 'of' ' or alternatively the use of apostrophe.**

object possessed mas.sg.	object possessed mas.pl.	case
room of Vidya vidyā kā kamrā विद्या का कमरा	rooms of Vidya vidya ke kamre विद्या के कमरे	direct
in Vidya's room vidyā ke kamre meṁ विद्या के कमरे में	in Vidya's rooms vidya ke kamroṁ meṁ विद्या के कमरों में	oblique
object possessed fem.sg.	**object possessed fem.pl.**	**case**
book of Vidya vidyā kī kitāb विद्या की किताब	books of Vidya vidya kī kitābeṁ विद्या की किताबें	direct
in book of Vidya vidyā kī kitāb meṁ विद्या की किताब में	in books of Vidya vidya kī kitāboṁ meṁ विद्या की किताबों में	oblique

Pronouns in Possessive Case

m.sg	m.pl	f.sg./pl.	English
merā मेरा	mere मेरे	merī मेरी	my, mine
hamārā हमारा	hamāre हमारे	hamārī हमारी	our, ours
terā तेरा	tere तेरे	terī तेरी	your, yours intimate
tumhārā तुम्हारा	tumhāre तुम्हारे	tumhārī तुम्हारी	your, yours informal
āpkā आपका	āpke आपके	āpkī आपकी	your, yours formal
uskā उसका	uske उसके	uskī उसकी	his/her/hers non-proximate
iskā इसका	iske इसके	iskī इसकी	his/her,hers proximate
unkā उनका	unke उनके	unkī उनकी	their/theirs non-proximate
inkā इनका	inke इनके	inkī इनकी	their/theirs proximate
kiskā किसका	kiske किसके	kiskī किसकी	whose (sg.)
kinkā किनका	kinke किनके	kinkī किनकी	whose (pl.)

1. यह उनका घर m.sg. है। — This is their house.
   yah unkā ghar m.sg. hai.
2. वे मेरे खिलौने m.pl. हैं। — Those are my toys.
   ve mere khilaune m.pl. haiṁ.

3. यह उसकी बेटी f.sg. है। — This is his daughter.
   yah uskī beṭī fsg. hai.
4. यह किसका छाता m.sg. है? — Whose (sg.)umbrella is this?
   yah kiskā chātā m.sg. hai?
5. ये किनके कमरे m.pl. हैं? — Whose (pl.) rooms are these?
   ye kinke kamre m..pl. haiṁ.

Ex. 1: Say in English

1. यह उसका कमरा m.sg है।
2. आप उसके कमरे m.sg में जाइए।
3. उसका भाई m.sg यहाँ रहता है।
4. क्या आप उसके भाई m.sg को जानते हैं?
5. यह हमारा छोटा–सा बाग़ीचा m.sg है।
6. ये हमारे छोटे–से बाग़ीचे m.sg की सब्जियाँ हैं।
7. यह लड़कियों का छात्रावास m.sg है।
8. इस लड़कियों के छात्रावास m.sg में कितनी लड़कियाँ रहती हैं?
9. मेरे अच्छे दोस्त को मिलिए।
10. उसके नए मकान का पता क्या है?

1. yah uskā kamrā hai.
2. āp uske kamre meṁ jāie.
3. uskā bhāī yahāṁ rahtā hai.
4. kyā āp uske bhāī ko jānte haiṁ?
5. yah hamārā choṭa-sā bāGīcā hai.
6. ye hamāre choṭe-se bāGīce kī sabziyāṁ haiṁ.
7. yah laṛkiyoṁ kā chātrāvās hai.
8. is laṛkiyoṁ ke chātrāvās meṁ kitnī laṛkiyāṁ rahtī haiṁ?
9. mere acche dost ko milie.
10. uske nae makān kā patā kyā hai?

Ex. 2: Say in Hindi:

1. It is her problem, not mine.
2. This is a good book. Is it yours?
3. This is not my pen. Mine is the black one.
4. These are not my shoes. Those ones are mine.
5. This is not their house. That one is theirs.
6. Whose camera is this? Is this Sushma's?

7. This is your work. Not mine.
8. Hindi is my mother tongue. What is your mother tongue?
9. "Is this your final decision?" "Yes, this is our final decision."

Ex.3: Fill in the blanks with suitable possessive forms of the pronouns.

1. यह चित्र .... है? (कौन)
2. ये खिलौने ....हैं। (तुम)
3. क्या ये लेख ....है। (आप)
4. यह पत्रिका ....है। (हम)
5. वे दोनों तोते .... हैं। (बग़लवाले)
6. सुमैया अपने मंगेतर (m.) को ....यहां मिली। (कौन)
7. वह संगमरमर का भवन (f.)......................... ? (तुम)
8. लड़का ज़ोर–ज़ोर से ....पुकार रहा है। (किसी)
9. .... महिला .... बेटा मर गया है। (यह)
10. ....नाम क्या है? (तुम)

1. yah citra ....hai? (kaun)
2. ye khilaune...haiṁ. (tum)
3. kyā ye lekh .... haiṁ. (āp)
4. yah patrikā .... hai. (ham)
5. ve donoṁ tote ....hai. (baGalvāle)
6. sumaiyā apne maṅgetar ko .....ke yahāṁ milī. (kaun)
7. vah saṅgmarmar kā bhavan ....? (tum)
8. laṛkā zor-zor se ....pukār rahā thā. (kisī)
9. ....mahilā................beṭā mar gayā hai. (yah)
10. -------------bhāī------------------- nām kyā hai? (tum)

Key 1

1. This is her room.
2. You go in his room.
3. His/ Her brother lives here.
4. Do you know his/her brother?
5. This is our rather small garden.
6. These are vegetables from our rather small garden.
7. This is a girls' hostel.
8. How many girls live in this girls' hostel?
9. Meet my good friend.
10. What is the address of his new house?

Key 2

1. यह उसकी समस्या है, मेरी नहीं।
2. यह अच्छी किताब है। क्या यह तुम्हारी है?
3. यह मेरा क़लम नहीं। मेरा कालावाला है।
4. ये मेरे जूते नहीं। वेवाले मेरे हैं।
5. यह उनका घर नहीं। वहवाला उनका है।
6. यह किसका कैमरा है? क्या यह सुष्मा का है?
7. यह तुम्हारा काम है, मेरा नहीं।
8. हिन्दी मेरी मातृभाषा है। आपकी मातृभाषा क्या है?
9. "क्या यह आप लोगों का अन्तिम फ़ैसला है?"
   "जी हाँ, यह हमारा अन्तिम फ़ैसला है।"

1. yah uskī samasyā hai, merī nahīṁ.
2. yah acchī kitāb hai. kyā yah tumhārī hai?
3. yah merā qalam nahīṁ. merā kālāvālā hai.
4. ye mere jute nahīṁ. vevāle mere haiṁ.
5. yah unkā ghar nahīṁ. vahvālā unkā hai.
6. yah kis kā kaimerā hai? kyā yah sushmā kā hai?
7. yah tumhārā kām hai, merā nahīṁ.
8. hindī merī matṛbhāṣā$^{f.sg}$ hai. āpkī matṛbhāṣā kyā hai?
9. "kyā yah āp logoṁ kā antim faislā hai?"
   "ji hāṁ, yah hamārā antim faislā hai."

Key 3

1. किसका	2. तुम्हारे	3. आपका
4. हमारी	5. बग़लवालों के	6. किसके
7. तुम्हारा	8. किसीको	9. इस महिला का
10. तुम्हारे भाई का		

1. kiskā	2. tumhāre	3. āpkā
4. hamārī	5. baGalvāloṁ ke	6. kiske
7. tumhārā	8. kisiko	9. is....kā
10. tumhāre bhāī kā		

21 अपना, अपने, अपनी
apnā, apne, apnī

अपना, अपने, अपनी apnā, apne, apnī (one's own) are used as reflexive adjective when the object belongs to the subject.

1. आप अपना काम कीजिए। — You do your work.
   āp apnā kām kījie.
2. मैं अपनी किताब से पढ़ूँगा। — I will read from my book.
   maiṁ apnī kitāb se paṛhūṁgā
3. आप अपनी किताब से पढ़िए। — You read from your book.
   āp apnī kitāb se paṛhie.

☞ Other possessive pronouns are used when the object belongs to someone other then the subject. **Compare and comprehend:**

1. मैं अपने घर जा रहा हूँ। — I am going to my (own) house.
   maim apne ghar jā rahā hūṁ
2. वह मेरे घर आ रहा है। — He is coming to my house.
   vah mere ghar ā rahā hai.
3. मैंने अपने अध्यापक से पूछा। — I asked my(own) teacher.
   maiṁne apne adhyāpak se pūchā.
4. पिता जी ने मेरे अध्यापक से पूछा। — Father asked my teacher.
   pitā. jī ne mere adhyāpak se pūchā.

Repetitive use of अपना– अपना, apnā-apnā

1. अपने–अपने घर जाओ। — Go to your respective homes.
   apne-apne ghar jāo.
2. अपनी–अपनी पुस्तक खोलो। — Open your respective books.
   apnī-apnī pustak kholo.
3. अपना–अपना काम करो। — Do your respective tasks.
   apnā-apnā kām karo.

अपने से **'apne se'** अपने आप **'apne āp'** /अकेले ही **akele hī**
= by oneself, by myself, by yourself, by ourselves, by themselves etc. Adverbial use.
☞ **Alternatively** स्वयम् **'svayaṁ'**, खुद **'khud' are used.**

1. वे अपने–से यहाँ आए।
   ve apne-se yahāṁ āe.
   They came here by themselves.
2. वह अपना खाना अपने–आप बनाना चाहती है।
   vah apnā khānā apne-āp banānā cāhtī hai.
   She wants to cook her meals herself.

Ex. 1: Translate into English:

1. उसने मुझे अपनी कहानी सुनाई।
2. आप सब अपने–अपने सामान का घ्यान रखिए / रखें ।
3. आज मैं अपने दोस्तों के साथ बाहर खा रहा हूँ ।
4. अपनी कार यहाँ खड़ी मत करो।
5. दोनों मित्रों ने अपनी–अपनी पत्नी की प्रशंसा की।

1. usne mujhe apnī kahānī sunāī.
2. āp sab apne-apne sāmān kā dhyān rakhie./ rakheṁ.
3. āj maiṁ apne dostoṁ ke sāth bāhar khā rahā hūṁ.
4. apnī 'kār' yahāṁ khaṛī mat karo.
5. donoṁ mitroṁ ne apnī-apnī patnī kī praśaṃsā kī.

Ex. 2: Say in Hindi: one of many

1. She lent me a book of hers.
2. He married a classmate of his.
3. We went on a picnic with some friends of ours.
4. She invited a few friends of hers to lunch.
5. I will go leisure wandering with a colleague of mine.

Ex.3: Fill in the blanks with suitable forms of अपना, अपने, अपनी **and preposition if required.**

1. उसने मुझे .... एक पत्रिका पढ़ने को दी।
2. प्रतिभा ने .... एक सहपाठी से शादी की।
3. मैं .... एक सहकर्मी के साथ केदारनाथ जाने की सोच रही हूँ।

4. क्या ये सब यहाँ से वहाँ तक उनके........... ....खेत हैं?
5. आज मैं .... नई 'कार' से पुराने स्कूल जाऊँगी।
6. उन्होंने .... मकान ....बनवाया है।
7. कल शर्मा जी .... .अपने अधिकारी के साथ हमारे यहाँ आए।
8. आप लोग .... चीज़ों को सँभालकर रखिए।

1. usne mujhe .... ek patrikā paṛhne ko dī.
2. pratibhā ne .... ek sahpāṭhī se śādī kī.
3. maiṁ .... ek sahkarmī ke sāth kedārnāth jāne kī soc rahī hūṁ.
4. kyā yah sab yahāṁ se vahāṁ tak unke ....khet haiṁ?
5. āj maiṁ ....purāne skūl jāūṁgī.
6. unhoṁne .... makan ....banvāyā hai.
7. kal śarmā jī .... adhikārī ke sāth yahāṁ āe.
8. āp log ....cīzoṁ ko saṁbhālkar rakhie.

Ex. 4: Translate into Hindi: Use: अपने से **apne se' '** अपने आप **apne āp '**

1. One should do one's work by oneself.
2. Did she cook all this by herself?
3. He keeps sitting there for hours by himself.
4. The door opened by itself.

Ex. 5: Translate into English:

1. क्या तुम स्कूल अपने–से जाते हो?
2. उन्होंने अपना घर अपने–से रंगा है।
3. मैं यह भारी संदूक अपने–से नहीं ले जा पाऊँगा।
4. मैंने यह घड़ी अपने–से ठीक की।

1. kyā tum skūl apne-se jāte jo?
2. unhoṁne apnā ghar apne-se raṁgā hai.
3. maiṁ yah bhārī sandūk apne-se nahīṁ le jā pāūṁgā.
4. maiṁne yah ghaṛī apne-se ṭhīk kī.

Key 1

1. She / He told me her / his story.
2. All of you take care of your baggage.
3. Today I am eating out with my friends.
4. Don't park your car here.
5. Both the friends praised their respective wives.

Key 2

1. उसने मुझे अपनी एक पुस्तक उधार दी।
2. उसने अपनी एक सहपाठिन के साथ विवाह किया।
3. हम अपने कुछ मित्रों के साथ पिकनिक पर गए।
4. उसने अपने कुछ दोस्तों को दिन के खाने पर बुलाया।
5. मैं अपने एक सहकर्मी के साथ घूमने जाऊँगा।

1. usne mujhe apnī ek pustak udhār dī.
2. usne apnī ek sahpāṭhin ke sāth vivāh kiyā.
3. ham apne kuch mitroṁ ke sāth picnic par gae
4. usne apne kuch dostoṁ ko din ke khāne par bulāyā.
5. maiṁ apne ek sahkarmī ke sāth ghūmne jāūṁgī.

Key 3

1. अपनी	2. अपने	3. अपने
4. अपने	5. अपने	6. अपना, अपने–आप
7. अपने	8. अपनी–अपनी	

1. apnī	2. apne	4. apne
4. apne	5. apne	6. apnā, apne.āp
7. apne	8. apnī-apnī	

Key 4

1. व्यक्ति को अपना काम अपने–से करना चाहिए।
2. क्या उसने यह सब अपने–से पकाया?
3. वह वहाँ घण्टों अपने–से बैठा रहता है।
4. दरवाज़ा अपने–से खुल गया।

1. vyakti ko apnā kām apne-se karnā cāhie.
2. usne yah sab apne-se pakāyā?
3. vah vahāṁ ghaṇṭoṁ apne-se baiṭhā rahā.
4. darvāzā apne-se khul gāyā.

Key 5

1. Do you go to school by yourself?
2. They have painted their house themselves.
3. I will not be able to carry this heavy box by myself.
4. I repaired this watch myself.

22 जानना, आना
jānanā, ānā
मालूम होना, पता होना
mālūm honā, patā honā

to know

subject + object + जानना jānanā + होना honā
nom.case — agree with the subject in the required tense

☞ जानना **is be used for knowing a person, or having knowledge about something, knowing how to do something.**

1. मैं रौनक़ को जानता हूँ।
   maiṁ raunaq ko jāntā hūṁ.
   I know Raunaq.
2. मैं जानता हूँ कि रौनक़ विदेश जा रहा है।
   maiṁ jāntā hūṁ ki raunaq videś jā rahā hai.
   I know Raunaq is going abroad.
3. मैं हिन्दी जानता हूँ।
   maiṁ hindī jāntā hūṁ
   I know Hindi.

subject + ko + object + मालूम mālūm / पता patā + होना honā in the required tense

☞ मालूम होना mālūm honā, पता होना patā honā is be used for having knowledge about something.

मुझको पता है / मालूम है कि रौनक़ विदेश जा रहा है।
mujhko patā hai / mālūm hai ki raunaq videś jā rahā hai.
I know Raunaq is going abroad.

(subject + को ko) + object + आना ānā + होना honā

agree with the object in the required tense

☞ आना **ānā is be used for knowing how to do something.**

मुझको हिन्दी बोलनी आती है। I know how to speak
mujhko hindī bolnī ātī hai. Hindi.
क्या तुम्हें कार चलाना आता है? Do you know car driving.
kya tumheṁ 'car' calānā ātā hai?

Ex.:Translate into English :

1. मैं उसे जानता हूँ, परन्तु मेरा मित्र नहीं जानता।
2. वह भारतीय संस्कृति जानती है, लेकिन मैं नहीं जानती।
3. आपको पता है, कल बिजली कर्मचारियों की हड़ताल हैं?
4. मुझे मालूम है, वह परसों शाम की उड़ान से आ रही है।
5. क्या आपको तैरना आता है?
6. मुझे जर्मन भाषा आती है।

1. maiṁ use jāntā hūṁ parantu merā mitra nahīṁ jāntā.
2. vah bhārtīyă saṃskṛti jāntī hai, lekin maiṁ nahīṁ jāntī.
3. āpko patā hai, kal bijlī karmcāriyoṁ kī haṛtāl hai?
4. mujhe mālūm hai, vah parsoṁ śām kī uṛān se ā rahī hai.
5. kyā āpko tairnā ātā hai?
6. mujhe 'jarman' bhāṣā ātī hai.

Glossary:

भारतीय संस्कृति (f.)	bhārtīyă saṁskṛti	Indian culture
बिजली कर्मचारी (m.)	bijlī karmcārī	electricity workers
हड़ताल (f.)	haṛtāl	strike

Key

1. I know him / her, but my friend doesn't.
2. She knows Indian culture, but I don't.
3. Do you know theelectricity employees are on strike tomorrow?
4. I know she is coming the day after by evening flight.
5. Do you know how to swim ?
6. I know German language.

23 पसन्द करना pasand karnā / पसन्द होना pasand honā / पसन्द आना pasand ānā / अच्छा लगना acchā lagnā — to like

पसन्द करना **pasand karnā**

subject +	object +	pasand karnā +	honā
Nom. case		पसन्द करना	होना
			in the required tense to agree with the subject

1. क्या तुम (m.) सिनेमा देखना पसन्द करते हो?
   kyā tum (m.) 'sinemā' dekhnā pasand karte ho?
   Do you like to watch movies?
2. मेरी मित्र घर का काम करना पसन्द नहीं करती थी।
   merī mitra ghar kā kām karnā pasand nahīṁ kartī thī.
   My friend didn't use to like to do household chores.

पसन्द आना **pasand ānā**

(subject+ को ko) +	object +	पसन्द आना pasand ānā*	+ होना
			in the required tense to agree with the object

* Liking or not liking is expressed after first hand experience with the situation:

1. मुझे फ़िल्म (f.) बहुत पसन्द आई। — I liked the film very much.
   mujhe film (f.) bahut pasand āī.
2. तुम्हें भारत अवश्य पसन्द आएगा। — You will certainly like India.
   tumheṁ bhārat avaśyă pasand āegā.

पसन्द होना pasand honā; अच्छा लगना acchā lagnā

(subj.+ **को** ko) + obj. + पसन्द pasand / + होना honā
अच्छा लगता[m.sg] acchā lagtā
अच्छे लगते[m.pl.] acche lagte
अच्छी लगती[f.sg./pl.] acchī lagtī
in the required tense
to agree with the object

Remember:

- pasand honā and acchā lagnā agree with the number of the object.
  Use **hai** with verb infinitive or singular object;
  Use **haiṁ** with plural object.

Examples:

1. छात्रों को खेलना पसन्द है। The students like to play.
   chātroṁ ko khelnā pasand hai.
   = छात्रों को खेलना अच्छा लगता है।
   chātroṁ ko khelnā acchā lagtā hai.
2. उसे एकाकीपन (m.) पसन्द है। She likes solitude.
   use ekākīpan pasand hai.
   = उसे एकाकीपन (m.) अच्छा लगता है।
   use ekākīpan acchā lagtā hai.

Ex. 1: Say in English:

1. क्या आप (m.) शतरंज खेलना पसन्द करते हैं?
2. वे लोग हवाई जहाज़ से सफ़र करना पसन्द करेंगे।
3. तुम (m.) यहाँ क्या पसन्द करते हो?
4. मेरी मित्र मसालेदार भोजन पसन्द नहीं करती थी।
5. मुझे बनारस के मंदिर बहुत पसन्द आए।
6. मुझे यात्रा करना सदैव पसन्द आता है।
7. मुझे मोलभाव (m.) करना अच्छा लगता है।
8. उसे लाल रंग की 'कार' (f.sg.) अच्छी लगेगी।
9. उसको चिंतापरक भाषण पसन्द नहीं , परन्तु उसकी बहन को पसंद हैं।
10. वह शोधपरक फ़िल्में पसन्द नहीं करता, परन्तु उसके भाई करते हैं।

1. kyā āp (m.) śatrañj khelnā pasand karte haiṁ?
2. ve log (m.) havāī jahāz se safar karnā pasand kareṁge.
3. tum (m.) yahāṁ kyā pasand karte ho?.
4. merī mitra (f.) masāledār bhojan pasand nahīṁ kartī thī.
5. mujhe banāras ke mandir bahut pasand āe.
6. mujhe yātrā karnā sadaiv pasand ātā hai.
7. mujhe mol bhāv karnā acchā lagtā hai.
8. use lāl raṅg kī' kār' (f.) acchī lagegī.
9. usko cintāparak bhāṣaṇ pasand nahīṁ, parantu uskī bahan ko pasand haiṁ.
10. vah śodhparak filmeṁ pasand nahīṁ kartā, parantu uske bhāī karte haiṁ.

चिंतापरक	cintāparak	thoughtful
शोधपरक	śodhparak	research based

Ex.2: : Complete the sentences using appropriate forms of पसन्द आना pasand ānā + होना 'honā'.

1. मुझे होटल का खाना (m.)अक्सर पसन्द नहीं.............. । (pres. indef.)
2. क्या आपको 'फ़्लैट' (m.) पसन्द ....? (past simple)
3. मुझे यह किताब (f.) बहुत पसन्द .... । (past simple)
4. तुम्हें भारत अवश्य पसन्द .... । (fut. simple)

1. mujhe hoṭal kā khānā aksar pasand nahīṁ......... (pres. indef.)
2. kyā āpko flaiṭ (m.) pasand .... (past simple)
3. mujhe yah kitāb bahut pasand............................ (past simple)
4. tumheṁ bhārat avaśyă pasand .... (future simple)

Ex. 3: Complete the sentences with पसन्द होना pasand honā **and change them to अच्छा लगना** acchā lagnā **as shown :**

> मुझको तैरना **पसन्द** है।
> ⇨ मुझको तैरना **अच्छा लगता** है।

1. माता जी को घर में रहना ....
⇨ ....
2. पिता जी को घूमना ....
⇨ ....
3. आपको क्या ....
⇨ .... ?

4. मेरे मित्र को प्रेमचन्द के उपन्यास (m.pl.)..................................

⇨ ....

> mujhko tairnā pasand hai.
> ⇨ mujhko tairnā acchā lagtā hai.

1. mātā jī ko ghar meṁ rahnā ....

⇨ ....

2. pitā jī ko ghūmnā pasand ....

⇨ ....

3. āpko kyā pasand ....?

⇨ ....

4. mere mitra ko premcand ke upanyās ....

⇨ ....

Key 1

1. Do you like to play chess?.
2. They will like to travel by air.
3. What do you like here?
4. My friend didn't use to like spicy food.
5. I liked the temples of Benares very much.
6. I always like to travel.
7. I like to bargain. = Bargaing pleases me.
8. She will like red color car. = Red color car will please her.
9. She does not thoughtful speeches but her sister does.
10. He does not like research based filmed but his brothers do.

Key 2

1. आता।	2. आया।	3. आई।	4. आएगा।
1. ātā	2. āyā	3. āī	4. āegā

Key 3

1, 2, 3,	पसन्द है।	pasand hai
4	पसन्द हैं।	pasand haiṁ
1, 2, 3	अच्छा लगता है।	acchā lagtā hai.
4	अच्छे लगते हैं।	acche lagte haiṁ.

24 Frequentative

(v.r. + आ ā / या yā) + करना karnā + होना honā

■ Frequentative language structures are used as alternative to present simple, past habitual, future simple and imperatives. It implies enhanced frequency during a certain period.

subj. +	obj. +	(v.r. + आ ā / या yā) +	करना karnā + होना honā
nom. case	(if any)	(invariable)	agree with N and G of the subj. in the required tense.

Present Simple Tense

1. जब–जब मैं भारत में होता हूँ, मैं सिर्फ़ हिन्दी बोला करता हूँ।
   jab-jab maiṁ bhārat meṁ hotā hūṁ, maiṁ sirf hindī bolā kartā hūṁ.
   Whenever I am in India, I speak only Hindi.
2. अनिल यहाँ तस्वीरें खींचा करता है।
   anil yahāṁ tasvīreṁ khīṁcā kartā hai.
   Anil takes pictures here.

Past Habitual Tense

1. जब मैं भारत में था, मैं सिर्फ़ हिन्दी बोला करता था।
   jab maiṁ bhārat meṁ thā , maiṁ sirf hindī bolā kartā thā.
   When I was in India, I used to speak only Hindi.
2. वह अध्यापक (m.) हमें विज्ञान पढ़ाया करता था।
   vah adhyāpak hameṁ vigyān paṛhāyā kartā thā.
   That teacher used to teach us science.

Future Simple Tense

1. जब मैं भारत जाऊँगा, मैं सिर्फ़ हिन्दी बोला करूँगा।
   jab maiṁ bhārat jāūṁgā, maiṁ sirf hindī bolā karūṁgā.
   When I go to India, I will speak only Hindi.
2. मैं (f.) बाहर की गन्दी चीज़ें नहीं **खाया करूँगी**।
   maiṁ (f.) bāhar kī gandī cīzeṁ nahīṁ khāyā karūṁgī.
   I will not eat junk food from outside.

Imperative

1. जब आप भारत जाते हैं, आप सिर्फ़ हिन्दी बोला कीजिए।
   jab āp bhārat jāte haiṁ, āp sirf hindī bolā kījie.
   When you go to India, you(make it your habit to) speak only Hindi.

2. ध्यान लगाकर **अपना काम किया करो।**
   dhyān lagākar apnā kām kiyā karo.
   Do your work attentively.

Ex.1 Translate into English:

1. धोबी (m.sg.)इस घाट पर कपड़े **धोया करता है।**
2. मोर (m.pl.) बाग़ीचे में सब्ज़ी **खाया करते हैं।**
3. रेलकर्मचारी (m.pl.) प्रायः हड़ताल **किया करते हैं।**
4. मेरी बेटी (f.) बचपन में बहुत शैतानी **किया करती थी।**
5. हम लोग (m.pl.) तालाब में **मछली पकड़ा करते थे।**
6. मैं (f.) प्रतिदिन रिक्शे से स्कूल **जाया करती थी।**
7. मैं हर रोज़ व्यायाम **किया करूँगा।**
8. वे (m.sg. hon.) अपने शिष्यों का मार्गदर्शन किया **करेंगे।**
9. विपुल अपने माता–पिता की सेवा **किया करेगा।**
10. व्यर्थ समय न **गँवाया करो।**
11. सप्ताह में कम–से–कम दो बार व्यायामशाला **जाया करो।**.
12. अपनी चीज़ों को संभालकर **रखा कीजिए।**

1. dhobī is ghāṭ par kapṛe dhoyā kartā hai.
2. mor bāGīce meṁ sabzī khāyā karte haiṁ.
3. rel karmcārī prāyaḥ haṛtāl kiyā karte haiṁ.
4. merī beṭī bacpan meṁ bahut śaitānī kiyā kartī thī.
5. ham log tālāb meṁ machlī pakṛā karte the.
6. maiṁ pratidin rikśe se skūl jāyā kartī thī.
7. maiṁ har roz vyāyām kiyā karūṁgā.
8. ve apne śiśyoṁ kā mārgdarśan kiyā kareṁge.
9. vipul apne mātā-pitā kī sevā kiyā karegā.
10. vyarth samay na gaṁvāyā karo.

11. saptāh meṁ kam-se-kam do bār vyāyāmśālā jāyā karo.

12. apnī cīzoṁ ko saṁbhālkar rakhā kījie.

Glossary

धोबी (m.)	dhobī	washerman
मोर (m.)	mor	peacock
बाग़ीचा (m.)	bāGīcā	park
सब्ज़ी (f.)	sabzī	vegetable
रेलकर्मचारी (m.pl.)	rel karmcārī	rail- employees
प्रायः (adv.)	prāyaḥ	usually
हड़ताल (f.)	haṛtāl	strike
बचपन (m.)	bacpan	childhood
शैतानी (f.)	śaitānī	mischief
मछली (f.)	machlī	fish
पकड़ना (v.t.)	pakaṛnā	to catch
प्रतिदिन (adv.)	pratidin	every day
व्यायाम करना (v.t.)	vyāyām karnā	to do gymnastics
शिष्य (m.)	śiṣyă	pupil
मार्गदर्शन (m.)	mārgdarśan	mentorship
सेवा (f.)	sevā	service
गँवाना (v.t.)	gaṁvānā	to lose, to waste
व्यायामशाला (f.)	vyāyāmśālā	gym

Ex. 2: Translate into Hindi . Use frequentative :

1. I (m.) collect stamps.
2. She goes for morning walk every day.
3. This hotel didn't use to be here.
4. She didn't use to have short hair.
5. Will you always study like this?
6. Will they go to the beach in summer?
7. Learn classical music!
8. Watch at least one Hindi movie every weak?

Glossary:

to collect	इकट्ठा करना (v.t.)	ikaṭṭhā karnā
stamps.	डाक टिकट (m.)	ḍāk ṭikaṭ
morning walk	सुबह की सैर (f.)	subah ki sair
classical music	शस्त्रीय संगीत (m.)	śāstrīyă saṅgīt
every weak	हर हफ़्ते (adv.)	har hafte

Ex. 3: Rewrite the sentences given below using the frequentative in the required tense as shown:

> मैं अक्सर नदी में **नहाता हूँ**।
> ⇨ मैं अक्सर नदी में **नहाया करता हूँ**।

1. बच्चे (m.pl.) शाम को मैदान में खेलते हैं।
2. विद्यार्थी (m.pl.) प्रति रविवार को पिकनिक पर जाते हैं।

> बच्चे (m.pl.) सप्ताहान्त पर तालाब में **तैरते थे**।
> ⇨ बच्चे (m.pl.) सप्ताहान्त पर तालाब में **तैरा करते थे**।

3. हम (m.pl.) पहले एक गाँव में रहते थे।
4. सुनीता (f.) अंग्रेज़ी सीखती थी।

> अब मैं भारत में पढ़ूँगी।
> ⇨ अब मैं भारत में **पढ़ा करूँगी**।

5. विदेश जाकर मैं स्वयं खाना बनाऊँगी।
6. अब वे (f. sg. hon.) नौकरानी से कपड़े धुलवाएँगी।

> आप समय पर दफ़्तर आइए।
> ⇨ आप समय पर दफ़्तर **आया कीजिए**।

7. तुम रोज़ सुबह सैर करने **जाओ**।.
8. रात को देर तक न **पढ़िए**।

maiṁ aksar nadī meṁ nahātā hūṁ.
⇨ maiṁ aksar nadī meṁ nahāyā kartā hūṁ.

1. bacce śām ko maidān meṁ khelte haiṁ.
2. vidyārthī ravivār ko picnic par jāte haiṁ .

bacce saptāhānt par tālāb meṁ tairte the.
⇨ bacce saptāhānt par tālāb meṁ tairā karte the.

3. ham pahle ek gāṁv meṁ rahte the.
4. sunītā angrezī sīkhtī thī.

ab maiṁ bhārat meṁ paṛhūṁgī.
⇨ ab maiṁ bhārat meṁ paṛhā karūṁgī.

5. videś jā kar maiṁ svayaṁ khānā banāūṁgī.
6. ab ve naukarānī se kapṛe dhulvāeṁgī.

āp samay par daftar āie.
⇨ āp samay par daftar āyā kījie.

7. āp roz subah sair karne jāie.
8. rāt ko der tak na paṛhie.

Key 1

1. The washerman washes clothes at this ghat.
2. The peacocks eat vegetables in the garden.
3. The railway employees often go on strike.
4. My daughter used to make much mischief in her childhood.
5. We used to catch fish in the pond.
6. I used to go to school every day by rikshaw.
7. I will do gymnastics every day.
8. He will mentor his students.
9. Vipul will look after his parents.
10. Don't waste time in vain.
11. Go to the gym at least twice a week.
12. Keep your things safely.

Key 2

1. मैं (m.) डाक टिकट इकट्ठे किया करता हूँ।
2. वह (f.) रोज़ सुबह सैर करने जाया करती है।
3. यह 'होटल' (m.) यहाँ नहीं हुआ करता था।
4. उसके बाल (m.pl.) छोटे नहीं हुआ करते थे।
5. क्या तुम (m.) हमेशा ऐसे पढ़ा करोगी?
6. क्या वे (m.pl./hon.) गर्मी में समुद्रतट पर जाया करेंगे?
7. तुम (f.) शस्त्रीय संगीत सीखा करो।
8. तुम (f.) हर हफ़्ते कम–से–कम एक हिन्दी फ़िल्म देखा करो।

1. maiṁ (m.) ḍāk ṭikaṭ ikaṭṭhe kiyā kartā hūṁ.
2. vah (f.)roz subah sair karne jāyā kartī hai.
3. yah hoṭal (m.) yahāṁ nahīṁ huā kartā thā .
4. uske bāl (m.pl.) choṭe nahīṁ huā karte the.
5. kyā tum (m.) hameśā aise paṛhā karogī?
6. kyā ve (m.pl./hon.) garmī meṁ samudra taṭ par jāyā kareṁge?
7. tum (f.)śāstrīyă saṅgīt sīkhā karo.
8. tum (f.) har hafte kam-se-kam ek hindī film dekhā karo.

Key 3

1. खेला करते हैं।
2. जाया करते हैं।
3. रहा करते थे।
4. सीखा करती थी।
5. बनाया करूँगी।
6. धुलवाया करेंगी।
7. जाया करो।
8. पढ़ा कीजिए।

1. khelā karte haiṁ.
2. jāyā karte haiṁ.
3. rahā karte the.
4. sikhā kartī thī.
5. banāyā karūṁgī.
6. dhulvāyā kareṁgī.
7. jāyā karo.
8. paṛhā kījie.

Rhyme words in Hindi:
Native hindi speakers often use rhyme words the second part of which has no meaning. Examples:

शादी–वादी	sādi vādi	=	marriage
खाना–वाना	khānā-vānā	=	meal
काम–वाम	kām-vām	=	work

25 Suffix vālā/ vāle/vālī

वाला, वाले, वाली

noun + **vālā**/vāle/**vālī** = the doer of an activity

दुकानवाला duk**ā**nv**ā**l**ā** = **shopkeeper**

Ex. 1: Say in English:

1. अण्डेवाला
2. बसवाला
3. फूलवाला
4. सब्ज़ीवाला
5. अख़बारवाला
6. मकानवाला

1. aṇḍevālā
2. basvālā
3. phūlvālā
4. sabzīvālā
5. akhbārvālā
6. makānvālā

noun + (v.r. +ne) +**vālā**/vāle/**vālī** = the doer of the activity

कपड़े धोनेवाला kapṛe dhonev**ā**l**ā**

= the one who washes clothes (washerman)

Ex. 2: Say in English:

1. कपड़े सीनेवाला
2. सामान उठानेवाला
3. जूते ठीक करनेवाला
4. खाना पकानेवाला
5. खाना पकानेवाली
6. दूध बेचनेवाला
7. इतिहास पढ़ानेवाला
8. बाल बनानेवाला
9. सफ़ाई करनेवाली
10. कपड़े सीनेवाली

1. kapṛe sīnevālā
2. sāmān uṭhānevālā
3. jūte ṭhīk karnevālā
4. khānā pakānevālā
5. khānā pakānevālī
6. dūdh becnevālā
7. itihās paṛhānevālā
8. bāl banānevālā
9. safāī karnevālī
10. kapṛe sīnevālī

Ex.3: Write imperative sentences as per example using the verbs in the parentheses and a postposition if required :

> छोटावाला कमरा .... जाना
> छोटेवाले कमरे में जाओ / जाइए।

1. बग़लवाला कमरा .... (प्रतीक्षा करना)
2. नयावाला अतिथिगृह .... (ठहराना)
3. पीछेवाला उद्यान .... (खेलना)
4. नीचेवाला स्नान–घर .... (नहाना)
5. ऊपरवाली मंज़िल .... (रहना)

1. baGalvālā kamrā ....(pratīkṣā karnā)
2. nayāvālā atithigṛh .... (ṭhahrnā)
3. pīchevālā udyān .... (khelnā)
4. nīcevālā snān-ghar .... (nahānā)
5. ūparvālī manzil .... (rahnā)

> pronoun /adective/ adverb + **vālā** /**vāle**/ **vālī**
> = to specify the noun
> यहवाला yahv**ālā** = **this one**
> पीछेवाला pichev**ālā** = **the one behind**
> कौन–सा वाला kaun-s**ā vālā** = **which one**

Ex.4: Translate into English:

1. यहवाला दूरदर्शन यंत्र महँगा है।
2. मैं सामनेवालों के यहाँ जा रही हूँ।
3. यहवाला कमरा बड़ा है।
4. वहवाली दीवार नीची है।
5. मुझको यहवाली पोशाक पसन्द है।

1. yahvālā dūrdarśan yantra mahṁgā hai.
2. maiṁ sāmnevāloṁ ke yahāṁ jā rahī hūṁ.
3. yahvālā kamrā baṛā hai.
4. vahvālī dīvār nīcī hai.
5. mujhko yahvālī pośāk pasand hai.

दूरदर्शन यंत्र	durdarśan yantra	television set
दीवार (f.)	dīvār	wall
नीची (adj.)	nīcī	low
पोशाक (f.)	pośāk	dress
येवाले	yevāle	these ones
वेवाले	vevāle	those ones
सामनेवाले	sāmnevāle	the ones in front

(verb root + ने ne) + वाला vālā / वाले vāle / वाली vālī

= something is about to happen

पहुँचनेवाले	pahuṁcnevāle	about to arrive
उबलनेवाली	ubalnevālī	about to boil

Ex.5: Say in English:

1. माताजी कहाँ जानेवाली हैं?
2. पुस्तक (f.) मेज़ से गिरनेवाली है।
3. बच्चा (m.) पेड़ से गिरनेवाला है।
4. वर्षा (f.) होनेवाली हैं।
5. बर्फ़ (f.) पड़नेवाली है।
6. मंत्री जी मंच छोड़कर जानेवाले हैं।
7. गाड़ी (f.) छूटनेवाली है।

1. mātā jī kahāṁ jānvālī haiṁ?
2. pustak (f.) mez se girnevālī hai.
3. baccā (m.) peṛ se girnevālā hai.
4. varṣā (f.) honevālī hai.
5. barf (f.) paṛnevālī hai
6. mantrī jī mañc choṛkar jānevāle haiṁ.
7. gāṛī (f.) chūṭnevālī hai.

Glossary:

जानेवाला, –वाले, –वाली	jānevālā, -e, -ī	about to go
गिरनेवाला, –वाले, –वाली	girnevālā, -e, -ī	about to fall
वर्षा (f.)	varṣā	rain
होनेवाला, –वाले, –वाली	honevālā, -e, -ī	about to happen
पड़नेवाला, –वाले, –वाली	*paṛnevālā, -e, -ī	about to happen
मंत्री (m)	mantrī	minister

*See use of 'paṛnā' as weather verb pg. 208

मंच (m)	mañc	stage
छूटनेवाला, –वाले, –वाली	chūṭnevālā, -e, -ī	about to depart

subj. + तो to + (v.r. + ने ne) + वाला, –वाले, –वाली vālā, -e, -ī + था, थे, थी, थीं

= something was supposed to or expected to take place but didn't.

1. आप तो कल आनेवाले थे !
   āp to kal āne vāle the!
   You were supposed to come yesterday.
2. आज तो छोटे डॉकटरों की हड़ताल होनेवाली थी।
   āj to choṭe ḍaukṭroṁ kī haṛtāl honevālī thī.
   There was to be the junior doctors' strike today.(but didn;t)

Ex.6: Say in Hindi:

1. The children are about to go to the playground.
2. Strong storm with thunder and lightning is about to come.
3. Concert is about to end.
4. The chief guest is about to arrive.
5. The air-plane is about to take off.
6. Mother is about to return from the US.
7. The clock is about to fall off the wall.
8. The minister's speech is about to begin.

Glossary:

playground	खेल का मैदान (m.)	khel kā maidān
strong	तेज़ (adj.)	tez
storm	आँधी (f.)	āṁdhī
thunder	गरज (f.)	garaj
lightning	चमक (f.)	camak
concert	गोष्ठी (f.)	goṣṭhī
chief guest	मुख्य अतिथि (m.)	mukhyă atithi
about to arrive	पहुँचनेवाला,[m] –वाली	pahuṁcnevālā, -ī
air-plane	हवाई जहाज़ (m.)	havāī jahāz

about to take off	छूटनेवाला,[m] –वाली	chūṭnevālā/-vālī
about to return	लौटनेवाला,[m]–वाली[f.]	lauṭnevālā, -ī
clock	घड़ी (f.)	ghaṛī
off the wall	दीवार से	dīvār se
minister	मंत्री (m.)	mantrī
speech	भाषण (m.)	bhāṣaṇ

Ex.7: Say in Hindi:

1. I like that kurta.
- Which one?
- The one with a green and pink border.

2 Do you like that picture?
- Which one?
- The one on the wall above the window.

3. Give me that pen.
- Which one?
- The one with golden streaks.

4. He wants to be friends with that young man.
- Which one?
- The one in blue trousers and white shirt.

Key 1

1. the egg seller
2. the bus driver
3. the flower seller
4. the vegetable seller
5. the newspaper seller
6. the house owner.

Key 2

1. tailor (m.)
2. porter
2. shoe maker
4. cook (m.)
5. cook (f.)
6. milkman
7. history teacher
8. barber
9. the cleaning lady
10. tailor (f.)

Key 3

1. बग़लवाले कमरे में प्रतीक्षा करो / प्रतीक्षा काजिए।
2. नएवाले अतिथिगृह में ठहरो / ठहरिए।
3. पीछेवाले उद्यान में खेलो / खेलिए।
4. नीचेवाले स्नान–घर में नहाओ / नहाइए।
5. ऊपरवाली मंज़िल में रहो / रहिए।

1. baGalvāle kamre meṁ pratīkṣā karo / kījie.
2. naevāle atithigṛh meṁ ṭhahro / ṭhaharie.
3. pīchevāle udyān meṁ khelo / khelie.
4. nīcevāle snān-ghar meṁ nahāo / nahāie.
5. ūparvālī manzil meṁ raho / rahie.

Key 4

1. This television set is expensive.
2. I am going to my neigh bors in front(across from us).
3. This room is big.
4. That wall is low.
5. I like this dress.

Key 5

1. Where is mother about to go?
2. The book is about to fall from the table.
3. The child is about to fall from the tree.
4. It is about to rain.
5. It is about to snow.
6. The minister is about to leave the stage and go.
7. The train is about to depart.

Key 6

1. बच्चे^m.pl. खेल के मैदान में जानेवाले हैं।
2. गरज–चमक के साथ तेज़ आँधी^f आनेवाली है।
3. संगीत गोष्ठी ^f. समाप्त होनेवाली है।
4. मुख्य अतिथि^m.hon. पहुँचनेवाले हैं।
5. हवाई जहाज़^m छूटनेवाला है।
6. माता जी अमरीका से लौटनेवाली हैं।
7. घड़ी ^f..sg. दीवार से गिरनेवाली है।
8. मंत्री का भाषण शुरू होनेवाला है।

1. bacce khel ke maidān meṁ jānevāle haiṁ.
2. garaj-camak ke sāth tez āṁdhī ānevālī hai.
3. saṅgit goṣṭhī smāpt honevālī hai.
4. mukhyă atithi pahuṁcnevāle haiṁ.
5. havāī jahāz chūṭnevālā hai.
6. mātā ji amrīkā se lauṭnevālī haiṁ.
7. ghaṛī dīvār se girnevālī hai.
8. mantrī kā bhāṣaṇ śurū honevālā hai.

Key 7

1. मुझे वह कुर्ता पसन्द है।
- कौन–सा वाला?
- वह हरे और गुलाबी किनारेवाला।

2. क्या तुम्हें वह चित्र पसन्द है?
- कौन–सा वाला?
- वह वाला जो दीवार पर खिड़की के ऊपर है।

3. मुझे वह क़लम दो।
- कौन–सा वाला?
- सुनहली धारियोंवाला।

4. वह उस युवक से दोस्ती करना चाहता है।
- कौन–से वाले से?
- उस नीली पैण्ट और सफ़ेद कमीज़वाले से।

1. mujhe vah kurtā pasand hai.
- kaun-sā vālā?
- vah hare aur Gulābī kinārevālā.

2. kyā tumheṁ vah citra pasand hai?
- kaun-sā vālā?
- vahvālā jo dīvār par khiṛkī ke ūpar hai.

3. mujhe vah qalam do.
- kaun-sā vālā?
- sunhailī dhāriyoṁvālā.

4. vah us yuvak se dostī karnā cāhtā hai.
- kaun-se vāle se?
- us nīlī 'paiṇt' aur safed kamīz vāle se.

26 कर (kar)- conjunct

कर (kar)-conjunct is used to join the sentences having the same subject doing various activities following one another.

☞ subject (direct or oblique) of the final activity is used only once at the beginning of the compound sentence.
In past simple, present or past perfect tense, if the final activity is transitive, the subject + ने (ne) comes at the beginning of the sentence and the verb of the final activity agrees with the object. (E. 7)

☞ verb root + कर 'kar' is used for all preceding activ**ities.**

☞ If the verb root is कर 'kar', only के 'ke' follows it.

1. बैठो। पढ़ो। baiṭho. paṛho. Sit. Study.

⇨ बैठकर पढ़ो। baiṭh**kar** paṛho. Sit **and** study.

2. किताब बन्द कीजिए। किताब ताक पर रखिए।
kitāb band kījie! kitāb tāk par rakhie!
Shut the book. Put the book on the shelf.

⇨ किताब बन्द करके ताक पर रखिए।
kitāb band **karke** tāk par rakhie.
Shut the book and put it on the shelf.

3. मैं सुबह उठती हूँ। मैं चाय बनाती हूँ।
maiṁ subah uṭhtī hūṁ. maiṁ cāy banātī hūṁ.
I get up in the morning. I make tea.

⇨ मैं सुबह उठकर चाय बनाती हूँ।
maiṁ subah **uṭhkar** cāy banātī hūṁ.
I get up in the morning and make tea.

4. बच्चे स्कूल जाते हैं। बच्चे विज्ञान पढ़ते हैं

bacce skūl jāte haiṁ. bacce vigyān paṛhte haiṁ.

The children go to school. The children study science.

⇨ बच्चे स्कूल **जाकर** विज्ञान पढ़ते हैं।

bacce skūl **jākar** vigyān paṛhte haiṁ.

The children go to school and study science.

5. वह सुबह पाँच बजे उठती थी। वह नाश्ता बनाती थी। वह दफ़्तर जाती थी।

vah subah pāṁc baje uṭhtī thī. vah nāśtā banātī thī. vah daftar jātī thī.

She used to get up at five o'clock in the mornng. She used to prepare breakfast. She used to go to office.

⇨ वह सुबह **उठकर,** नाश्ता **बनाकर** दफ़्तर जाती थी।

vah subah **uṭhkar,** nāśtā **banākar** daftar jātī thī.

She used to get up in the morning, prepare breakfast and go to office.

6. मैंने एक उपहार ख़रीदा। मैं अपनी बहन के घर गई।

maiṁne ek uphār kharīdā. maiṁ apnī bahan ke ghar gaī.

I bought a gift. I went to my sister's house

⇨ मैं एक उपहार **ख़रीदकर** अपनी बहन के घर गई।

maiṁ ek uphār **kharīdkar** apnī bahan ke ghar gaī

I bought a gift **and** went to my sister's house.

7. पिता जी बैंक गए। पिता जी ने पैसे निकाले। पिता जी ने खिलौने ख़रीदे।

pitā jī baiṅk gae. pitā jī ne paise nikāle. pitā jī ne khilaune kharīde

Father went to the bank. Father withdrew money. Father bought toys.

⇨ पिता जी ने बैंक **जाकर**, पैसे **निकालकर** खिलौने ख़रीदे।

pitā jī ne baink **jākar**, paise **nikāl** kar khilaune kharīde.

Father went to the bank, withdrew money and bought toys

8. मैं दक्षिण भारत जाऊँगी। मैं तमिल सीखूँगी।

maiṁ dakṣiṇ bhārat jāūṁgī. maiṁ tamil sīkhūṁgī.

I will go to South India. I will learn Tamil.

⇨ मैं दक्षिण भारत जाकर तमिल सीखूँगी।

maiṁ dakṣiṇ bhārat jākar tamil sīkhūṁgī.

I will go to South India and learn Tamil.

Ex. 1: Translate into English

1. माता बच्चे का घाव देखकर छटपटाई।
2. पुलिस ने झूठे आरोप लगाकर आठ युवकों को बन्दी बनाया।
3. वे घर बन्द करके घूमने जा रहे थे।
4. उसने भारत आकर दर्शनशास्त्र पढ़ा।
5. आप उनको बुलाकर समझाइए।

1. mātā bacce kā ghāv dekhkar chaṭpaṭāī.
2. pulis ne jhūṭhe ārop lagākar āṭh yuvkoṁ ko bandī banāyā.
3. ve ghar band karke ghūmne jā rahe the.
4. usne bhārat ākar darśanśāstra paṛhā.
5. āp unko bulākar samjhāie.

Glossary:

घाव (m.)	ghāv	wound
छटपटाना (v.i.)	chaṭpaṭānā	to suffer
झूठा (adj.)	jhūṭhā	false, untrue
आरोप (m.)	ārop	blame
युवक (m.)	yuvak	young man
बन्दी (m.)	bandī	prisoner
दर्शनशास्त्र (m.)	darśanśāstra	Indian Philophy.
समझाना (v.t.)	samajhānā	to explain

Ex. 2: Translate into Hindi :

1. Put on your shoes and socks and go out.
2. We often have a bath in the Ganges, sit on the ghāṭ and drink tea.
3. She stood on the terrace and began to shout.
4. He heard my story and became happy.
5. I(m.) will meet the doctor and bring medicine for you.
6. You go to market and bring vegetables, fruit etc.
7. They will be very pleased to meet you.
8. I(m.) will go to London and learn English.
9. We will watch the serial on television and go to sleep.
10. We will eat food and then have ice-cream.

Ex. 3: Join the sentences given below using the कर– conjunct:

1. बत्ती बुझाओ। सो जाओ। ....
2. हाथ–मुँह धोओ। आराम करो। ....
3. वन्दिता नाश्ता बनाती है। वन्दिता नाश्ता खाती है। वन्दिता स्कूल जाती है। ....
4. विभा कपड़े धोती है। विभा कपड़े सुखाती है। विभा कपड़े अलमारी में रखती है।
   ....
5. श्रुति दौड़ी। श्रुति मेरे पास आई। ....
6. पुलिस आई। पुलिस ने चोर को पकड़ा। पुलिस चोर को ले गई।
   ....
7. बच्चे बस में बैठे हैं। बच्चे स्कूल गए हैं।
   ....
8. उसने दरवाज़े पर ताला लगाया था। वह काम पर जा रहा था।
   ....
9. वे (f.hon.)अगले हफ़्ते आगरा आएँगी। वे आपसे मिलेंगी।
   ....
10. मैं अगले साल स्पेन जाऊँगी। (शायद) मैं स्पेनी भाषा सीखूँगी।
    ....

1. battī bujhāo. so jāo. ....
2. hāth-muṁh dho'o. ārām karo..
3. vanditā nāśtā banātī hai. vanditā nāśtā khātī hai. vanditā skūl jātī hai. ....
4. vibha kapṛe dhotī hai. vibha kapṛe sukhātī hai. vibha kapṛe almārī meṁ rakhtī hai. ....
5. śruti dauṛī. śruti mere pās āī. ....
6. pulis āī. pulis ne cor ko pakṛā. 'pulis' cor ko le gaī.
   ....
7. bacce 'bas' meṁ baiṭhe haiṁ. bacce skūl gae haiṁ.
   ....
8. usne darvāze par tālā lagāyā thā. vah kām par jā rahā thā.
   ....
9. ve (f.hon.)agle hafte āgrā āeṁgī. ve āpse mileṁgī.
   ....
10. maiṁ agle sāl 'spen' jāūṁgī. (sāyad) maiṁ 'spenī' bhāṣā sīkhūṁgī.
    ....

Key 1

1. Mother saw the child's wound and became restless.
2. Police falsely accused eight young men and made them prisoners.
3. They had shut the house and were going out.
4. He came to India and studied Indian Philophy.
5. You call them and explain to them.

Key 2

1. अपने जूते–मोज़े पहनकर बाहर जाओ। 2. हम अक्सर गंगा में स्नान करके, घाट पर बैठकर चाय पीते हैं। 3. वह छत पर खड़ी होकर चिल्लाने लगी। 4. वह मेरी बात सुनकर ख़ुश हआ। 5. मैं चिकित्सक से मिलकर आपके लिए दवाई लाऊँगा। 6. आप बाज़ार जाकर सब्ज़ी–फल आदि लाइए। 7. वे आपसे मिलकर बहुत खुश होंगे। 8. मैं लंदन में जाकर अंग्रेज़ी सीखूँगा। 9. हम दूरदर्शन पर धारावाहिक देखकर सोएँगे। 10. हम खाना खांकर आइस–क्रीम खाएँगे।

1. apne jūte-moze pahankar bāhar jāo. 2. ham aksar gaṅgā meṁ snān karke , ghāṭ par baiṭhkar cāy pīte haiṁ. 3. vah chat par khaṛī hokar cillāne lagī. 4. vah merī bāt sunkar khuś huā. 5. maiṁ cikitsak se milkar āpke lie davāī lāūṁgā. 6. āp bāzār jākar sabzī-phal ādi lāie. 7. ve āpse milkar bahut khuś hoṁge. 8. maiṁ 'landan' jākar aṅgrezī sīkhūṁgā. 9. ham dūrdarśan par dhārāvāhik dekhkar soeṁge. 10. ham khānā khākar āis krīm' khāeṁge.

Key3

1. बत्ती बुझाकर सो जाओ।
2. हाथ–मुँह धोकर आराम करो।
3. वन्दिता नाश्ता बनाकर, खाकर स्कूल जाती है।
4. विभा कपड़े धोकर, सुखाकर अलमारी में रखती है।
5. श्रुति दौडकर मेरे पास आई।
6. पुलिस आकर, चोर को पकड़कर ले गई।
7. बच्चे बस में बैठकर स्कूल गए हैं।
8. वह दरवाज़े पर ताला लगाकर काम पर जा रहा था।
9. वे अगले हफ़्ते आगरा आकर आपसे मिलेंगी।
10. शायद मैं अगले साल स्पेन जाकर स्पेनी भाषा सीखूँ।

1. battī bujhākar so jāo.
2. hāth-mumh dhokar ārām karo.
3. vanditā nāśtā banākar, khākar skūl jātī hai.
4. vibhā kapṛe dhokar, sukhākar almārī meṁ rakhtī hai.
5. śruti dauṛkar mere pās āī.
6. pulis ākar , cor ko pakaṛkar le gaī.
7. bacce 'bas' meṁ baiṭhkar skūl gae haiṁ.
8. vah darvāze par tālā lagākar kām par jā rahā thā.
9. ve agle hafte āgrā ākar āpse mileṁgī.
10. sāyad maiṁ agle sāl 'spen' jākar 'spenī' bhāṣā sīkhūṁ.

Use of some abstract nouns and their adjectival form:

☞ **subject + adj. + honā (to agree with the subject in the required tense)**

मैं निराश हूँ ।	maiṁ nirāś hūṁ	I am disappointed.
वह भयभीत है ।	vah bhaybhīt hai.	She/He is afraid
वे संतुष्ट हैं ।	ve santuṣṭ haiṁ.	They are satisfied.
आप अनुभवी हैं ।	āp anubhavī haiṁ.	You are experienced

☞ **(subject + ko) + noun + honā**

मुझको निराशा है।	mujhko nirāśā hai.	I have disappointment.
उसको भय है ।	usko bhay hai.	She/ He has fear.
उनको संतोष है ।	unko santoṣ hai.	They have satisfaction
आपको अनुभव है ।	āpko anubhav hai.	You have experience

27 चाहना cāhnā (to want)

subject + object *+ चाहना + होना

agree with N and G of the subject in the appropriate tense

* object desired may be some noun or activity. If object is some activity, infinitive form of the verb is used.

■ when object wanted is activity:

1.	मैं^f हिन्दी सीखना चाहती हूँ। maiṁ hindī sīkhnā cāhtī hūṁ.	I want to learn Hindi. **(Present simple)**
2.	हम^m स्वीडन जाना चाहते थे। ham swīḍan jānā cāhte the.	We wanted to go to Sweden. **(Past habitual)**
3.	मैंने सदैव अपने देश में रहना चाहा है। maiṁne sadaiv apne deś meṁ rahnā cāhā hai.	I have always wanted to live in my **country.** **(Present perfect)**
4.	दादा जी उद्यान में घूमना चाहेंगे। dādā jī udyān meṁ ghūmnā cāheṁge.	Grandfather would want to walk in the garden. **(Future simple)**

■ when object wanted is a noun:

1.	मैं^m चार कमरों का फ़्लैट चाहता हूँ। maiṁ cār kamroṁ kā 'flaiṭ' cāhtā hūṁ.	I want a four room flat. **(Present Simple)**
2.	वह^m क्या चाहता था ? vah kyā cāhtā thā?	What did he want? **(Past habitual)**

3. वह^{m} एक नई 'कार' चाहता था। vah ek naī 'kār' cāhtā thā. — He wanted a new car.

4. आप^{m} क्या चाहेंगे? āp kyā cāheṁge? — What would you want? **(Future simple)**

Ex.1: Say in English:

1. वह$^{m.}$ आपसे मिलना चाहता है। 2. कौन$^{m..hon.}$ इस होटल में रहना चाहते हैं? 3. मैं$^{m..}$ यहाँ दो दिन / एक महीना रहना चाहता हूँ। 4. क्या आप$^{m..hon.}$ विदेश में नहीं बसना चाहते? 5. मेरी सहेली$^{f.}$ स्पेनी भाषा सीखना चाहती थी। 6. मैं^{f} उबला पानी पीना चाहती थी। 7. हम$^{m..pl}$ अपना घर नीला रंगना चाहते थे। 8. क्या तुम^{m} अपने लिए नए जूते ख़रीदना चाहोगे? 9. वे$^{m..hon.}$ आज का समाचारपत्र पढ़ना चाहेंगे। 10. क्या वह हमारे साथ विश्व भ्रमण करना चाहेगा?

1. vah āp se milnā cāhtā hai. 2. kaun is hoṭal meṁ rahnā cāhte haiṁ? 3. maiṁ yahāṁ do din / ek mahīnā rahnā cāhtā hūṁ. 4. kyā āp videś meṁ nahīṁ basnā cāhte? 5. merī sahelī spenī bhāṣā sīkhnā cāhtī thī .6. maiṁ ublā pānī pīnā cāhtī thī. 7. ham apnā ghar nīlā raṁgnā cāhte the. 8. kyā tum apne lie nae jūte kharīdnā cāhoge? 9. ve āj kā samācār patra paṛhnā cāheṁge. 10. kyā vah hamāre sāth viśva bhramaṇ karnā cāhegā?

Ex. 2: Say in Hindi:

1. He^{m} wants to talk to you. 2. I want to change jobs. 3. He wants to buy a new car. 4. He wants to sell all his belongings. 5. What do you$^{m.form.}$ want to do on the weekend? 6. Where did you^{m} want to go yesterday? 7. I^{m} wanted to live longer in India. 8. We^{m} wanted to do a boatride. 9. I^{m} want to watch some good film today . 10. I want to visit my maternal grandparents. 11. Today we want to eat out somewhere. 12. My daughter wants to learn painting. 13. My mother wanted to establish an old people's home. 14. My paternal grand parents would want to donate their eyes.

Ex. 3: Change present simple to ' चाहना cāhnā + होना honā' in the required tense:

1. वह **संगीत सीखता** है। वह **संगीत सीखना चाहता** है।
2. मैं इतिहास **पढ़ाती हूँ।** ....
3. तुम क्या **करते हो?** ....
4. हम अकसर ताश **खेलते हैं।** ....

5. विद्यार्थी रोज़ शाम को व्यायामशाला **जाते थे**।.... ....
6. हम लगभग रोज़ दादी जी से कहानी **सुनते थे**।.....................................
7. मेरा परिवार हर साल गरमी में पहाड़ पर **जाएगा**। ....
8. मैं सदैव बड़ों की सलाह **लूँगा**। ....

1. vah hindī sīkhtā hai. vah hindī sīkhnā cāhtā hai.
2. maiṁ itihās paṛhātī hūṁ. ....
3. tum kyā karte ho. ....
4. ham aksar tāś khelte haiṁ...
5. vidyārthī roz śām ko vyāyāmśālā jāte the. ....
6. ham lagbhag roz dādī jī se kahānī sunte the. ....
7. merā parivār har sal garmī meṁ pahāṛ par jāegā. ....
....
8. maiṁ sadaiv baṛoṁ kī salāh lūṁgā.. ....

Key 1

1. He wants to meet you. 2. Who wants to stay in this hotel? 3. I want to stay here for two days/ one month. 4. Don't you want to settle abroad? 5. My friend wanted to learn Spanish language. 6. I wanted to drink boiled water. 7. We wanted to paint our house blue. 8. Would you like to buy new shoes for yourself? 9. He would like to read today's newspaper.10. Would he want to do do a world tour with us.

Key 2

1. वह[m..] आपसे बात करना चाहता है। 2. मैं[m.] अपना काम बदलना चाहता हूँ। 3. वह [m.] नई कार ख़रीदना चाहता है। 4. वह [m]अपना सब सामान बेचना चाहता है। 5. आप[m..hon.] सप्ताहान्त पर क्या करना चाहते हैं? 6. आप[m..hon.] कल कहाँ जाना चाहते थे? 7. मैं[m..hon.] भारत में और रहना चाहता था। 8. हम[m..pl] नौका विहार करना चाहते थे।। 9. आज मैं[m.] कोई अच्छी फ़िल्म देखना चाहता हूँ। 10. मैं [m..]अपने ननिहाल जाना चाहता हूँ। 11. आज हम[m...pl] कहीं बाहर खाना चाहते हैं। 12. मेरी बेटी[f.sg.] चित्रकला सीखना चाहती है। 13. मेरी माता जी[m..hon.] वृद्ध आश्रम स्थापित करना चाहती थीं। 14. मेरे दादा–दादी[f..hon.] अपनी आंखें दान करना चाहेंगे।

1. vah āpse bāt karnā cāhtā hai. 2. maiṁ apnā kām badalnā cāhtā hūṁ. 3. vah naī kār kharīdnā cāhtā hai. 4. vah apnā sab sāmān becnā cāhtā hai. 5. āp saptāhānt par kyā karnā cāhte haiṁ? 6. āp kal kahāṁ jānā cāhte the?

7. maiṁ bhārat meṁ aur rahnā cāhtā thā. 8. ham nauka vihar karnā cāhte the. 9. āj maiṁ koī acchī film dekhnā cāhtā hūṁ. 10. maiṁ apne nanihāl jānā cāhtā hūṁ. 11. āj ham kahīṁ bāhar khānā cāhte haiṁ. 12. merī beṭī citrakalā sīkhnā cāhtī hai.13. merī mātā jī vṛdh āśram sthāpit karnā cāhtī thīṁ.14. mere dādā-dā dī apnī āṁkheṁ dān karnā cāheṁge.

Key 3

2. मैं इतिहास **पढ़ाना चाहती हूँ।**
3. तुम क्या **करना चाहते हो?**
4. हम अकसर ताश **खेलना चाहते हैं।**
5. विद्यार्थी रोज़ शाम को व्यायामशाला **जाना चाहते थे।**
6. हम लगभग रोज़ दादी जी से कहानी **सुनना चाहते थे।**
7. मेरा परिवार हर साल गरमी में पहाड़ पर **जाना चाहेगा।**
8. मैं सदैव बड़ों की सलाह **लेना चाहूँगा।**

2. maiṁ itihās paṛhānā cāhtī hūṁ.
3. tum kyā karnā cāhte ho?
4. ham aksar tāś khelnā cāhte haiṁ.
5. vidyārthī roz śām ko vyāyāmśālā jānā cāhte the.
6. ham lagbhag roz dādī jī se kahānī sunanā cāhte the.
7. merā parivār har sāl garmī meṁ pahāṛ par jānā cāhegā.
8. maiṁ sadaiv baṛoṁ kī salāh lenā cāhūṁgā.

कब का, कब के, कब की kab kā, kab ke, kab kī = since long ....

का, के, की kā, ke, kī, **agrees** with the subject if the subject is in the nominative case. (E. 1) These agree with the object If the subject is followed by a postosition. (E. 2):

1. एक औरत कब की आपका इन्तज़ार कर रही है।

   ek aurat kab k**ī** āp kā intzār kar rah**ī** hai.

   A woman has been waiting for you since long.
2. उसने कब का धूम्रपान करना छोड़ दिया।

   usne kab kā dh**ū**mrapān karnā cho**ṛ** diyā.

   He gave up smoking long ago.

E. = example

28 saknā सकना / pānā पाना

(can or be able to do something)

subj. + obj. + v.r. + सकना saknā / पाना pānā + होना honā
in the required tense
to agree with N and G of subject

☞ सकना **saknā** is used to talk about one's physical or mental ability to do some task.

☞ **पाना pānā instead of सकना saknā is used when one is able to manage to do something by putting in some extra effort or alternatively unable to do something despite extra effort.**

1. मैं[f] तैर सकती हूँ। maiṁ[f] tair saktī hūṁ	I can swim. (present simple tense)
2. वे[f] नहीं तैर सकतीं। 've[f] nahīṁ tair saktīṁ.	They cannot swim. (present simple tense)
3. वह[m.] सिलाई कर सकता था। vah [m] silāī kar saktā thā. (past habitual tense)	He used to be able to sew.(past habitual tense)
5. हम[f] शतरंज नहीं खेल सकीं। ham [f] śatrañj nahīṁ khel sakīṁ.	We couldnot play chess. (past simple tense)
4. वेद[m] नाव नहीं चला सकेगा। ved [m] nāv nahīṁ calā sakegā.	Ved will not be able to row a boat. (future simple tense)
6. मैं दूध की मिठाइयाँ नहीं पचा पाती। maiṁ dūdh kī miṭhāiyāṁ nahīṁ pacā pātī.	I am not able to digest milk-sweets. (present simple tense)
7. मैं बिल्कुल नहीं चल पाई। maiṁ bilkul nahīṁ cal pāī.	I was absolutely not able to walk.(past simple)

Ref. सकना saknā and passive see pg. 183

8. हम पर्वत पर नहीं चढ़ पाएँगे। ham parvat par nahīṁ caṛh pāeṁge. — We will not be able to climb up the mountain.

Some other uses of **सकना sakna** in Hindi:

- **For asking or giving permission:**

1. क्या मैं अन्दर आ सकता हूँ ? kyā maiṁ andar ā saktā hūṁ? — May I come in?
2. अब तुम जा सकते हो। ab tum jā sakte ho. — You may go now.

- **Probability:**

1. शाम को बारिश आ सकती है। śām ko bāriś ā saktī hai. — It might rain in the evening.
2. महँगाई और बढ़ सकती है। mahṁgāī aur baṛh saktī hai. — Inflation could go higher still.

- **Apprehension:**

1. वे तुम्हें मार भी सकते थे। ve tumheṁ mār bhī sakte the. — They could have even killed you.
2. तुम्हें चोट लग सकती है। tumheṁ coṭ lag saktī hai. — You could get injured.

Ex. 1: Translate into English:

1. क्या वह (f.) अंदर आ सकती है? 2. क्या तुम (m.) मुझको अपना शब्दकोश दे सकते हो? 3. क्या मैं (m.) यहाँ बैठ सकता हूँ? 4. क्या आप (m.) अंग्रेज़ी का अख़बार पढ़ सकते हैं? 5. क्या आप (m.) मुझे उनके घर का रास्ता बता सकते हैं? 6. क्या वे (f.) कल सुबह आठ बजे मुझे मिल सकेंगी? 7. क्या वे (m.)हमारे साथ संगीत गोष्ठी में चल सकेंगे। ? 8. हम सब (m.) एक कमरे में नहीं रह पाएँगे। 9. हम (m.) उनकी मदद नहीं कर पाएँगे।। 10. मैं (f.) अपनी बेटी के लिए कोई उपहार नहीं ख़रीद पाई। 11. क्या न्यायालय (f.) बलात्कारी को मृत्यु दण्ड दे पाएगा? 12. वे लोग (m.) यहाँ कैसे पहुँच पाएँगे? 13. मैं तैरना सीखना चाहती हूँ परन्तु **सीख नहीं सकती**। 14. वह डॉक्टर बनना चाहती थी लेकिन **बन नहीं सकी**। 15. अंकिता अध्यापिका बनना चाहती है लेकिन **बन नहीं सकेगी**।

1. kyā vah[f.] andar ā saktī hai? 2. kyā tum[m.sg.] mujhko apnā śabdkoś de sakte ho? 3. kyā maiṁ[m.] yahāṁ baiṭh saktā hūṁ? 4. kyā āp[m.form.] aṅgrezī kā akhbār[m.] paṛh sakte haiṁ? 5. kyā āp[m.form.] mujhe unke ghar kā rāstā batā sakte haiṁ? 6. kyā ve[f.form.] kal subah āṭh baje mujhe mil sakeṁgī? 7. kyā ve hamāre sāth saṅgīt gosṭhī meṁ cal sakeṁge? 8. ham[m.pl.] sab ek kamre meṁ nahīṁ rah pāeṁge. 9. ham[m.] unkī madad nahīṁ kar pāeṁge. 10 maim [f.sg] apnī beṭī ke lie koī uphār nahīṁ k͟harīd pāī. 11. kyā nyāyālay balātkārī ko mṛtyudaṇḍ de pāegā.? 12.ve log (m.) yahāṁ kaise pahuṁc pāeṁge? 13.maiṁ tairnā sīkhnā cāhtī hūṁ parantu **sīkh nahīṁ saktī.** 14. vah ḍaukṭar banānā cāhtī thī lekin ban **nahīṁ** sakī. 15. ankitā adhyāpikā banānā cāhtī hai **lekin** ban **nahīṁ** sakegī.

न्यायालय[m]	nyāyālay	law court
बलात्कारी [m]	balātkārī	rapist
मृत्युदण्ड [m.]	mṛtyudaṇḍ	death sentence

Ex.2: Translate into Hindi:

1. She cannot sew clothes.
2. Father cannot travel alone.
3. Her mother cannot stand up without support.
4. She cannot speak fluent German.
5. My husband can swim but I can't.
6. I cannot go to the market today; will you (f.) be able to shop for me?
7. Who can sing in your house?
8. Can I come with you to the cinema?
9. Can you hear me properly?
10. Today I could not understand a word in class.

Ex.3: Complete the sentences given below using the verb given in the brackets and 'सकना' in the required tense :

1. मैं (f.) हिन्दी अच्छी तरह पढ़ **सकती हूँ**। **(Pres. indef.)** (पढ़ना)
2. वह (m.) सब प्रकार के व्यंजन .... । (बनाना)
3. क्या तुम (f.) समुद्र में.. । (तैरना)
4. हसन बहुत बढ़िया छायाचित्र **बना सका**। **(Past simple)**
5. हमारे बच्चे (m.pl.) इस स्कूल में प्रवेश नहीं .... । (पाना)
6. क्या आपके छात्र (m.pl) खेल में भाग .... । (लेना)

7. हमारा इतिहास का शिक्षक (m.)आज नहीं **पढ़ा सकेगा** ।**(Fut. simple)**
8. क्या आप आज (f.) मेरे साथ फ़िल्म ....? (देखना)
9. सरकार आपदाग्रस्तों को समय से राहत नहीं .... । (पहुँचाना)
10. क्या उनको समस्या से छुटकारा (m.) ....? (मिलना)

1. maiṁ (f) hindī acchī tarah paṛh saktī hūṁ. (paṛhnā - Pres.Indef.)
2. vah (m.) sab prakār ke vyañjan............... (banānā)
3. kyā tum samudra meṁ (f.) .... ? (tairnā)
4. hasan bahut baṛhiyā chāyācitra **banā sakā.** (banānā - Past simple)
5. hamāre bacce (m.pl.) is skūl meṁ praveś nahīṁ .... (pānā)
6. kyā āpke chātra (m.pl.) khel meṁ bhāg ....? (lenā)
7. hamārā itihās kā śikṣak (m.) āj nahīṁ **paṛhā sakegā**. (paṛhānā - Fut. simple)
8. kyā āp āj mere sāth film ....? (dekhnā)
9. sarkār āpdāgrastoṁ ko samay se rāhat nahīṁ .... (pahuṁcānā)
10. kyā unko samasyā se chuṭkārā (m.) ....? (milnā)

आपदाग्रस्त (adj.)	āpdāgrast	beset by disaster
राहत (f)	rāhat	relief
पहुँचाना (v.t.)	pahuṁcānā	to reach
छुटकारा (m.)	chuṭkārā	riddance

Key1

1. Can she come in? 2. Can you give me your dictionary? 3. May I sit here? 4. Can you read the English newspaper? 5. Could you tell me the way to their house? 6. Will she be able to meet me tomorrow at eight o'clock in the morning. 7. Will they be able to come with us to the music concert? 8.All of us will not be able to live in one room. 9. We won't be able to help them. 10. I could not buy any gift for my daughter. 11. Will the judiciary be able to sentence the rapist to death? 12. How will they be able to get here? 13. I want to learn swimming but I can not learn. 12. She wanted to become a doctor but could not become one. 13. Ankita wants to become a teacher but will not be able to.

Key 2

1. वह कपड़े नहीं सी सकती।
2. पिता जी अकेले सफ़र नहीं कर सकते।
3. उसकी माता जी बिना सहारे के खड़ी नहीं हो सकतीं।
4. वह धाराप्रवाह जर्मन नहीं बोल सकती।

5. मेरे पति तैर सकते हैं, परन्तु मैं नहीं।
6. मैं आज बाजार नहीं जा सकती, क्या तुम (f.) मेरे लिए ख़रीदारी कर पाओगी?
7. आपके घर में कौन गा सकता हैं?
8. क्या मैं आपके साथ सिनेमा चल सकता / सकती हूँ?
9. क्या आप मुझे ठीक से सुन सकते / सकती हैं?
10. आज कक्षा में मैं एक शब्द भी समझ नहीं पाया।

1. vah kapṛe nahīṁ sī saktī.
2. pitā jī akele safar nahīṁ kar sakte.
3. uskī mātā jī binā sahāre ke khaṛī nahīṁ ho saktīṁ.
4. vah dhārāpravāh 'german' nahīṁ bol saktī.
5. mere pati tair sakte haiṁ parantu maiṁ nahīṁ.
6. maiṁ āj bāzār nahīṁ jā saktī. kyā tum mere lie kharīdārī kar pāogī?
7. āpke ghar meṁ kaun gā saktā hai?
8. kyā maiṁ āpke sāth cinemā cal saktā/saktī hūṁ?
9. kyā āp mujhe ṭhīk se sun sakte/saktī haiṁ?
10. āj maiṁ kakṣā meṁ ek śabd bhī nahīṁ samajh pāyā.

Key 3

2. बना सकता है। 3. तैर सकती हो? 5. पा सके।
6. ले सके? 8. देख सकेंगे। 9. पहुँचा सकेगी।
10. मिल सकेगा?

2. banā saktā hai. 3. tair saktī ho? 5. pā sake.
6. le sake. 8. dekh sakeṁge. 9. pahuṁcā sakegī.
10. mil sakegā?

29 चाहिए Cāhie

(need)

(subject + को)	+ noun object	+	चाहिए cāhie	+	honā

* **'honā' in required tense (if necessary) to agree with the N and G of the object.**

* **Alternatively, to express need, Hindi uses** 'की आवश्यकता होना' **kī āvaśyaktā honā** / 'की ज़रूरत होना' **kī zarūrat honā' instead of** चाहिए **cāhie, :**

Examples:

1. मुझको एक कम्बल चाहिए। mujhko ek kambal cāhie. — I need a blanket. (Need in the Present)

1a. मुझको एक कम्बल की ज़रूरत है। mujhko ek kambal kī zarūrat hai.

2. मुझको एक रज़ाई चाहिए थी। mujhko ek razāī cāhie thī. — I needed a quilt. (Need in the Past)

2a. मुझको एक रज़ाई की ज़रूरत थी। mujhko ek razāī **kī** zarūrat thī.

3. मुझको एक और कम्बल चाहिए होगा। mujhko ek aur kambal c**āhie** hog**ā**. — I will need one more blanket. (Need in the Future)

3a. मुझको एक और कम्बल की आवश्यकता होगी। mujhko ek aur kambal **kī āvaśyaktā** hogī.

Ex.: Rewrite the sentences given below replacing 'चाहिए' with **की आवश्यकता / की ज़रूरत होना** kī āvaśyaktā/ kī zarūrat honā as per example:

> मुझे निजी 'कम्प्यूटर' चाहिए।
> ⇨ मुझे निजी कम्प्यूटर **की आवश्यकता / की ज़रूरत है।**

1. मेरी बहन को कुछ नई पोशाकें चाहिए।
2. हमें तुरन्त एक नया दूरदर्शन यंत्र चाहिए।
3. आपको उनसे कौन–कौन–से दस्तावेज़ चाहिए?
4. उसे विवाह के लिए बहुत से आभूषण और वस्त्र चाहिए थे।
5. इस नौकरी के लिए क्या–क्या योग्यताएँ चाहिए थीं?
6. मुझे इन दस्तावेज़ों की छह–छह छायाप्रतियाँ चाहिए होंगी।
7. मुझे खाना खाते ही कुछ मीठा चाहिए होगा।

> mujhe nijī 'computer' cāhie.
> ⇨ mujhe nijī 'computer' kī āvaśyaktā / kī zarūrat hai.

1. merī bahan ko kuch naī pośākeṁ cāhie.
2, hameṁ turant ek nayā dūrdarśan yantra cāhie.
3. āpko unse kaun-kaun-se dastāvez cāhie?
4. use vivāh ke lie bahut se ābhūṣaṇ aur vastra cāhie the.
5. is naukrī ke lie kyā-kyā yogyătāeṁ cāhie thīṁ.
6. mujhe in dastāvzoṁ kī chah-chah chāyāpratiyāṁ cāhie hoṁgī.
7. mujhe khānā khāte hī kuch mīṭhā cāhie hogā.

आभूषण (m.)	ābhūṣaṇ	ornaments
दस्तावेज़ (m.)	dastāvez	documents
योग्यताएँ (f.pl.)	yogyătāeṁ	qualifications
छायाप्रति (f.)	chāyāprati	photocopy

Key

1. मेरी बहन को नई पोशाकों की आवश्यकता / की ज़रूरत है।
2. हमें तुरन्त एक नए दूरदर्शन यंत्र की आवश्यकता / की ज़रूरत है।
3. आपको उनसे किन–किन दस्तावेज़ों की आवश्यकता / की ज़रूरत है।
4. उसे विवाह के लिए बहुत से आभूषणों और वस्त्रों की आवश्यकता / की ज़रूरत थी।

5. इस नौकरी के लिए किन–किन योग्यताओं की आवश्यकता/ की ज़रूरत थी?
6. मुझे इन दस्तावेज़ों की छह–छह छायाप्रतियों की आवश्यकता/ की ज़रूरत होगी?
7. मुझे खाना खाते ही कुछ मीठे की आवश्यकता/ की ज़रूरत होगी।

1. merī bahan ko naī pośākoṁ kī āvaśyaktā/ kī zarūrat hai.
2, hameṁ turant ek nae dūrdarśan yantra kī āvaśyaktā/ kī zarūrat hai.
3. āpko unse kin-kin dastāvezoṁ kī āvaśyaktā/ kī zarūrat hai?
4. use vivāh ke lie bahut se ābhūṣṇoṁ aur vastroṁ kī āvaśyaktā/ kī zarūrat thī.
5. is naukrī ke lie kin-kin yogyătāoṁ kī āvaśyaktā/ kī zarūrat thī.
6. mujhe in dastāvzoṁ kī chah-chah chāyāpratiyoṁ kī āvaśyaktā/ kī zarūrat hogī?
7. mujhe khānā khāte hī kuch mīṭhe kī āvaśyaktā / kī zarūrat hogī.

कभी–कभार kabhī-kabhār..... rarely

यदा–कदा yadā-yadā .... once in a blue moon

शायद ही कभी sāyad hī kabhī--------hardly ever

1. हम कभी–कभार अंग्रेज़ी फ़िल्म देखते हैं।
   ham kabhī-kabhār aṅgrezī film dekhte haiṁ.
   We rarely watch an English film.
2. वे यदा–कदा हमारे यहाँ आते हैं।
   ve yadā-yadā hamāre yahāṁ āte haiṁ.
   They come to our place once in a blue moon.
3. वे बनारस में रहते हुए भी शायद ही कभी गंगा स्नान करते हैं।
   ve banāras meṁ rahte hue bhī śāyad hī kabhī gaṅgā snān karte haim.
   Despite living in Benares, they hardly ever have a bath in the Ganges.

30 चाहिए cāhie
(should/ ought to)

■ **Use of चाहिए cāhie in the sense of should/ought to do some thing i.e. to express moral obligation:**

subj. + obj. + v.r + ना nā * + चाहिए cāhie + होना honā*
+ को ने ne (if necessary)
नी nī

☛ *** If it is intransitive activity, use the verb infinitive E.1**

☛ *** v.r + ना nā, ने ne, नी nī and होना honā agree with the number and gender of the object. E.2**

☛ **Even in the case of transitive activities, if object is not clearly stated, use the infinitive (i.e.the verb ending in ना nā). E. 3**

1. अब आपको जाना चाहिए। — You ought to go now.
   ab āpko jānā cāhie.
2. आपको यह पत्रिका पढ़नी चाहिए थी। — You ought to have read this magazine.
   āpko yah patrikā paṛhnī cāhie thī.
3. मरीज़ को क्या खाना चाहिए? — What should the patient eat ?
   marīz ko kyā khānā cāhie?

Ex. 1: Translate into English:

1. मेरे विचार में तुम्हें अब अपना धंधा बदल लेना चाहिए।
2. मेरे विचार में तुम्हें यहवाला 'कैमरा' ख़रीद लेना चाहिए।
3. क्या आपको लगता है कि मुझे यहवाली साड़ी ख़रीद लेनी चाहिए?
4. क्या आपको लगता है कि हमें उन्हें मिलने जाना चाहिए था?
5. मेरी राय में तुम्हें उन्हें मिलने नहीं जाना चाहिए था।
6. उन्हें मुझे अपने साथ आने देना चाहिए था।

1. mere vicār meṁ tumheṁ apnā dhandhā badal lenā cāhie.
2. mere vicār meṁ tumheṁ yahvālā 'kaimrā' kharīd lenā cāhie.

3. kyā āpko lagtā hai ki mujhe yahvālī sāṛī kharīd lenī cāhie?
4. kyā āpko lagtā hai ki hameṁ unheṁ milne jānā cāhie thā?
5. merī rāy meṁ tumheṁ unheṁ milne nahīṁ jānā cāhie thā.
6. unheṁ mujhe apne sāth āne denā cāhie thā.

Glossary:

मेरे विचार में	mere vicār meṁ	I think
क्या आपको लगता है	kyā āpko lagtā hai	Do you think
मेरी राय में	meri rāy meṁ	In my opinion
मिलना	milnā	to meet
आने देना	āne denā	to let come

Ex.2: Say in Hindi as per example:

You ought to be careful. आपको सावधान रहना चाहिए।
āpko sāvdhān rahnā cāhie.

⇨ You ought to have been careful. आपको सावधान रहना चाहिए था।
āpko sāvdhān rahnā cāhie thā

1. He ought not to read this book.
=> He ought not to have read this book.
2. He ought not to waste money.
=> He ought not to have wasted money.
3. You should consult a doctor and take necessary medicine.
=> You should have consulted a doctor and taken necessary medicine.
4. You should look both ways and then cross the road.
=> You should have looked both ways and then crossed the road.

Glossary:

careful	सावधान (adv,)	sāvdhān
to waste	बर्बाद करना (v.t.)	barbād karnā
consult	सलाह लेना (v.t.)	salāh lenā
necessary	ज़रूरी (adj,)	zarūrī
medicine	दवाई (f.)	davāī
on both sides	दोनों ओर (adv)	donoṁ or
street	सड़क (f.)	saṛak
to cross (road, river etc)	पार करना (v.t.)	pār karnā

Ex.3: Change as per example, beginning the sentences with `X' को चाहिए कि....' `X' ko cāhie ki......:

> आपको अच्छी तरह **पढ़ना चाहिए।**
>
> ➪**आप को चाहिए कि** आप अच्छी तरह **पढ़ें।**

1. तुम्हें इनको शीघ्र अस्पताल ले जाना चाहिए।
2. उसे यथासंभव हिन्दी बोलनेवालों से मिलना.जुलना चाहिए।
3. आपको गाड़ी का टिकट पहले से ख़रीद लेना चाहिए।
4. उनको प्रतिदिन दूरदर्शन पर हिन्दी के समाचार और धारावाहिक देखने चाहिए।
5. आपको अधिक–से–अधिक भारतीय मित्र बनाने चाहिए।

> āpko acchī tarah paṛhnā cāhie.
>
> ➪ āpko cāhie ki āp acchī tarah paṛheṁ.

1. tumheṁ inko śīghra aspatāl le jānā cāhie.
2. use yathāsambhav hindī bolnevāloṁ se milnā-julnā cāhie
3. āpko gāṛī kā tikeṭ pahle se kharīd lenā cāhie.
4. unko pratidin dūrdarśan par hindī ke samācār aur dhārāvāhik dekhne cāhie.
5. āpko adhik-se-adhik bhārtīyă mitra banāne cāhie.

Glossary:

शीघ्र (adv.)	śīghra	quickly
सर्दी (f.)	sardī	winter
प्रतिदिन (adv.)	pratidin	every day
समाचार (m.)	samācār	news
धारावाहिक (m.)	dhārāvāhik	serial
भारतीय(adj./n.)	bhārtīyă	Indian
समय (m.)	samay	time
बिताना (v.i..)	bitānā	to spend(time)

Key 1

1. I think you should change jobs now.
2. I think you should buy this camera.

3. Do you think I should buy this sari?
4. Do you think we should have gone to meet them?
5. In my opinion you ought not to have gone to meet them.
6. They should have let me come with them.

Key 2

1. उसे यह किताब नहीं पढ़नी चाहिए।
=> उसे यह किताब नहीं पढ़नी चाहिए थी।
2. उसे पैसा बर्बाद नहीं करना चाहिए।
=> उसे पैसा बर्बाद नहीं करना चाहिए था।
3. आपको डाक्टर से मिलकर ज़रूरी दवाई लेनी चाहिए।
=> आपको डाक्टर से मिलकर ज़रूरी दवाई लेनी चाहिए थी।
4. आपको दोनों ओर देखकर सड़क पार करनी चाहिए ।
=> आपको दोनों ओर देखकर सड़क पार करनी चाहिए थी।

1. use yah kitāb nahīṁ paṛhnī cāhie.
=> use yah kitāb nahīṁ paṛhnī cāhie thī.
2. use paisā barbād nahīṁ karnā cāhie.
=> use paisā barbād nahīṁ karnā cāhie thā.
4. āpko 'daukṭar' se milkar zarūrī davāī lenī cāhie.
=> āpko 'daukṭar' se milkar zarūrī davāī lenī cāhie thī.
5. āpko donoṁ or dekhkar saṛak pār karnī cāhie.
=> āpko donoṁ or dekhkar saṛak pār karnī cāhie thī.

Key 3

1. तुम्हें चाहिए कि तुम इनको शीघ्र अस्पताल ले जाओ।
2. उसे चाहिए कि वह यथासंभव हिन्दी बोलनेवालों से मिले–जुले।
3. आपको चाहिए कि आप गाड़ी का टिकट पहले से ख़रीद लें।
4. उनको चाहिए कि वे प्रतिदिन दूरदर्शन पर हिन्दी के समाचार और धारावाहिक देखें।
5. आपको चाहिए कि आप अधिक–से–अधिक भारतीय मित्र बनाएँ।

1. tumheṁ cāhie ki tum inko śīghra aspatāl le jāo.
2. use cāhie ki vah yathāsambhav hindī bolnevāloṁ se mile-jule
3. āpko cāhie ki āp gāṛī kā 'tikaṭ' pahle se kharīdeṁ .
4. unko cāhie ki ve pratidin dūrdarśan par hindī ke samācār aur dhārāvāhik dekheṁ
5. āpko cāhie ki āp adhik-se-adhik bhārtīyă mitra banāeṁ

31 (v.r + ते te + ही hi)

jaise hī जैसे ही ....vaise hī वैसे ही

('as soon as' ....)

Hindi uses के ke + (v.r. + ते te + ही hī) or only (v.r. + ते te + ही hī) to express activities happening or done almost simultaneously. ☞ Corresponding English clause is 'as soon as'.

☞ The subject of two clauses may be different or the same.

☞ Regardless of the tense in question, (v.r. + ते te + ही hī) clause is invariable. Conjugated verb of the corresponding simultaneous activity is the key to the tense.

के ke + (v.r. + ते te + ही hī) is used when the noun subject of two sentences is different and living: E. 1-3

1. माता आती है। बच्चा हँसता है । mātā ātī hai. baccā haṁstā hai.	Mother comes. The child laughs.
⇨ माता के आते ही बच्चा हँसता है। mātā ke āte hī baccā haṁstā hai .	As soon as mother comes, the child laughs.
2. माता आई। बच्चा हँसा। mātā āī . baccā haṁsā .	Mother came. The child laughed.
⇨ माता के आते ही बच्चा हँसा। mātā ke āte hī baccā haṁsā.	As soon as mother came, the child laughed.
3. माता आएगी। बच्चा हँसेगा। mātā āegī. baccā haṁsegā .	Mother will come. The child will laugh.
⇨ माता के आते ही बच्चा हँसेगा। mātā ke āte hī baccā haṁsegā	As soon as mother comes, the child will laugh.

☞ **When subject of the (v.r. + ते te + ही hī) clause happens to be one of the pronouns such as मैं maiṁ, हम ham, तू tū, तुम tum, then their ए e- ending possessive pronomial form i.e. मेरे mere, हमारे hamāre, तेरे tere, तुम्हारे tumhāre** + (v..r. +ते **te** + **ही hī)is used: E. 4, 5.**

4. मैं पढ़ने बैठी। बिजली चली गई। — I sat down to study.The electricity went.
maiṁ paṛhne baiṭhī. bijlī calī gaī.

⇨ मेरे पढ़ने बैठते ही बिजली चली गई। — As soon as I sat down to study, electricity went.
mere paṛhne baiṭhte hī bijlī calī gaī.

5. हम घर में घुसे। तेज़ आँधी आ गई। — we entered the house. A strong storm came.
ham ghar meṁ ghuse. tez āṁdhī ā gaī.

⇨. हमारे घर में घुसते ही तेज़ आँधी आ गई। — As soon as we entered the house, a strong storm came.
hamāre ghar meṁ ghuste hī tez āṁdhī ā gaī.

> ☞ **When the subject of 'as soon as' clause is non living.**
> **only (v.r. + ते te + ही hī) is used: E. 6**

6. बारिश बन्द हुई। हम बाहर निकले। — It stopped raining. We came out.
bāriś band huī. ham bāhar nikle.

⇨ बारिश बन्द होते ही हम बाहर निकले। — As soon as it stopped raining we came out
bāriś band hote hī ham bāhar nikle.

> ☞ **When the subject of both the sentences is living and the same:**
> **The subject is used only once at the beginning of the 'as soon as' clause, or at the beginning of the following clause as shown below. E. 7 given below.**
>
> ☞ **In case this common subject happens to be in different cases, then the subject- form of the following activity is used once at the beginning of the 'as soon as' clause . E. 8, 9 given below.**

7. बच्चे घर आते हैं। बच्चे खेलते हैं। bacce ghar āte haiṁ. bacce khelte haiṁ. — The children come home. The children play.

⇨ बच्चे घर आते ही खेलते हैं। bacce ghar āte hī khelte haiṁ. — As soon as the children come home, they play.

or

घर आते ही बच्चे खेलते हैं।

ghar āte hī bacce khelte haiṁ.

8. सविता दफ़्तर पहुँची। सविता ने काम करना शुरू किया। savitā daftar pahuṁcī. savitā ne kām karnā śurū kiyā. — Savita arrived at the office. Savita began to work.

⇨ सविता ने दफ़्तर पहुँचते ही काम करना शुरू किया। savitā ne daftar pahuṁcte hī kām karnā śurū kiyā. — As soon as Savita reached the office, she began to work.

9. मैं घर आई। मुझको सिर में दर्द होने लगा। maiṁ ghar āī. mujhko sir meṁ dard hone lagā. — I reached home. I began to have a head ache.

⇨. मुझको घर आते ही सिर में दर्द होने लगा। mujhko ghar āte hī sir meṁ dard hone lagā. — As soon as I came home, I began to have a head-ache.

Ex.1: Say in English:

1. पावनी माँ को देखते ही रो पड़ी।
2. शरद ऋतु शुरू होते ही मेरे शहर में बहुत पर्यटक आने लगते हैं।
3. नवीन ने एम.बी.बी. एस. की परीक्षा में उत्तीर्ण होते ही शादी कर ली।
4. मेरे पलंग पर लेटते ही किसीने द्वार पर खटखटाया ।
5. बड़ों के घर से निकलते ही बच्चे शोर मचाने लगे।
6. आप खाना मेज़ पर लगते ही हमें बुला लीजिएगा।

7. वे निर्णय लेते ही हमें सूचित करेंगे।
8. मैं (m.)भारत पहुँचते ही हिन्दी बोलना सीखूँगा।

1. pāvnī māṁ ko dekhte hī ro paṛī.
2. śarad ṛtu śurū hote hī mere śahar meṁ bahut paryaṭak āne lagte haiṁ.
3. navīn ne MBBS kī parīkṣā meṁ uttīrṇ hote hī śādī kar lī.
4. mere palaṅg par leṭte hī kisīne dvār par khaṭkhaṭāyā.
5. baṛoṁ ke ghar se nikalte hī bacce śor macāne lage.
6. āp khānā mez par lagte hī hameṁ bulā lījiegā
7. ve nirṇay lete hī hameṁ sūcit kareṁge.
8. maiṁ (m.) bhārat pahuṁcte hī hindī bolnā sīkhūṁgā.

शरदऋतु (f.)	śarad ṛtu	winter season
पर्यटक (m.)	paryaṭak	tourist
शोर मचाना (v.t.)	śor macānā	to make a noise
खटखटाना (v.t.)	khaṭkhaṭānā	to knock at
निर्णय लेना (v.t.)	nirṇay lenā	to decide
सूचित करना (v.t.)	sūcit karnā	to inform

Alternatively जैसे ही ....वैसे ही **jaise hī --- vaise hī** can be used instead of (v.r. + ते + ही*).

Use of वैसे ही vaise hī is not obligatory.

1. माता के आते ही बच्चा हँसता है। — As soon as mother comes, the child laughs.(Pres. indef.)
   mātā ke āte hī baccā haṁstā hai .

➪ जैसे ही माता आती है बच्चा हँसता है।

jaise hī mātā ātī hai, baccā haṁstā hai .

2. माता के आते ही बच्चा हँसा। — As soon as mother came, the child laughed.
   mātā ke āte hī baccā haṁsā

➪ जैसे ही माता आई, वैसे ही बच्चा हँसा। . (Past simple)

jaise hī mātā āī, vaise hī baccā haṁsā.

3. माता के आते ही बच्चा हँसेगा। — As soon as mother comes, the child will laugh.
   mātā ke āte hī baccā haṁsegā

➪ जैसे ही माता आएगी, वैसे ही बच्चा हँसेगा। .(Fut. simple)

jaise hī mātā āegī, vaise hī baccā haṁsegā

Ex. 2: Translate into English:

1. जैसे ही अधिकारी आता है, (वैसे ही) कर्मचारी काम करने लगते हैं।
2. जैसे ही छह बजते हैं, मैं दूरदर्शन पर समाचार देखता हूँ।
3. जैसे ही हमारा बेटा डाक्टर को देखता है, वह रोने लगता है।
4. जैसे ही स्कूल बन्द हुआ, (वैसे ही) छात्र खेलने को चले गए।
5. जैसे ही बैठक ख़त्म हुई, (वैसे ही) सभागार खाली हो गया।
6. जैसे ही उसने 'ई–मेल' पढ़ी, वह बेहोश हो गई।
7. जैसे ही अभिनेत्री मंच पर आई, दर्शकों ने तालियों से उसका स्वागत किया।
8. जैसे ही मेरी नौकरी लगेगी, मैं एक नया घर किश्तों पर ख़रीदूँगी।

1. jaise hī adhikārī ātā hai, (vaise hi) karmcārī kām karne lagte haiṁ.
2. jaise hī chah bajte haiṁ , maiṁ dūrdarśan par samācār dekhtā hūṁ.
3. jaise hī hamārā beṭā ḍaukṭar ko dekhtā hai, vah rone lagtā hai.
4. jaise hī skūl band huā, (vaise hī) chātra khelne ko cale gae.
5. jaise hī baiṭhak khatam huī, (vaise hī) sabhāgār khālī ho gayā.
6. jaise hī usne 'e-mail' paṛhī, vah behoś ho gaī.
7. jaise hī abhinetrī mañc par āī, darśakoṁ ne tāliyoṁ se uskā svāgat kiyā.
8. jaise hī merī naukrī lage gī, maiṁ ek nayā ghar kiśtoṁ par kharīdūṁgī.

Ex. 3: Change as per example using 'के + (v.r. + ते + ही*):

1. जैसे ही प्रवक्ता ने बोलना शुरू किया, श्रोतागण एक दम शान्त हो गए।

⇨ प्रवक्ता के बोलना शुरू करते ही श्रोतागण एक दम शान्त हो गए।

2. जैसे ही बरसात का मौसम आता है, (वैसे ही) छातों और बरसातियों की बिक्री बढ़ जाती है।

⇨ ....

3. जैसे ही आपका सन्देश मिला (वैसे ही) हम वहाँ से चल पड़े।

⇨ ....

4. जैसे ही हम लेटे, (वैसे ही) पड़ोस से ज़ोर ज़ोर से आवाज़ें आने लगीं।

⇨ ....

5. जैसे ही मैं अमरीका जाऊँगी (वैसे ही) मैं अपने लिए एक कार ख़रीदूँगी।

⇨ ....

6. जैसे ही खिलाड़ी ने चौके–छक्के लगाए, प्रशंसक जीत का जशन मनाने लगे।

⇨ ....

1. jaise hī pravaktā ne bolnā śurū kiyā, śrotśāgaṇ ek dam śānt ho gae.

⇨ gāṛī pleṭfaurm par pahuṁcte hī yātrī uskī or dauṛte haiṁ.

2. jaise hī barsāt kā mausam ātā hai, (vaise hī) chātoṁ aur barsātiyoṁ kī bikrī baṛh jātī hai.

⇨ ....

3. jaise hī āpkā sandeś milā, (vaise hī) ham vahāṁ se cal paṛe.

⇨ ....

4. jaise hī ham leṭe, (vaise hī) paṛos se zor-zor se āvāzeṁ āne lagīṁ.

⇨ ....

5. jaise hī maiṁ amrīkā jāūṁgī, (vaise hī) maiṁ apne lie ek 'kār' kharīdūṁgī.

⇨ ....

6. jaise hī khilārī ne cauke chakke lagae, (vaise hī) praśaṃsak jīt kā jaśan manāne lage.

⇨ ....

Glossary:

प्रवक्ता (m.)	pravaktā	speaker
श्रोतागण (m.pl)	śrotāgaṇ	audience
एक दम (adv.)	ek dam	absolutely
शान्त (adj.)	śānt	peaceful
बरसात का मौसम (m.)	barsāt kā mausam	rainy season
छाता (m.)	chātā	umbrella
बरसाती (f.)	barsātī	raincoat
बिक्री (f.)	bikrī	sale
बढना (v.i.)	baṛhnā	to grow
चल पडना (v.i.)	cal paṛnā	to set off
मेज़ पर खाना लगना (v.i.)	mez par khānā lagnā	table be laid
पड़ोस (m.)	paṛos	neighborhood
ज़ोर ज़ोर से (adv.)	zor-zor se	loudly
आवाज़ें (f.pl)	āvāzeṁ	sounds
चौके–छक्के (m.pl)	cauke-chakke	groups of four-six
प्रशंसक (m.)	praśaṃsak	admirer(s)
जशन मनााना (v.t.)	jaśan manānā	to rejoice

Key 1

1. As soon as Pavni saw her mother, she burst out crying.
2. Many tourists begin to come to my city as soon as the winter season begins.
3. Navin married as soon as he passed his MBBS exam.
4. As soon as I lay on bed, someone knocked at the door.
5. As soon as the elders left the house, the children began to make noise.
6. Please call us as soon as the food is laid on the table.
7. As soon as we decide, we will inform you.
8. As soon as I arrive in India, I will learn to speak Hindi

Key 2

1. As soon as the boss comes , the employees begin to work.
2. As soon as it is six o'clock, I watch news on t.v.
3. As soon as our son sees the doctor, he begins to cry.
4. As soon as the school closed, the students went to play.
5. As soon as the meeting ended, the hall became empty.
6. As soon as she read the e-mail, she fainted.
7. As soon as the actress came on the stage, the viewers welcomed her with an applaud.
8. As soon as I get a job, I will buy a new house on installments.

Key 3

1. प्रवक्ता के बोलना शुरू करते ही श्रोतागण एक दम शान्त हो गए।
2. बरसात का मौसम आते ही छातों और बरसातियों की बिक्री बढ़ जाती है।
3. आपका सन्देश मिलते ही हम वहाँ से चल पड़े।
4. हमारे लेटते ही पड़ोस से ज़ोर ज़ोर से आवाज़ें आने लगीं।
5. अमरीका जाते ही मैं अपने लिए एक कार ख़रीदूँगी।
6. खिलाड़ी के चौके–छक्के लगाते ही प्रशंसक जीत का जशन मनाने लगे।

1. pravaktā ke bolnā śurū karte hi śrotśāgaṇ ek dam śānt ho gae.
2. barsāt kā mausam āte hī chātoṁ aur barsātiyoṁ kī bikrī baṛh jātī hai.
3. āpkā sandeś milte hī ham vahāṁ se cal paṛe.
4. hamāre leṭte hī paṛos se zor-zor se āvāzeṁ āne lagīṁ.
5. amrīkā jāte hī maiṁ apne lie ek 'kār' kharīdūṁgī.
6. khilārī ke cauke-chakke lagāte hī praśaṃsak jīt kā jaśan manāne lage.

32 No sooner ....than

subj. + v.r. + ā,-e, i + hi + thā, -e, -ī ki ....

जैसे ही मैं सोई, कोई द्वार खटखटाने लगा।
jaise hī maiṁ soī, koī dvār khaṭ-khaṭāne lagā.

- **मेरे सोते ही** कोई द्वार खटखटाने लगा।
mere sote hi koī dvār khaṭ-khaṭāne lagā.
As soon as I slept, someone began to knock at the door.
- **मैं सोई ही थी कि** कोई द्वार खटखटाने लगा।
maiṁ soī hī thī ki koī dvār khaṭ-khaṭāne lagā.
No sooner had I slept, than someone began to knock at the door.

Ex.1: Change as per example given above.

1. **जैसे ही** फ़िल्म शुरू हुई, बिजली चली गई।
....
2. **जैसे ही** प्रधानमंत्री का भाषण शुरू हुआ, दर्शक नारे लगाने लगे।
....
3. **जैसे ही** हमने अपना घर ख़रीदा, पिता जी का स्थानान्तरण हो गया।
....
4. **जैसे ही** गाड़ी की आवाज़ सुनाई दी, लोग सामान उठाकर इधर–उधर दौड़ने लगे।
....
5. **जैसे ही** सभा समाप्त हुई, सभापति उठकर चले गए।
....
6. **जैसे ही** हम घर से निकले, बर्फ़ पड़ने लगी।
....
7. **जैसे ही** उसे वेतन मिला, उसने सब ख़र्च डाला।
....

1. jaise hī film śurū huī, bijlī calī gaī.

2. jaise hī pradhān mantrī kā bhāṣaṇ śurū huā, darśak nāre lagāne lage
3. jaise hī hamne apnā nayā ghar kharīdā, pitā jī kā sthānāntaraṇ ho gayā.
4. jaise hī gāṛī kī āvāz sunāī dī, log sāmān uṭhākar idhar udhar dauṛne lage.
5. jaise hī sabhā smāpt huī, sabhāpati uṭhkar cale gae.
6. jaise hī ham ghar se nikle, barf paṛne lagī.
7. jaise hī use vetan milā, usne sab kharc ḍālā.

Key

1. • film śurū hote hī, bijlī calī gaī.
   • film śurū huī hī thī ki bijlī calī gaī.
2. • pradhān mantrī kā bhāṣaṇ śurū hote hī darśak nāre lagāne lage
   • pradhān mantrī kā bhāṣaṇ śurū huā hī thā ki darśak nāre lagāne lage.
3. • hamāre apnā nayā ghar kharīdte hī, pitā jā kā sthānāntaraṇ ho gayā.
   • hamne apnā nayā ghar kharīdā hī thā ki pitā jī kā sthānāntaraṇ ho gayā.
4. • gāṛī kī āvāz sunāī dete hī, log sāmān uṭhākar idhar udhar dauṛne lage.
   • gāṛī kī āvāz sunāī dī hī thī ki log sāmān uṭhākar idhar udhar dauṛne lage.
5. • sabhā smāpt hote hī sabhāpati uṭhkar cale gae.
   • sabhā smāpt huī hī thī ki sabhāpati uṭhkar cale gae.
6. • hamāre ghar se nikalte hī, barf paṛne lagī.
   • ham ghar se nikle hī the ki barf paṛne lagī.
6. • usne vetan milte hī sab <u>kh</u>arc ḍālā.
   • use vetan milā hī thā ki usne sab <u>kh</u>arc ḍālā.

दर्शक (m.)	darśak (m.)	viewers
नारे लगाना (v.t.)	nāre lagānā	to shout slogans
स्थानान्तरण (m.)	sthānāntaraṇ	change places
सभापति (m.)	sabhāpati	chairman
वेतन (m.)	vetan	salary
ख़र्चना (v.t.)	<u>kh</u>arcnā	to spend

33 Participial Constructions

Perfective Participial Construction

v.r.	+	आ, ए, ई +	हुआ, हुए, हुई
		ā, e, ī	huā, hue, huī

☞ **It can be used as adjective, adverb or noun.**
Like any ā -ending adjective, it changes to '-e, -ī-ending to agree with the number and gender of the noun. For example:

खुला हुआ दरवाज़ा	khulā huā darvāzā	open door
खुले हुए दरवाज़े	khule hue darvāze	open doors
खुली हुई खिड़की	khulī huī khiṛkī	open window
खुली हुई खिड़कियाँ	khulī huī khiṛkiyāṁ	open windows

☞ As adverbs, they are best used in the neuter ए e-ending. See E. 7.

☞ **When it is used as nouns, it takes the place of nouns it modifies.**

☞ **Use of हुआ huā, हुए hue, हुई huī is not obligatory.**

1. टूटा हुआ फूलदान फेंक दो। (adj.)
   ṭūṭā huā phūldān pheṁk do.
   Throw away the broken flower vase.
2. औरत लेटी हुई / लेटे हुए पढ़ रही थी। (adverb)
   aurat leṭī huī paṛh rahī thī.
   The woman was reading while lying down.
3. आपका कहा हुआ एक–एक शब्द मुझे याद है।
   apkā kahā huā ek-ek śabd mujhe yād hai.(noun)
   I remember every single word of what you said.

Repetitive use of the past participle:
(v.r. + आ ā, ए e, ई ī) + (v.r. +आ ā, ए e, ई ī) . It is used as adverb.

ppc = perfective participial construction

4. वह सोई–सोई / सोए–सोए बोल रही थी। — She was talking while asleep.

vah soī-soī / soe-soe bol rahī thī.

- **Predicative use of *ppc:**

subject + ppc* + honā to agree with the subject:

1. खिड़की[f.pl] खुली हुई है। — The window is open.

khiṛkī khulī huī hai.

2. किताब[sg.] यहाँ पड़ी हुई है। — The book is lying here.

kitāb yahāṁ paṛī huī hai

Ex.1: Translate into English:

1. उनके सामनेवाले उद्यान में बहुत मुरझाए हुए फूल हैं।
2. ये फटे हुए काग़ज़ किसने मेरे अध्ययन कक्ष में रखे?
3. इस खुली हुई खिड़की से चोर अन्दर आ सकता है।
4. मुझे टूटे हुए प्याले में चाय मत दो।
5. डॉक्टर की कही हुई बातों पर ग़ौर करो।
6. मुझे अपना देश छोड़े हुए महीनों हो गए हैं।
7. वह बेंच पर बैठा–बैठा चाँद की ओर देख रहा था।
8. मेरी बेटी हमेशा लेटे–लेटे संगीत सुनती है।

1. unke sāmnevāle udyān meṁ bahut murjhāe hue phūl haiṁ.
2. ye phaṭe hue kāGaz kisne mere adhyayan kakṣ meṁ rakhe?
3. is khulī huī khiṛkī se cor andar ā saktā hai.
4. mujhe ṭūṭe hue pyāle meṁ cāy mat do.
5. ḍaukṭar kī kahī huī bātoṁ par Gaur karo.
6. mujhe apnā deś choṛe hue mahīnoṁ ho gae haiṁ.
7. vah 'baiñc' par baiṭhā-baiṭhā cāṁd kī or dekh rahā thā.
8. merī beṭī hameśā leṭe-leṭe sangīt suntī hai.

Glossary:

मुरझाए हुए (ppc)	murjhāe hue	withered
सामनेवाला (adj.)	sāmnevālā	the one in front
उद्यान (m.)	udyān	garden
अध्ययन कक्ष (m.)	adhyayan kakṣ	study room

काग़ज़ (m.)	kāGaz	papers
कहना (v.t.)	kahnā	to say
बातें (f.pl.)	bātem̐	spoken words
ग़ौर करना (v.t.)	Gaur karnā	to heed
महीनों (adv.)	mahīnom̐	months
चाँद (m.)	cām̐d	moon
लेटे–लेटे (ppc.)	leṭe-leṭe	lying down

Ex. 2 Translate into Hindi:

1. Where did you buy these over ripe bananas[m.pl].
2. Whose is this recently painted house[m.sg]?
3. Where did you keep the blossomed roses[m.pl]?
4. They took away the fallen tree.
5. I like the music written by him.
6. Pick up these scattered papers.
7. In India I (f.) always drink boiled water
8. Don't you get bored lying on bed all day?
9. This water is boiled.

be ripe	पका, पके, पकी होना	pakā, pake, pakī honā
over ripe	ज़्यादा पके हुए (ppc)	zyādā pake hue
recently	हाल में (adv.)	hāl mem̐
to paint	रंगना (v.t.)	ram̐gnā
to blossom	खिलना (v.i.)	khilnā
to be blossomed	खिला होना (v.i.)	khilā honā
rose	गुलाब (m.)	gulāb
take away	ले जाना (comp. verb)	le jānā
music	संगीत (m.)	saṅgīt
written by X	X का लिखा हुआ (ppc)	X kā likhā huā
to pick up	उठाना (v.t.)	uṭhānā

scattered	बिखरे हुए (ppc.)	bikhre hue
always	सदैव (adv.)	sadaiv
to get bored	ऊबना (v.i.)	ūbnā

Key 1

1. There are many withered flowers in their front garden.
2. Who put these torn papers in my study room?
3. A thief could come in through this open window.
4. Don't give me tea in the broken cup.
5. Pay heed to the things the doctor said.
6. It has been months since I left my country.
7. He looked in the direction of the moon while sitting on the bench.
8. My daughter always listens to music while lying down.

Key 2

1. तुमने ये ज़्यादा पके हुए केले m.pl कहाँ ख़रीदे?
2. यह हाल में रंगा हुआ घरm. किसका है?
3. तुमने खिले हुए गुलाबm.pl कहाँ रखे?
4. वे गिरे हुए पेड़ m.sg.. को ले गए।
5. मुझे उसका लिखा हुआ संगीतm. पसन्द हैं।
6. ये बिखरे हुए काग़ज़ उठा लो।
7. भारत में मैं f सदैव उबला हआ पानीm. पीती हूँ।
8. तुम f. दिन भर पलंग पर पड़ी–पड़ी ऊबती नहीं हो?
9. यह पानी m.sg. उबला हुआ है।

1. tumne ye zyādā pake hue kele kahāṁ <u>kh</u>arīde?.
2. yah hāl meṁ raṁgā huā ghar kiskā hai?
3. tumne khile hue gulāb kahāṁ rakhe?
4. ve gire hue peṛ ko le gae.
5. mujhe uskā likhā huā saṅgīt pasand hai.
6. ye bikhre hue kāGaz uṭhā lo.
7. bhārat meṁ maiṁ sadaiv ublā huā pānī pītī hūṁ.
8. tum dinbhar palaṅg par paṛī-paṛī ūbtī nahīṁ ho?
9. yah pānī ublā huā hai.

Imperfective Participial Construction

v.r. + ता, ते, ती + हुआ, हुए, हुई

tā, te, tī — huā, hue, huī

☞ **Use of हुआ huā, हुए hue, हुई huī is not obligatory**

☞ **It can be used as adjective, adverb or noun.**

☞ **When it is used as nouns, it takes the place of noun it modifies**

☞ **Like any ā -ending adjective it changes to '-e, -ī-ending to agree with the number and gender of the noun. e.g.**

1. **मैंने उसे चलती हुई** गाड़ी[f.] में चढ़ते देखा। maiṁne use caltī huī gāṛī meṁ carhte dekhā. (adj.)	I saw him getting on a moving bus.
2. शराबी[m] **बड़बड़ाता हुआ** आया। śarābī baṛbaṛātā huā āyā. (adverb)	The drunkard came babbling.
3. **खातों** को मत टोको। khātoṁ ko mat ṭoko. (noun)	Dont' interrupt the ones who are eating

■ **Repetitive use of present participle** :

(v.r. + ता tā, ते te, ती tī) + (v.r. + ता tā, ते te, ती tī)

☞ **This is used as adverb.**

4. मैं[m] चाय पीते–पीते अख़बार पढ़ता हूँ । maiṁ[m] cāy pīte-pīte- akhbār paṛhtā hūṁ	I read the newspaper while drinking tea.
5. वह अचानक बोलते–बोलते रुक गया। vah acānak bolte-bolte ruk gayā.	He suddenly stopped while talking.

■ Two very specific uses of IPC are:

subj. + (v.r. + ते te)+(v.r. + ते te,) + बचना bacnā,

☞ बचना bacnā used when an accident almost happened.

☞ बचना bacnā agrees with the N & G of the subj. in the past tense.

1. फूलदान गिरते–गिरते बचा। phūldān girte-girte bacā.	The vase almost fell.
2. मेरी कार पेड़ से टकराते–टकराते बची। merī 'kār' peṛ se ṭakrāte-ṭakrāte bacī.	My car almost hit against the tree.

subj. + (v.r. + ते te)+(v.r. + ते te,) + रह जाना rah jānā

☞ रहना rahnā is used when an activity due to some last minute obsruction remains unfulfilled..

☞ रहना rahnā, agrees with the N &G of the subject.

1. मेरा काम होते होते रह गया। merā kām hote-hote rah gayā.	My work almost got done!
2. वह भारत जाते–जाते रह गई। vah bhārat jāte-jāte rah gaī.	She almost went to India!

देखते–ही–देखते dekhte-hī-dekhte = in no time

1. देखते–ही–देखते सड़क ख़ाली हो गई। dekhte-hī-dekhte saṛak khālī ho gaī.	In no time, the road became empty.

Ex. 1 Translate into English:

1. लड़के गाते हुए जा रहे थे।
2. उसने झेंपते हुए कहा।
3. वह बिखरे हुए काग़ज़ों को समेटती हुई बोली।
4. आज मेरे साथ एक बड़ा हादसा होते–होते बचा।

5. देखते–ही–देखते उसने इतनी ज़मीन–जायदाद बना ली।
6. पिछले महीने उसकी शादी होते–होते रह गई।
7. मुझे यह काम मिलते–मिलते रह गया।

1. laṛke gāte hue jā rahe the.
2. usne jheṁpte hue kahā.
3. vah bikhre hue kaGzoṁ ko sameṭtī huī bolī.
4. āj mere sāth ek baṛā hādsā hote-hote bacā.
5. dekhte-hī-dekhte usne itnī zamīn-jāydād banā lī!
6. pichle mahīne uskī śādī hote-hote rah gaī.
7. mujhe yah kām milte-milte rah gayā.

Glossary:

झेंपना (v.i.)	jheṁpnā	be embarrassed
बिखरना (v.i.)	bikharnā	to scatter
समेटना (v.t.)	sameṭnā	to gather together
हादसा (m.)	hādsā	accident
ज़मीन–जायदाद (f.)	zamīn- jāydād	landed property

Ex. 2: Translate into Hindi:

1. The young woman was singing while dancing.
2. The dog was following the thief while barking.
3. I am tired studying continuously since the morning.
4. I am bored with doing the same chores every day.
5. Everything was sold out in no time.
6. The crowd dispersed in no time and the field became empty.
7. The car almost collided with the truck.
8. The house got almost burnt.

Glossary:

young woman	युवती (f.)	yuvatī
to dance	नाचना (v.i.)	nācnā
to bark	भौंकना (v.i.)	bhauṁknā
to follow	पीछा करना (v.t.)	pīchā karnā
continuously	निरन्तर (adv.)	nirantar
be bored	ऊबना (v.i.)	ūbnā

chores	काम–काज (m.)	kām-kāj
crowd	भीड़ (f.)	bhīṛ
disperse	तितर–बितर होना (v.i.)	titar-bitar honā
field	मैदान (m.)	maidān
empty.	ख़ाली (adj.)	<u>kh</u>ālī
to collided with	टकराना (v.i.)	ṭakrānā

Key 1

1. The boys were going while singing.
2. He said while feeling embarrassed.
3. She spoke while gathering together the scattered papers.
4. I almost met a big accident today.
5. In no time he made so much landed property!
6. She/ He almost got married last month.
7. I almost got this job.

Key 2

1. युवती नाचते हुए गा रही थी।
2. कुत्ता भौकते हुए चोर का पीछा कर रहा था।
3. मैं सुबह से निरन्तर पढ़ते–पढ़ते थक गई हूँ।
4. मैं रोज़ वही घरेलू कामकाज करते–करते ऊब गई हूँ।
5. देखते–ही–देखते सब कुछ बिक गया।
6. देखते–ही–देखते भीड़ तितर बितर हो गई और मैदान ख़ाली हो गया।
7. कार 'ट्रक' में भिड़ते–भिड़ते बची।
8. घर जलते–जलते बचा।

1. yuvatī nācte hue gā rahī thī.
2. kuttā bhauṁkte hue cor kā pīchā kar rahā thā.
3. maiṁ subah se paṛhte-paṛhte thak gaī hūṁ.
4. maiṁ roz vahī gharelū kām-kāj karte-karte ūb gaī hūṁ.
5. dekhte- hī- dekhte sab kuch bik gayā.
6. dekhte- hī- dekhte bhīṛ titar-bitar ho gaī, aur maidān <u>kh</u>ālī ho gayā.
7. 'car' 'truck' se bhiṛte-bhiṛte bacī.
8. ghar jalte-jalte bacā.

34 Relative Clauses

जो jo is used in the direct case.
जिस jis sg. / जिन jin pl. followed by suitable postposition are used in the oblique case.
In Hindi use of को ko is not obligatory when the object is non living. In this case जो can be used in the oblique case.

Examples :

1. जो लोग मेले में खोए हैं, उन्हे ढूँढ़ना आसान नहीं। jo log mele meṁ khoe haiṁ, unheṁ ḍhūṁḍhnā āsān nahīṁ.	The people who got lost in the fair, are not easy to find.
2. जो अकारण क्रोध करता है, वह बाद में पछताता है। jo akāraṇ krodh kartā hai, vah bād meṁ pachtātā hai.	The one who gets angry for no reason, regrets later.
3. मैं उस देश में नहीं रहती जिस में मैं पली–बड़ी। maiṁ us deś meṁ nahīṁ rahtī jis meṁ maiṁ palī-baṛhī.	I don't live in the country where I grew up.
4. यही वे चित्र हैं जिन्हें मैं सालों से ढूँढ़ रही हूँ।। yahī ve citra haiṁ jinheṁ maiṁ sāloṁ se ḍhūṁḍh rahī hūṁ.	These are the pictures that I have been looking for for years.
6. जिस मकान में अब आप रहते हैं, उसमें पहले मैं रहती थी। jis makān meṁ ab āp rahte haiṁ, us meṁ pahle maiṁ rahtī thī.	The house in which you live now, formerly I used to live in it .

Ex.1: Translate into English.

1. जो सामान नीचे गिरा हुआ है, उसको उठा लीजिए।
2. जो कपड़े धुले हुए हैं, उन्हें सुखा दो।
3. जो पुस्तकें मेंज़ पर पड़ी हुई हैं, उन्हें अलमारी में रख दो।
4. वह शब्दकोश जो ताक पर पड़ा हुआ है, किसका है ?
5. क्या वह तुम्हारा 'कोट' है जो सामनेवाली दीवार पर टँगा हुआ है ?
6. जो बातें आपने मुझे समझाई थीं, मैं उन्हें कभी नहीं भूलूँगा।
7. जो पुस्तकें रागिनी ने तुम्हें दी हैं, वे बहुत उपयोगी हैं।
8. जिस किराए के मकान में हम रहते हैं, वह बहुत जीर्ण–शीर्ण अवस्था में है।
9. मैं जिन व्यक्तियों से बात कर रही थी, वे मेरे सहकर्मी हैं।
10. जिस गुण्डे ने कल मुझ पर हमला किया, वह पकड़ लिया गया है।
11. जिस बूढ़े आदमी ने तुम्हें अभी–अभी आशीर्वाद दिया, वे मेरे शवसुर है।

1. jo sāmān nīce girā huā hai, usko uṭhā lījie.
2. jo kapṛe dule hue haiṁ, unheṁ sukhā do.
3. jo pustakeṁ mez par paṛī huī haiṁ, unheṁ almārī meṁ rakh do.
4. vah śabdkoś jo tāk par paṛā huā hai, kiskā hai?
5. kyā vah tumhārā 'coat' hai jo sāmnevālī dīvār par ṭaṁgā huā hai?
6. jo bāteṁ āpne mujhe samjhāī thīṁ, maiṁ unheṁ kabhī nahīṁ bhūlūṁgā.
7. jo pustakeṁ rāginī ne tumheṁ dī haiṁ, ve bahut upyogī haiṁ.
8. jis kirāe ke makān meṁ ham rahte haiṁ , vah bahut jīrṇ-śīrṇ avasthā meṁ hai.
9. maiṁ jin vyaktiyoṁ se bāt kar rahī thī, ve mere sahkarmī haiṁ.
10. jis guṇḍe ne kal mujh par hamlā kiyā, vah pakaṛ liyā gayā hai.
11. jis būṛhe ādmī ne tumheṁ abhī-abhī āśīrvād diyā , vah merā śvasur hai.

Glossary:

ताक (m.)	tāk	shelf
टँगा होना (v.i.)	ṭaṁgā honā	to be hanging
सामनेवाली (adj.)	sāmnevālī	the one in front
शब्दकोश (m.)	śabdkoś	dictionary
उपयोगी (adj.)	upyogī	useful

किराए का मकान (m.)	kirāe kā makān	rented house
जीर्ण–शीर्ण अवस्था में	jīrṇ-śīrṇ avasthā meṁ	dilapidated
आशीर्वाद (m.)	āśīrvād	blessing
शवसुर (m.)	śvasur	father in law

Ex. 2: Say in Hindi:

1. Did you write the story that you sent to me last week?
2. These are the stairs where I fell last month and almost broke my leg.
3. The advice **that** he gave me was very practical.
4. The picture **that** he showed me was of his wife.
5. The woman **who** lives upstairs is very rich.
6. The boy **that** is running towards us is very talented.
7. They have set up a branch office in India whose job is to give quick service to the customers.
8. That is my friend Dinesh, whose brother died in the air crash yesterday.
9. She sent me two boxes of chocolates by post, **neither of which** I have received yet.
10. Savita has five siblings, **not even one of whom** lives in India.

practical.	कारगर (adj.)	kārgar
stairs	सीढ़ियाँ (f.pl)	sīṛhiyāṁ
upstairs	ऊपर (adv.)	ūpar
talented	प्रतिभावान (adj.)	pratibhāvān
quick service	तवरित सेवा (adj. + f.)	tvarit sevā
air crash	हवाई दुर्घटना (adj. + f.)	havāī durghaṭnā
customer	गाहक (m.)	gāhak

Ex.3: Fill in the blanks with जो, जिस, जिन, जहाँ

1. ....आदमी हमारे कपड़े धोता है, वह दो महीने से बीमार है।
2. यही वह पुस्तक है ....के बारे में मैं आपको बता रही थी।
3. वह पहली महिला है ....एक उपयोगी सुझाव दिया है।
4. आप पहले व्यक्ति हैं ....मेरी बेटी प्रभावित है।
5. यही वह युवक है ....कई दिनों से मेरा पीछा कर रहा है।
6. यही वह युवती है .... सौंदर्य के चर्चे सब जगह हो रहे हैं।
7. यही वह नेता है .... हमारे इलाक़े का हर आदमी समर्थन देता है।

* the tree under which Lord Buddha did penance and got enlightened.

8. हमारे शहर में चार हवाई पुल बन रहे हैं, ...चौक को सीधे उपनगरों से जोड़ेंगे।
9. दावत में बहुत लोग आए ....मैं पहले कभी नहीं मिली थी।
10. यह बोधिवृक्ष* है...............नीचे बुद्ध को ज्ञान प्राप्त हुआ था।
11. वह एक मात्र खिलाड़ी है.............भारत का नाम विश्व में ऊँचा किया है।

1. .... ādmī hamāre kapṛe dhotā hai, vah do mahīne se bīmār hai.
2. yahī vah pustak hai ..... ke bāre meṁ maiṁ āpko batā rahī thī.
3. vah pahlī mahilā hai ....ek upyogī sujhāv diyā hai.
4. āp pahle vyakti haiṁ ....merī beṭī prabhāvit hai.
5. yahī vah yuvak hai.............kaī dinoṁ se merā pīchā kar rahā hai.
6. yahī vah yuvtī hai..........saundryă ke carce sab jagah ho rahe haim.
7. yahī vah netā hai .....hamāre ilāqe kā har ādmī samarthan deta hai.
8. hamāre śahar meṁ cār havāī pul ban rahe haiṁ...............cauk ko sīdhe upnagroṁ se joṛeṁge.
9. dāvat meṁ bahut log ae..........maiṁ pahle kabhī nahīṁ milī thī.
10. yah bodhivṛkṣ hai ....nīce buddh ko gyān prāpt huā thā.
11. vah ek mātra khilāṛī hai........bhārat kā nām visva meṁ ūṁcā kiyā hai.

प्रभावित करना (v.t.)	prabhāvit karnā	to impress
प्रशिक्षण (m.)	praśikṣaṇ	training
हेतु (ppn.)	hetu	for

Key 1

1. Pick up the stuff that has fallen down.
2. Dry the clothes that are washed.
3. Put the books that are lying on the table in the cupboard.
4. Whose is the dictionary that is lying on the shelf?
5. Is the coat that is hanging on the wall yours?
6. I will never forget the things that you had explained to me.
7. The books which Ragini has given to you are very useful.
8. The rented house in which we live is in dilapidated state.
9. The people I was talking to are my colleagues.
10. The hooligan who attacked me yesterday, has been arrested.
11. The old man who blessed you just now is my father–in–law.

Key 2

1. क्या वह कहानी आपने लिखी जो आपने मुझे पिछले सप्ताह पढ़ने को भेजी थी?
2. यही वे सीढ़ियाँ हैं जिनसे मैं पिछले महीने गिरी थी, और मेरी टाँग टूटते–टूटते बची थी।

3. जो सलाह उसने मुझे दी, बहुत कारगर थी।
4. जो चित्र उसने मुझे दिखाया, वह उसकी पत्नी का था।
5. जो औरत ऊपर रहती है, वह बहुत धनी है।
6. जो लड़का दौड़कर हमारी ओर आ रहा है, वह बहुत प्रतिभावान है।
7. उन्होंने अपने दफ़्तर की एक शाख़ा भारत में स्थापित की है जिसका काम गाहकों को त्वरित सेवा देना है।
8. यह मेरा मित्र दिनेश है जिसके भाई का कल हवाई–दुर्घटना में देहान्त हो गया।
9. उसने मुझे दो चाकलेट के डब्बे डाक से भेजे, जिनमें से मुझे अभी तक एक भी नहीं मिला।
10. सविता के पाँच भाई बहन हैं, जिनमें से एक भी भारत में नहीं रहता।

1. kyā vah kahānī āpne likhī jo āpne mujhe pichle saptāh paṛhne ko bhejī thī.
2. yahī ve sīṛhiyāṁ haiṁ jahāṁ maiṁ pichle mahīne girī thī aur merī ṭāṁg ṭūṭte-ṭūṭte bacī thī.
3. jo salāh usne mujhe dī, vah bahut kārgar thī.
4. jo citra usne mujhe dikhāyā, vah uskī patnī kā thā.
5. jo aurat ūpar rahtī hai, vah bahut dhanī hai.
6. jo laṛkā dauṛ kar hamārī or ā rahā hai, vah bahut pratibhāvān hai.
7. unhoṁne apne daftar kī ek śākhā bhārat meṁ sthāpit kī hai jiskā kām gāhkoṁ ko tvarit sevā denā hai.
8. yah merā mitra dineś hai jiske bhāī ka kal havāī durghaṭnā me dehānt ho gayā.
9. usne mujhe do' caukleṭ' ke ḍabbe ḍāk se bheje, jin meṁ se mujhe abhī tak ek bhī nahīṁ milā.
10. savitā ke pāṁc bhāī-bahan haiṁ, jin meṁ se ek bhī bhārat meṁ nahīṁ rahtā.

Key 3

1. जो	2. जिस	3. जिसने
4. जिनसे	5. जो	6. जिसके
7. जिसको	8. जो	9. जिनको
10. जिसके	11. जिसनैं	
1. jo	2. jis	3. jisne
4. jinse	5. jo	6. jiske
7. jisko	8. jo	9. jinko
10. jiske	11. jisne	

35 Compulsion Structure

■ **Hindi expresses compulsion in three diffent ways:**

(1) inner compulsion (2) outer compulsion (3) moral compulsion .

Inner Compulsion : v. intransitive

(subj. + को) +	v.inf.	+	होना honā
		in the required tense	

1. अब हमें सोना है। — We must sleep now.
   ab hameṁ sonā hai.
2. उस समय उन्हें तैरना था। — At that time they had to swim.
   us samay unheṁ tairnā thā.
3. आज मुझे डाकघर जाना होगा। — I will have to go to the post office today.
   āj mujhe ḍākghar jānā hogā.

Inner compulsion : v. transitive

(subj. + को ko) +	obj. +	v.r. + ना nā	+ होना honā
		ने ne	in the required
		नी nī	tense
		agree with the N and G of the obj.	

1. उसे भी यह पत्रिका (f.) पढ़नी है। — She also has to read this magazine.
   use bhī yah patrikā (f.) paṛhnī hai
2. पिता जी को अख़बार(m.) पढ़ना था। — Father had to read the newspaper.
   pitā jī ko akhbār paṛhnā thā.
3. मुझे अगले हफ़्ते पदयात्रा(f.) करनी होगी। — I will have to go trekking next week.
   mujhe agle hafte padyātrā karnī hogī.

Outer compulsion : verb intransitive

(subj. + को ko)	+	v.inf.	+	पड़ना	+	होना
				parṇā		honā
				in the required tense		

1. दादा जी को रोज़ सुबह जल्दी उठना पड़ता है।
   dādā jī ko roz subah jaldī uṭhnā paṛtā hai
   Grandfather has to get up early every morning (Pres. Indef.)
2. मुझे रात को देर तक जागना पड़ता था।
   mujhe rāt ko der tak jāgnā paṛtā thā.
   I used to have to stay awake late at night. (Past hab.)
3. कल मुझे चार किलोमीटर पैदल चलना पड़ा।
   kal mujhe cār 'kilometer' paidal calnā paṛā.
   Yesterday I had to walk four kilo meters. (Past simple)
4. हमें एक महीना कल्पवास* में रहना पड़ेगा।
   hameṁ ek mahīnā kalpvās meṁ rahnā paṛegā.
   We will have to remain in kalpvas* for one month. (Fut. simple)

Outer compulsion : verb transitive

(subj.+ को)	+	obj.	+	(v.r. + ना , ने , नी)	+	पड़ना	+	होना
				nā ne, n ī		parṇā		honā
						in the required tense		
						agree with N and G of the obj.		

1. मुझे ठंडा दूध[m.] पीना पड़ता है।
   mujhe ṭhaṇḍā dūdh pīnā paṛtā hai.
   I have to drink cold milk. (Pres. Indef.)
2. उनको रात्रि में काम[m.] करना पड़ता था।
   unko rātri meṁ kām karnā paṛtā thā.
   They used to have to work at night. (Past hab.)

kalpvās = residence of an ascetic on the banks of the Ganges during the month of 'Magh'(9th month of Hindu calendar)

3. मुझे दवाई खानी पड़ी। — I had to take medicine.
   mujhe davāī khānī paṛī. — (Past simple)

4. आज मुझे खाना^{m.} पकाना पड़ेगा। — I will have cook food
   āj mujhe khānā pakānā paṛegā — today. (Fut. simple)

> ☞ **Be it inner or outer compulsion, when verb transitive is used without mention of the object, use only m.sg. 'आ' ā form of the verb infinitive as well as that of the compound verb पड़ना paṛnā.**

Ex. 1: Translate into English:

1. मैं आज सुबह बैंक गया। मुझे कुछ पैसा निकालना था।
2. आपको ठीक कितने बजे जाना है?
3. तुम्हें कितने बजे हवाई अड्डे पर होना था?
4. मुझे अगले सप्ताह अपने ददिहाल जाना होगा।
5. मेरी निगाह कमज़ोर हैं। मुझे हर वक़्त ऐनक पहननी पड़ती है।
6. मुझे रोज़ सुबह बहुत जल्दी उठना पड़ता है।
7. आपको कितना समय मेरी प्रतीक्षा करनी पड़ी?
8. आपको कितनी दूर पैदल चलकर जाना पड़ा?
9. उनको मुझको सिनेमा देखने जाने देना पड़ा।
10. मुझको उसे अवकाश पर जाने देना पड़ेगा।
11. मुझे सूर्योदय से पहले पढ़ने लगना पड़ेगा।

1. maiṁ āj subah 'baiṅk' gayā . mujhe kuch paisā nikālnā thā.
2. āpko ṭhīk kitne baje jānā hai?
3. tumheṁ kitne baje havāī aḍḍe par honā thā?
4. mujhe agle saptāh apne dadihāl jānā hogā.
5. merī nigāh kamzor hai. mujhe har vaqt ainak pahnanī paṛtī hai.
6. mujhe roz subah bahut jaldī uṭhnā paṛtā hai.
7. āpko kitnā samay merī pratīkṣā karnī paṛī?
8. āpko kitnī dūr paidal calkar jānā paṛā?
9. unko mujhko 'cinema' dekhne jāne denā paṛā.
10. mujhko use avkāś par jāne denā paṛegā.
11. mujhe sūryoday se pahle paṛhne lagnā paṛegā.

Glossary:

पैसा निकालना (v.t.)	paisā nikālnā	to withdraw money
हवाई अड्डा (m.)	havāī aḍḍā	air port
X से मिलने जाना (v.i.)	X se milne jānā	to visit X
निगाह (f.)	nigāh	eyesight
कमज़ोर (adj.)	kamzor	weak
हर वक़्त (adv.)	har vaqt	all the time
ऐनक (f.)	ainak	glasses
पहनना (v.t.)	pahananā	to wear
प्रतीक्षा (f.)	pratīkṣā	waiting
पैदल (adv.)	paidal	on foot

Ex. 2: Translate into hindi: Use होना, पड़ना :

1. We have to go to a wedding this evening.
2. I have to get up early tomorrow.
3. I had to learn Hindi when I went to India.
4. I had to postpone the meeting for ten days.
5. You will have to change flights at Delhi.
6. This evening, I may have to stay late in the office.
7. We may have to stay in India for another year.
8. They may have to buy a new car very soon.

Glossary:

meeting	सभा (f.)	sabhā
to postpone	स्थगित करना (v.t.)	sthagit karnā
change flights	उड़ान बदलना (v.t.)	uṛān badalnā
to stay	ठहरना (v.i.)	ṭhaharnā
very soon	जल्दी ही (adv.)	jaldī hi

Key 1

1. I went to the bank this morning. I had to withdraw some money.
2. What time exactly do you have to go?
3. What time did you have to be at the airport?
4. I will have to visit my paternal grandparents next week.
5. My eyesight is weak. I have to wear glasses all the time.
6. I have to get up very early every morning.
7. How long did you have to wait for me?

8. How far did you have to go on foot?
9. They had to let me go to watch a movie.
10. I will have to let him go on vacation.
11. I will have to begin to study before sunrise.

Key 2

1. आज शाम को हमें एक शादी में जाना है।
2. कल सुबह मुझे जल्दी उठना है।
3. जब मैं भारत गया, मुझे हिन्दी सीखनी पड़ी।
4. मुझे दस दिन के लिए सभा स्थगित करनी पड़ी।
5. तुम्हें दिल्ली में उड़ान बदलनी पड़ेगी।
6. आज शाम को मुझे देर तक दफ़्तर में रुकना पड़ सकता है।
7. शायद हमें भारत में एक साल और ठहरना पड़े।
8. हो सकता है उन्हें जल्दी ही नई 'कार' ख़रीदनी पड़े।

1. āj śām ko hameṁ ek śādī meṁ jānā hai.
2. kal subah mujhe jaldī uṭhnā hai.
3. jab maim bhārat gayā, mujhe hindī sīkhnī paṛī.
4. mujhe das din ke lie sabhā sthagit karnī paṛī.
5. tumheṁ dillī meṁ uṛān badalnī paṛegī.
6. āj śām ko mujhe der tak daftar meṁ ruknā paṛ saktā hai.
7.. śāyad hameṁ bhārat meṁ ek sāl aur ṭhaharnā paṛe.
8. ho saktā hai unheṁ jaldī hī naī 'kār' kharīdnī paṛe.

'..भी .. भी' = as well as :	
1. वह बुद्धू भी है और कुरूप भी। vah budhū bhī hai aur kurūp bhī.	She is unintelligent as well as ugly.
3. वह धनी भी है और उदार भी। vah dhanī bhī hai aur udār bhī.	He is wealthy as well as generous.
4. बीरबल दयालु भी था और हाज़िरजवाब भी। bīrbal dayālu bhī thā aur hāzirjavāb bhī.	Birbal was kind as well as witty

कुरूप	*kurūp*	ugly	बुद्धू	*budhū*	unintelligent
धनी	*dhanī*	wealthy	उदार	*udār*	generous
दयालु	*dayālu*	kind	हाज़िरजवाब	*hāzirjavāb*	witty

36 Passive

(subj. + से / के द्वारा) + obj + (v.r.+ आ / या, ए, ई) + जाना + होना
se/ ke dvārā ā / yā, e, ī jānā + honā
in the appropriate tense
to agree with the N and G of object

1. भारत में कई भाषाएँ[f.pl.] बोली जाती है।	Many languages are spoken in India
bhārat meṁ kaī bhāṣāeṁ[f.sg] bolī jātī haiṁ.	(Pres.Indef. passive)
2. मेरे कपड़े[m.pl.]इस दर्ज़ी के द्वारा सीए जाते थे।	My clothes used to be stiched by this tailor.
mere kapṛe[m.pl] is darzī ke dvārā sīe jāte the.	(Past hab. passive)
3. पिछले सप्ताह छात्रों को लैपटाप'[f.pl.] दिए गए ।	Last week laptops were given to the students.
pichle saptāh chātroṁ ko laip ṭop[m.sg] die gae.	(Past simple passive)
4. यह भवन[m.sg] हाल में बनाया गया है।	This building has been made recently.
yah bhavan[m.sg] hāl meṁ banāyā gayā hai.	(Pres. perf. passive)
5. ये पेड़[m.pl.] कब काटे गए थे?	When had these trees been
ye peṛ[m.pl.] kab kāṭe gae the?	cut?(Past perf. passive)
6. संगोष्ठी[f.sg] कहाँ की जाएगी?	Where will the seminar be
saṅgoṣṭhī[m.sg] kahāṁ kī jāegī?	organized? (Fut. simple passive)

Ex.1: Translate into English:

1. डोसा और इडली चावल और दाल से बनाए जाते हैं।
2. कपड़े धोबी के द्वारा धोए जाते हैं।
3. हमारा घर प्रतिवर्ष रंगा जाता था।
4. क्या पत्र ग़लत पते पर भेजा गया?
5. कल रात को बैंक लूट लिया गया।
6. रेडियो का आविष्कार कब किया गया ?
7. हमारे 'गराज' की मरम्मत की जा रही है।
8. हमारे घर के सामने एक नई सड़क बनाई जा रही है।
9. सरकार के द्वारा अनेक नए रोज़गार पैदा किए गए हैं।
10. मध्यावधि चुनाव के लिए बहुत तैयारियाँ की गई हैं।
11. पिछले साल हमारे इलाक़े में एक नया सिनेमा घर बनाया गया था।
12. कुंभ में लोक कल्याण के लिए बड़ी बड़ी धन राशियाँ दान दी गई थीं।
13. अगले महीने गेहूँ की फ़सल काटी जाएगी।
14. अंतर्राष्ट्रीय गोष्ठी का उदघाटन कल किया जाएगा।

1. ḍosā aur iḍlī cāval aur dāl se banāe jāte haiṁ.
2. kapṛe dhobī ke dvārā dhoe jāte haiṁ.
3. hamārā ghar prativarṣ raṁgā jātā thā.
4. kyā patra Galat pate par bhejā gayā?
5. kal rāt ko 'baiṅk' lūṭ liyā gayā.
6. 'radio' kā āviṣkār kab kiyā gayā?
7. hamāre garāj kī marammat kī jā rahī hai.
8. hamāre ghar ke sāmne ek naī saṛak banāī jā rahī hai.
9. sarkār ke dvārā anek nae rozgār paidā kie gae haiṁ.
10. madhyāvdhi cunāv ke lie bahut taiyāriyāṁ kī gaī haiṁ.
11. pichle sāl hamāre ilāqe mem ek nayā 'sinemā ghar' banāyā gayā thā.
12. kumbh meṁ lok kalyāṇ ke lie baṛī-baṛī rāśiyāṁ dān dī gaī thīṁ.
13. agle mahīne gehūṁ kī fasal kāṭī jāegī.
14. antarrāṣṭrīyă goṣṭhī kā udghāṭan kal kiyā jāegā.

Glossary:

प्रतिवर्ष (adv.)	prativarṣ	every year
रंगना (v.t.)	raṁgnā	to paint
ग़लत (adj.)	Galat	wrong
पता (m.)	patā	address

भेजना (v.t.)	bhejnā	to send
लूटना (v.t.)	lūṭnā	to rob
आविष्कार (m.)	āviṣkār	invention
गराज (m.)	garāj	garage
मरम्मत (f.)	marammat	repair
के सामने (ppn.)	ke sāmne	in front of
सरकार (f.)	sarkār	government
पैदा करना (v.t.)	paidā karnā	to create
मध्यावधि चुनाव (m.)	madhyāvdhi cunāv	midterm elections
तैयारियाँ (f.pl.)	taiyāriyāṁ	preparations
धन राशि (f.)	dhan rāśi	amount of money
गेहूँ (m.)	gehūṁ	wheat
फ़सल (f.)	fasal	crop
काटना (v.t.)	kāṭnā	here: to harvest
गोष्ठी (f.)	goṣṭhī	seminar
उदघाटन (m.)	udghāṭan	inauguration

Ex.2: Translate into Hindi:

1. Dogs are treated here by vets.
2. The house was cleaned by the servant.
3. A new dress is being made by the tailor.
4. The plants are being watered by the gardener.
5. A meeting of the volunteers was held in this field today.
6. All educational institutions have been closed for three weeks.
7. The lawns had been mowed yesterday evening.
8. This new bridge had been built a few years ago .
9. The mail will not be delivered today.
10. The script for this film will be written by my friend.

Glossary:

to treat	इलाज करना (v.t.)	ilāj karnā
vet	पशु–चिकित्सक (m.)	paśu cikitsak
gardener	माली (m.)	mālī
plant	पौधा (m.)	paudhā
to water	पानी देना (v.t.)	pānī denā
to hold a meeting	बैठक करना (v.t.)	baiṭhak karnā
volunteers	स्वयंसेवक (m.)	svayaṁ sevak
educational institutions	शिक्षा संस्थान (m.)	śikṣā saṃsthān

bridge	पुल (m.)	pul
build	बनाना (v.t.)	banānā
to deliver	वितरित करना (v.t.)	vitrit karnā
cinema script	पटकथा (f.)	paṭkathā
to return	लौटाना (v.t.)	lauṭānā

Some Other Uses of Passive in Hindi:

- **Passive to express inability to do an intransitive activity*:**

(subject + se) + (intransitive v.r. + आ ā/ या yā) + jānā + honā

जाना + होना

in the required tense.

***:Alternatively, inability can be expressed with**

subject + v.r. + पाना pānā / सकना saknā

in the required tense to agree with subj.

☞ **In this use, the verb जाना jānā** changes like a regular verb to **जाया jāyā and not गया** gayā. See E.3

1. मुझसे सीढ़ियाँ नहीं चढी जातीं। — I can't climb up the stairs.
   mujhse sīṛhiyāṁ nahīṁ caṛhī jātīṁ. — (present simple passive)
   - मैं सीढ़ियाँ नहीं चढ़ पाता / पाती।
     maiṁ sīṛhiyāṁ nahīṁ caṛh pātā/pātī.
2. उनसे तेज़ नहीं दौड़ा गया। — They could not run fast
   unse tez nahīṁ dauṛā gayā. — (past simple passive)
   - वे तेज़ नहीं दौड़ पाए।
     ve tez nahīṁ dauṛ pāe.
3. मरीज़ से पैदल नहीं जाया* जाएगा। — The patient won't be able to go on foot.
   marīz se paidal nahīṁ jāyā* jāegā. — (future simple passive)

- मरीज़ पैदल नहीं जा पाएगा।

  marīz paidal nahīṁ jā pāegā.

Subjunctive Passive

> **The main verb in the mas. sg. past simple tense followed by जाय jāy. It corresponds to the English usage 'Let's v.inf....' or 'Shall we v.inf. ...?'**

1. अब सोया जाय।	ab soyā jāy.	Let's go to bed now.
• अब सोया जाय?	ab soyā jāy.?	Shall we go to bed now?
2. घूमने चला जाय।	ghūmne calā jāy.	Let's go for a walk.
• घूमने चला जाय?	ghūmne calā jāy?	Shall we go for a walk?

Ex.3: Substitute intransitive passive for inability structure with 'पाना' or 'सकना' :

1. रोमिला तैर नहीं सकती। ....
2. हम रात को देर तक नहीं जाग सकते।...........................
3. मैं कल जल्दी नहीं उठ सकी।
4. बच्चा रात भर सो नहीं पाया। ....
5. बुख़ार के कारण मैं दावत में नहीं आ सका। . ...

1. romilā tair nahīṁ saktī. ....
2. ham rāt ko der tak nahīṁ jāg sakte...........................
3. maiṁ kal jaldī nahīṁ uṭh sakī. ....
4. baccā rāt bhar nahīṁ so pāyā. ....
5. bukhār ke kāraṇ maiṁ dāvat .... meṁ nahīṁ ā sakā. ....

Ex.4 : Substitute subjunctive passive as shown:

1. आइए गर्म–गर्म चाय **पीएँ**। आइए, गर्म–गर्म चाय **पी जाए**।
2. चलो, कुछ **खाएँ**। ....
3. चलिए, **चलें**। ....
4. आइए, तनिक **आराम करें**। ....
5. आइए, अब दूरदर्शन **देखें**। ....

1. āie garam-garam cāy pīeṁ. āie garam-garam cāy pī jāe.

2. calo, kuch khāeṁ. ....
3. calie, caleṁ. ....
4. āie tanik ārām kareṁ. ....
5. āie, ab dūrdarśan dekheṁ. ....

Key 1

1 'Dosa' and 'idli' are made from rice and lentil.
2. Clothes are washed by the washerman.
3. Our house was painted every year.
4. Was the letter sent to the wrong address?
5. The bank was robbed last night.
6. When was the radio invented?
7. Our garage is being repaired.
8. A new road is being built in front of our house.
9. Many new jobs have been created by the government.
10. Many preparations have been made for the mid term elections.
11. A new cinema hall had been built in our locality last year.
12. At Kumbh large sums of money had been donated for welfare of the people
13. Wheat crop will be be harvested next month.
14. The international seminar will be inaugurated tomorrow.

Key 2

1. यहाँ पशु–चिकित्सकों के द्वारा कुत्तों का इलाज किया जाता है।
2. नौकर के द्वारा घर साफ़ किया जाता था ।
3. दर्जी के द्वारा नई पोशाक बनाई जा रही है।
4. माली के द्वारा पौधों को पानी दिया जा रहा है।
5. आज इस मैदान में स्वयंसेवकों की सभा की गई ।
6. सब शिक्षा संस्थान तीन स्ताह के लिए बन्द किए गए हैं।
7. घास के मैदान कल शाम को छीले गए थे।
8. कुछ साल पहले यह नया पुल बनाया गया था।
9. आज डाक वितरित नहीं की जाएगी।
10. इस फ़िल्म की पटकथा मेरी मित्र के द्वारा लिखी जाएगी।

1. yahāṁ paśu cikitsakoṁ ke dvārā kuttoṁ kā ilāj kiyā jātā hai.
2. naukar ke dvārā ghar sāf kiyā jātā thā.
3. darzī ke dvārā naī pośāk banāī jā rahī hai.
4. mālī ke dvārā paudhoṁ ko pānī diyā jā rahā hai.
5. āj is maidān meṁ svayaṁ sevkoṁ ki sabhā kī gaī.

6. sab śikṣā saṃsthān tīn saptāh ke lie band kie gae haiṁ.
7. ghās ke maidān kal śām ko chīle gae the .
8. kuch sāl pahle yah nayā pul banāyā gayā thā.
9. aj ḍāk vitrit nahīṁ kī jāegī.
10. is film kī paṭkathā merī mitra ke dvārā likhī jāegī.

Key 3

1. रोमिला से तैरा नहीं जाता।
2. हमसे रात को देर तक नहीं जागा जाता।
3. मुझसे कल जल्दी नहीं उठा गया।
4. बच्चे से रात भर सोया नहीं गया।
5. बुखार के कारण मुझसे दावत में नहीं आया गया।
1. romilā se tairā nahīṁ jātā.
2. hamse rāt ko der tak nahīṁ jāgā jātā.
2. mujhse kal jaldī nahīṁ uṭhā gayā.
4. bacce se rāt bhar soyā nahīṁ gayā.
5. bukhār ke kāraṇ mujhse dāvat meṁ nahīṁ āyā gayā.

Key 4

2. चलो, कुछ खाया जाए।
3. चलिए, चला जाए।
4. आइए, तनिक आराम किया जाए।
5. आइए अब दूरदर्शन देखा जाए।
2. calo, kuch khāyā jāe.
3. calie, calā jāe.
4. āie, tanik ārām kiyā jāe.
5. āie, ab dūrdarśan dekhā jāe.

37 Conditionals

Hindi uses अगर / यदि at the beginning of a conditional clause, and 'तो' at the beginning of dependant clause. Sentence structures vary according to the level of probability indicated.

Probable conditions: There is very high probability of fulfilment of the condition and hence that of the dependant clause, Hindi uses simple future tense in both the clauses.

1. अगर मैं$^{m.sg}$ बाज़ार जाऊँगा, तो मैं आपके लिए ज़रूर फल लाऊँगा। agar maiṁ$^{m.sg}$ bāzār jāūṁgā, to maiṁ āpke lie zarūr phal lāūṁgā.	If I go to the market, I will certainly bring fruit for you.
2. अगर उसे अच्छा पैसा $^{m.sg}$ मिलेगा, तो वह अवश्य यह काम करेगा। agar use acchā paisā$^{m.sg}$ milegā, to vah avaśyă yah kām karegā.	If he gets good money, he will certainly do this work.

Improbable conditions: The probability of fulfilment of the condition and hence that of the dependent clause is somewhat less, Hindi uses past tense in 'if' clause, and simple future in 'तो' clause.

1. यदि/अगर वह $^{m.sg}$ भारत आया, तो आपसे मिलेगा। yadi /agar vah $^{m.sg}$ bhārat āyā, to āpse milegā	If he came to India, he would meet you.
2. यदि बर्फ़$^{f.sg}$ पड़ी, तो हम घर पर ही रहेंगे। yadi barf$^{f.sg}$ paṛī, to ham ghar par hī raheṁge.	If it snowed, we would just stay at home.

Absurd / unrealistic conditions: Hindi uses the subjunctive to agree with the subject in the respective clauses.

1. यदि मैं कुबेर होऊँ, तो इस दुनिया में कोई ग़रीब न हो।
   yadi maiṁ kuber hoūṁ, to is duniyā meṁ koī Garīb na ho.
   If I were Kuber, in this world no one would be poor.
2. यदि मैं चिड़िया होऊँ, तो आकाश में ऊँची उड़ती रहूँ।
   yadi maiṁ ciṛiyā hoūṁ, to ākāś meṁ ūṁcī uṛtī rahūṁ.
   If I were a bird, I would keep flying high in the sky.

Impossible condition, where the condition failed to realise in the past, and hence the fulfilment of the dependent clause is impossible, Hindi uses:

- **Both the 'if' as well as the dependent clause has verb conjugation**
  (v.r. + आ ā, ए e, ई ī) + होता hotā, होते hote, होती hotī
  Alternatively the dependent clause has the verb conjugation
  v.r.+ ता tā, ते te ,ती tī E. 1 and 2 given below.

☞ **These agree with the subject in case of intransitive activity and the object in case of transitive activity.**
In case the object is not explicitly stated, it is always in mas. sg. आ ā-form.

1. अगर आपने हमारी मदद$^{f.sg}$ न ली होती, तो आपका काम$^{m.sg}$ समय पर ख़त्म न हुआ होता।/ न होता।
   agar āpne hamārī$^{f.sg}$ madad na lī hotī, to āpkā kām samay par <u>kh</u>atm na huā hotā./na hotā.
   If you had not taken our help, your work would not have been completed on time.
2. यदि तुम$^{f.sg}$ नमक डालना न भूली होतीं, तो सब्ज़ी$^{F.sg}$ बहुत स्वादिष्ट हुई होती /होती।
   yadi tum$^{f.sg}$ namak ḍālnā na bhūlī hotīṁ, to sabzī bahut svādiṣṭ huī hotī./ hotī.
   If you had not forgotten to put salt, vegetable would have been delicious.

Ex.1: Translate into English: probable case:

1. अगर मेरे पास पैसे होंगे, तो मैं यह मकान ख़रीद लूँगा।
2. अगर आप उसे आमंत्रित करेंगे, तो वह आएगी।
3. अगर आप उसे अच्छा पैसा नहीं देंगे, तो वह आपके लिए काम नहीं करेगी।
4. अगर मेरे पास आवश्यक योग्यताएँ होंगी, तो मैं इस काम के लिए आवेदन पत्र भेजूँगा।
5. अगर मुझे काम करने की अनुमति मिलेगी, तो मैं आस्ट्रेलिया में उत्प्रवास करूँगा।

1. agar mere pās paise hoṁge, to maiṁ yah makān <u>kh</u>arīd lūṁgā.
2. agar āp use āmantrit kareṁ ge, to vah āegī .
3. agar āp use acchā paisā nahīṁ deṁge, to vah apke lie kām nahīṁ karegī.
4. agar mere pās āvaśyak yogyatāeṁ[f.pl.] hoṁgī, to maiṁ is kām ke lie āvedan patra bhejūṁgā.
5. agar mujhe kām karne kī anumati milegī, to maiṁ 'austṛeliā meṁ utpravās karūṁgā.

Glossary:

आमंत्रित करना (v.t.)	āmantrit karnā	to invite
आवश्यक (adj.)	āvaśyak	necessary
योग्यताएँ (f.pl.)	yogyatāeṁ	qualifications
अनुमति (f.)	anumati	permission
उत्प्रवास (m.)	utpravās	emigration

Ex.2: Translate into English: Improbable condition

1. यदि तुम्हारा 'मोबाईल फ़ोन' खो गया, तो तुम क्या करोगी?
2. अगर तुम्हारे क्षेत्र में भूकम्प आ गया, तो तुम क्या करोगी?
3. अगर उसने परीक्षा दी, तो वह अवश्य उत्तीर्ण होगा।
4. अगर आप किसी मठ में ठहरे, तो आपको बहुत महँगा नहीं पड़ेगा।
5. अगर हमने उन्हें सच्चाई नहीं बताई, तो वे हमें सज़ा देंगे।

1. yadi tumhārā mobāīl fon kho gayā, to tum kyā karogī?
2. agar tumhāre kṣetra meṁ bhūkaṁp ā gayā, to tum kyā karogī?
3. agar usne parīkṣā dī, to vah avaśyā uttīrṇ hogā.

4. agar āp kisī maṭh meṁ ṭhahre, to āpko bahut mahṁgā nahiṁ paṛegā.
5. agar hamne unheṁ saccāī nahīṁ batāī, to ve hameṁ sazā deṁge.

Glossary:

भूकम्प (m.)	bhūkaṁp	earthquake
उत्तीर्ण होना (v.i.)	uttīrṇ honā	to pass (an exam)
मठ (m.)	maṭh	hermitage
ठहरना (v.i.)	ṭhaharnā	to stay
सच्चाई (f.)	saccāī	truth
सज़ा (f.)	sazā	punishment

Ex.3 Translate into Hindi: **—impossible cases**

1. यदि तुमने 'इन्डक्शन कुकर' ख़रीद लिया होता, तो तुम्हारा बिजली पर ख़र्च कम हुआ होता/ होता।
2. यदि वह ऊँचा बोली होती, तो हम उसे समझ पाए होते/ पाते।
3. अगर बारिश न हुई होती, तो 'मैच' खेला गया होता/ खेला जाता। .
4. यदि तुम्हारे घर में एक-दो कुत्ते रहे होते, तो यह डाका न पड़ा होता/ पड़ता।
5. अगर वह ज़मीन सस्ती हुई होती, तो उन्होंने ख़रीद ली होती।/तो वे ख़रीद लेते।

1. agar tumne 'induction cooker' kharīd liyā hotā, to tumhārā bijlī par kharc kam **huā hotā/ hotā**
2. yadi vah ūṁcā bolī hotī, to ham use samajh **pāe hote/ pāte.**
3. agar bāriś na huī hotī, to 'maic' **khelā gayā hotā / khelā jātā.**
4. yadi tumhāre ghar meṁ ek-do kutte rahe hote, to yah ḍākā na paṛā hotā/ na paṛtā.
5. agar vah zamīn sastī huī hotī , to unhoṁne kharīd lī hotī./ ve kharīd lete.

Ex.4: Translate into English: Unreastic condition

1. अगर आप अपने देश के प्रधान मंत्री हों/होते, तो आप क्या करें/ करते?
2. अगर मैं भारत का प्रधान मंत्री होऊँ/ होता, तो भ्रष्टाचार ख़त्म करूँ/ करता।
3. अगर आप विश्व के रचयिता हों / होते, तो विश्व में कौन–कौन से परिवर्तन लाएँ/लाते।
4. अगर मैं तुम्हारे स्थान पर होऊँ/होता, तो राजनीति में भाग न लूँ/न लेता।
5. अगर तुम करोड़पति होओ/होते, तो क्या करो/करते?

1. agar āp apne deś ke pradhānmantrī hoṁ/ hote , to kyā kareṁ / karte.
2. agar maiṁ bhārat kā pradhānmantrī hoūṁ/ hotā , to bhraṣṭācār khatm karūṁ / kartā
3. agar āp viśva ke racyitā hoṁ/ hote , to viśva meṁ kaun-kaun se parivartan lāeṁ/ lāte.
4. agar maiṁ tumhārī jagah hoūṁ/ hotā, to rājnīti meṁ bhāg na lūṁ / letā.
5. agar tum karoṛpati ho'o / hote, to kyā karo /karte?

Glossary:

भ्रष्टाचार (m)	bhraṣṭācār	corruption
विश्व (m.)	viśva	world
रचयिता (m.)	racyitā	creator
परिवर्तन (m.)	parivartan	changes
राजनीति (f.)	rājnīti	politics
भाग लेना (v.t.)	bhāg lenā	take part

Ex.5: Translate into Hindi: probable case:

1. If my visa is extended, I shall stay in India until the end of April.
2. If the price is reduced, we will buy it.
3. If the salary is good, I will accept the job.
4. If you have the necessary qualifications, you will certainly get the job.
5. If she works hard, she will pass the medical entrance test.

Glossary:

extend	बढ़ाना (v.t.)	baṛhānā
reduce	कम करना (v.t.)	kam karnā
salary	वेतन (m.)	vetan
accept	स्वीकार करना (v.t.)	svīkār karnā

Ex.6: Translate into Hindi: Improbable condition

1. I would buy this orchard if I had the money.
2. She would come if you invited her.
3. If you didn't pay her well, she would not work for you.
4. I would apply for this job if I had the necessary qualifications.
5. I would certainly learn Urdu language if I got a really good teacher.

Ex.7 Translate into Hindi: —impossible cases

1. If you had not reminded me, I would have totally forgotten.
2. If I had had the money, certainly I would have lent it to you.
3. If I had known that you have to get up early, certainly I would have woken you up on time.
4. If she had been given immediate medical aid, she would have survived.
5. If you had listened to my advice, you would not have suffered any loss.

to remind	याद दिलाना (v.t.)	yād dilānā
totally	कतई (adv.)	kataī
to forget	भूल जाना (v.i.)	bhūl jānā
to lend	उधार देना (v.t.)	udhār denā
to get up early	जल्दी उठना (v.i.)	jaldī uṭhnā
to wake s.o. up	को जगाना (v.t.)	ko jāgānā
medical help	चिकित्सा (f.)	cikitsā
to survive	बच जाना (v.i.)	bac jānā
to listen to s.o.	की बात मानना (v.t.)	kī bāt mānanā
suffer loss	हानि होना (v.i.)	hāni honā

Key 1

1. I^m. will buy this house if I have the money.
2. She will come if you invite her.
3. If you^m don't pay her well, she will not work for you.
4. I^m will apply for this job if I have the necessary qualifications.
5. I^m will emigrate to Australia if I get a work permit.

Key 2

1. What would you do if you lost your mobile phone?
2. What would you do if an earthquake came in your area.
3. If he took the test, he would certainly pass.
4. If you stayed in some monastry, it would not cost you much.
5. If we did not tell them the truth, they would punish us.

Key 3

1. If you had bought an induction cooker, your expenditure on electricity would not have been so much.
2. If she had spoken louder, we would have been able to understand her.

3. The match would have been played, if it had not rained.
4. If you had had a couple of dogs in your house, there would not have been this robbery.
5. If it had not snowed, we would have gone for skiing.
6. I wouldn't have married her, if I hadn't truly wanted to.
7. If that land had been cheaper, they would have certainly bought it.

Key 4

1. What would you do if you were the Prime Minister of your country?
2. If I were the Prime Minister of India, I would end corruption.
3. If you were the creator of the universe, what changes would you make?
4. If I were you, I would not take part in politics.
5. What would you do if you were a multi-millionaire?

Key 5

1. अगर मेरा 'वीसा' बढ़ा दिया जाएगा, तो मैं अप्रैल के अन्त तक भारत में रहूँगा/रहूँगी।
2. यदि दाम कम कर दिया जाएगा, तो हम इसे ख़रीद लेंगे/लेंगी।
3. यदि वेतन अच्छा होगा, तो मैं यह नौकरी स्वीकार कर लूँगा।
4. यदि तुम्हारे पास आवश्यक योग्यताएँ होंगी, तो तुम्हे अवश्य यह काम मिलेगा।
5. अगर वह परिश्रम करेगी, तो चिकित्सा प्रवेश परीक्षा में उत्तीर्ण होगी।

1. agar merā 'vīsā' baṛhā diyā jāegā , to maiṁ 'aprail' ke ant tak bhārat meṁ rahūṁgā/ rahūṁgī.
2. yadi dām kam kar diyā jāegā, to ham ise <u>kh</u>arīd leṁge/ leṁgī.
3. yadi vetan acchā hogā, to maiṁ yah naukrī svīkar kar lūṁgā.
4. yadi tumhāre pās āvaśyak yogyatāeṁ hoṁgī, to tumheṁ avaśyă yah kām milegā.
5. agar vah pariśram karegī, to cikitsā praveś parīkṣā meṁ uttīrṇ hogī.

Key 6

1. अगर मेरे पास पैसे हुए, तो मैं यह फलवाटिका ख़रीद लूँगा/ख़रीद लूँगी।
2. अगर आपने उसे आमंत्रित किया, तो वह आएगी।
3. अगर आपने उसे अच्छा पैसा नहीं दिया, तो वह आपके लिए काम नहीं करेगी।
4. अगर मेरे पास आवश्यक योग्यताएँ हुईं, तो मैं इस काम के लिए आवेदन पत्र भेजूँगा/ भेजूँगी।
5. अगर मुझे सच में अच्छा अध्यापक मिला तो मैं उर्दू भाषा अवश्य सीखूँगा।

1. agar mere pās paise hue, to maiṁ yah phalvāṭikā kharīd lūṁgā/ kharīd lūṁgī.
2. agar āpne use āmantrit kiyā, to vah āegī .
3. agar āpne use acchā paisā nahīṁ diyā, to vah āpke lie kām nahīṁ karegī.
4. agar mere pās āvaśyak yogyătāeṁ huīṁ, to maiṁ is kām ke lie āvedan patra bhejūṁgā / bhejūṁgī.
5. agar mujhe sac meṁ acchā adhyāpak milā, to maiṁ urdū bhāṣā avaśyă sīkhūṁgā.

Key7

1. यदि तुमने मुझे याद नहीं दिलाया होता, तो मैं कतई भूल गया होता।/ भूल जाता।
2. अगर मेरे पास पैसे हुए होते, तो मैंने अवश्य तुम्हें उधार दे दिए होते।/मैं अवश्य तुम्हें उधार दे देता।
3. अगर मुझे पता होता कि तुम्हें जल्दी उठना है, तो अवश्य मैंने तुम्हें समय पर जगा दिया होता।/मैं तुम्हें समय पर जगा देता।
4. अगर उसकी चिकित्सा तत्काल हुई होती, तो वह बच गई होती।/ बच जाती।
5. यदि तुमने मेरी सलाह मान ली होती, तो तुम्हारी हानि न हुई होती ।/ न होती।

1. yadi tumne mujhe yād nahīṁ dilāyā hotā, to **maiṁ** kataī **bhūl gayā hotā./ bhūl jātā.**
2. agar mere pās paise hue hote, to **maiṁne** avaśyă tumheṁ udhār **de die hote./maiṁ** avaśyă tumheṁ udhār **de detā**
3. agar mujhe patā hotā ki tumheṁ jaldī uṭhnā hai, to avaśyă **maiṁne** tumheṁ samay par **jagā diyā hotā./ maiṁ** tumheṁ samay par **jagā detā.**
4. agar uskī cikitsā tatkāl huī hotī, to **vah bac gaī hotī./bac jātī.**
5. yadi tumne merī salāh mān lī hotī, to tumhārī hāni **na huī hotī./ na hotī.**

38 Wishing! काश !

Wishing for present

काश kāś ....v.r. + ता tā, ते te, ती tī (agree with subject)

1. काश मैं नाच सकती। — I wish I could dance!
   kāś maiṁ nāc saktī.
2. काश वह इतनी निर्दयी न होती। — I wish she were not so cruel!
   kāś vah itnī nirdayī na hotī.

Wishing for past

काश kāś ....v.r. + आ ā, ए e, ई ī + होता tā, होते te, होती hotī * agree with subject when verb intransitive * agree with object when verb transitive and the subject has ' ne' after it.

3. काश कल बारिश न हुई होती। — I wish it hadn't rained yesterday.
   kāś kal bāriś na huī hotī.
4. काश मैंने इतने लोगों को न बुलाया होता। — I wish I had not invited so many people!
   kāś maiṁne itne logoṁ ko na bulāyā hotā.

Wishing for future

काश kāś ....v.r. + ऊँūṁ, ओ o, ए e, एं eṁ (agree with subject)

5. काश वे हमेशा यहाँ रहें। — I wish they would always stay here.
   kāś ve hameśā yahāṁ raheṁ.
6. काश तुम सदैव इतने खुश लगो। — I wish you would always look so happy.
   kāś tum sadaiv itne khuś lago.

Ex. 1: Translate into English:

1. काश वह इतनी भुलक्कड़ न होती!
2. काश तुम मेरे जनम दिन की दावत में आए होते।
3. काश तुम इस शहर में न बसे होते।
4. काश आप मेरी सलाह को गम्भीरता से लें।
5. काश यहाँ इतना शोर न हो।

1. kāś vah itnī bhulakkaṛ na hotī.
2. kāś tum mere janam din kī dāvat meṁ āe hote.
3. kāś tum is śahar meṁ na base hote.
4. kāś āp merī salāh ko gambhīrtā se leṁ.
5. kāś yahāṁ itnā śor na ho.

Ex. 2: Translate into Hindi:

1. I wish you[m.] kept your study table clean.
2. I wish my daughter were with me today.
3. I wish you had taught me Hindi.
4. I wish I had grown up in a big city.
5. I wish these children would stop making noise.

Key 1

1. I wish she wasn't so forgetful !
2. I wish you had come to my birthday party.
3. I wish you had not settled in this city.
4. I wish you would take my advice seriously.
5. I wish there wouldn't be so much noise here.

Key 2

1. काश तुम अपनी पढ़ने की मेज़ साफ़ रखते।
2. काश मेरी बेटी आज मेरे पास होती।
3. काश आपने मुझे हिन्दी पढ़ाई होती।
4. काश मैं बड़े शहर में पला–बड़ा होता।
5. काश ये बच्चे शोर मचाना छोड़ दें।

1. kāś tum apnī paṛhne kī mez sāf rakhte.
2. kāś merī beṭī āj mere pās hotī.
3. kāś āpne mujhe hindī paṛhāī hotī.
4. kāś maiṁ [m.] baṛe śahar meṁ palā-baṛā hotā.
5. kāś ye bacce śor macānā choṛ deṁ.

39 Verb formation

Infinitives

In Hindi, all the infinitive verbs*, transitive or intransitive have ‘ ना na’=ending.

Verb transitive has a direct object, an answer to the question what? Examples:

खाना khānā (to eat) पीना pīnā (to drink)
पढ़ना paṛhnā (to sleep देखना dekhnā (to see).

Verb intransitive has no direct object as answer to the question what? Examples:

सोना sonā (to sleep) रोना ronā (to cry)
दौड़ना dauṛnā (to run) बैठना baiṭhnā (to sit).

The subject in the nominative or oblique case does these activities

1. माता जी ने खाना **बनाती हैं।** Mother **cooks** food.
   mātā jī khānā banātī haiṁ.
2. हमने कॉफ़ी **पी।** We **drank** coffee.
   hamne kaufī pī.
3. आप सो जाइए। Go to sleep.
   āp so jāie.
4. मुझको भारत अच्छा लगता है। I like India
   mujhko bhārat acchā lagtā hai.

Causative 1

Hindi speakers derive this verb form usually by infixing ‘‘आ ā’ between ‘v.r.’ and ‘ ना nā’ ending . This indicates that the subject made s.o.do something, For example:

खिलाना khilānā (to feed /offer s.o. s.th. solid to eat)
पिलाना pīlānā (to feed / /offer s.o. s.th. liquid to drink)
सुलाना sulānā (to put s.o. to sleep = X makes Y sleep)
दिखाना dikhānā (to show s.o. s.th. = X makes Y see)

*Ref. pg. 7-8 ;

1. माता जी ने हमको खाना **खिलाया**। mātā jī ne hamko khānā khilāyā. — Mother **offered** us food.
2. उन्हों ने हमें कॉफ़ी **पिलाई**। unhomne hamem kaufī pilāī — They **offered** us coffee.
3. आप बच्चे को सुलाइए। āp bacce ko sulāie. — Put the child to sleep.

Causative 2

When the subject uses an intermediary agent to get something done, Hindi speakers derive a verb form usually by infixing ''वा vā' between 'v.r.'- and ' ना nā' ending . Sometimes there is slight modifica tion of the spellings. For example:

खिलवाना khilvānā (to have s.o. fed by somebody)
पिलवाना pīnā (to have s.o. offered a drink by somebody)

1. कृपया यह काम दो दिन में करवा दीजिए।
   kṛpayā yah kām do din meṁ karvā dījie.
   Please get this work done in two days.
2. आप सामान्यता अपने कपड़े कहाँ धुलवाती हैं?
   āp sāmānyătā apne kapṛe kahāṁ dhulvātī haiṁ?
   Where do you normally get your clothes washed ?
3. मुख्य मंत्री बाढ़–ग्रस्त लोगों को पर्याप्त राहत पहुँचवा रहे हैं।
   mukhyă mantrī bāṛh-grast logoṁ ko paryāpt rāhat pahuṁcā rahe haiṁ.
   The Chief Minister is having suffient relief reach the flood victims.
4. अनिल ने पिछले हफ़्ते अपना स्कूटर गराज में ठीक करवाया।
   anil ne pichle hafte apnā skūṭar garāj meṁ ṭhīk karvāyā.
   Last week Anil had his scooter repaired in a garage.
5. केन्द्र सरकार कम आय के लोगों के लिए बहुत–से घर बनवाएगी।
   kendra sarkār kam āya ke logoṁ ke lie bahut se ghar banvāe gī.
   The central government will get many houses built for the low-income people.
6. हमें अगले साल एक और घर बनवाना होगा।
   hameṁ agle sāl ek aur ghar banvānā hogā.
   We will have to get one more house built next year.

7. मुझे कल तक इन दस्तावेज़ों का सत्यापन करवाना पड़ेगा।
   mujhe kal tak in dastāvezoṁ kā satyāpan karvānā paṛegā.
   I will have to get these documents verified by tomorrow.
8. आपको सत्यापित दस्तावेज़ों की दो –दो छायाप्रतियाँ करवानी होंगी।
   āpko satyāpit dastāvezoṁ kī do-do chāyāpratiyāṁ karāvānī hoṁgī.
   You will have to get the two photocopies each made of the verified documents .
9. हो सकता है मुझे इसी साल अपने पिता जी के घुटनों का 'आपरेशन' करवाना पड़े।
   ho saktā hai mujhe isī sāl apne pitā jī ke ghuṭnoṁ kā auperaśan karvānā paṛe.
   I may have to get my father's knees operated this year itself.

Compound Verbs

Compound verbs are (root of the main verb + one of the several verbs) such as जाना jānā, लेना lenā , and देना denā., चुकना cuknā, बैठना baiṭhnā, उठना uṭhnā, पड़ना paṛnā , डाल़ना ḍālnā etc. These can be used in all tenses, but more so in the past simple, present as well as past perfect tense.

☞ Meaning is given by the root of the main verb.

☞ The second verb in the compound does not lend its meaning at all. It just adds to ' emphasis' and 'nuance' and is conjugated to agree with the subject or object as required in the appropriate tense.

☞ The compound verbs are used both in interrogative and affirmative sentences, but not in negative sentences.

- **jānā जाना as compound verbs highlights the completion of action, change of state. It is used only with intransitive activities.**

1. अन्दर आ जाइए। Come in.
   andar ā jāie
2. दही जम गया है। The yogurt is set.
   dahi jam gayā hai.

- **लेना lenā and देना denā convey completion of a transitive activity.**

☞ **लेना lenā is used when the activity is to the favor of the doer.**

1. मक्खन ख़रीद लीजिए। — Please buy butter.
   makkhan <u>kh</u>arīd lījie.
2. मैंने दूध पी लिया है। — I have already had milk.
   maiṁne dūdh pī liyā hai.

☞ **देना denā is used when the activity benefits someone other than the doer.**

1. नौकर ने चाय बना दी है। — The servant has made tea.
   naukar ne cāy banā dī hai.
2. शिक्षक ने पाठ[m.spl.] पढ़ा दिया हैं। — The teacher has taught the lesson.
   śikṣak ne pāṭh paṛha[m.sg..pl.]
   diyā hai.

- Alternatively चुकना cuknā is used instead of जाना jānā, लेना lenā, देना denā. to convey the completion of transitive as well as intran sitive activities. It agrees with the N and G of the subject in all tenses.

1. छात्र आ गए हैं। — The students have already left.
   chātra ā gae haiṁ
   = छात्र आ चुके हैं।
   chātra ā cuke haiṁ.
2. डाकिये ने डाक[f.sg.] बाँट दी है। — The postman has delivered the mail.
   dākiye ne ḍāk bāṁṭ dī hai.
   = डाकिया डाक[f.sg.] बाँट चुका है।
   dākiyā ḍāk bāṁṭ cukā hai

- **Use of the verbs पड़ना paṛnā, उठना uṭhnā for sudden , rash and impulsive actions**

1. लड़की खिड़की से कूद पड़ी। — The girl jumped out of the window.
   laṛkī khiṛkī se kūd paṛī.
2. एक ईंट मेरे सिर पर गिर पड़ी। — A brick fell on my head.
   ek īṁt mere sir par gir paṛī.

3. वह मारे दर्द के कराह उठा। — He cried out of pain.
   vah māre dard ke karāh uṭhā.
4. बच्चा बीच में बोल उठा। — The child interrupted.
   baccā bīc meṁ bol uṭhā. — (The child cut in.)

- **Use of डालना ḍālnā, बैठना baiṭhnā, for rash, impulsive, inappropriate action:**

1. उसने मेरे कपड़े फाड़ डाले। — He tore my clothes.
   usne mere kapṛe phāṛ ḍāle.
3. वह अपने चाचा की जायदाद का मालिक बन बैठा है। — He has become the owner of his uncle's property.
   vah apne cācā kī jāydād kā mālik ban baiṭhā hai.

- **Inability expression (verb root + पाना) imply ability with some special effort or inability despite effort.** **(see pg. 141)**

1. मैं पैदल नहीं चल पाऊँगा। — I will not be able to walk.
   maiṁ paidal nahīṁ cal pāūṁgā.
2. आज वे बैठक में नहीं जा पाए। — They could not go to the meeting today.
   āj ve baiṭhak meṁ nahīṁ jā pāe.

- **(verb root + सकना) is used for ability, probability.** **Ref. pg.142**

Conjunct Verbs

- **को + noun / adjective+ verb**

X को पसन्द[f.] करना	X ko pasand karnā	to like X
X को शुरू[m.] करना	X ko śurū karnā	to start X
X को ख़त्म[adj.] करना	X ko khatm karnā	to finish
X को क्षमा[f.] करना	X ko kṣamā karnā	to forgive X
X को पसन्द[f.] आना	X ko pasand ānā	for X to like s.th.
X को नींद[f.] आना	X ko nīṁd ānā	to feel sleepy
X को मज़ा[m.] आना / आनन्द[m.] आना	X ko mazā ānā/ ānand ānā	to enjoy " "

X को Y (activity) आना	X koY(activity) ānā	for X to know how to do Y
X को नज़र[f.] आना	X ko nazar ānā	to be visible to X
X को नुकसान[m.] पहुँचाना	ko nuksān pahuṁcānā	cause harm to X
X को मार[f.] पड़ना	X ko mār paṛnā	for X to be beaten
X को बेवकूफ बनाना	X ko bevkūf banānā	to befool X

- **की + noun (f.)+ verb**

X की हानि[f.] करना	X kī hāni karnā	to cause loss to X
X की मरम्मत[f.] करना	X kī marammat karnā	to repair X
X की देखभाल[f.] करना	X kī dekhbhāl karnā	to look after X
X की सहायता[f.] करना	X kī sahāyatā karnā	to help X

- **का + noun + verb**

X का आयोजन[m.] करना	X kā āyojan karnā	to organise X
X का फ़ैसला[m.] करना	X kā faislā karnā	to decide X
X का इन्तज़ार[m.] करना	X kā intzār karnā	to wait for X
X का इलाज[m.] करना	X kā ilāj karnā	to treat X
X का निश्चय[m.] करना	X kā niścay karnnā	to resolve to do X
X का ध्यान[m.] रखना	X kā dhyān rakhnā	to take care of X

- **से + noun + verb**

X से बदला लेना	X se badlā lenā	to revenge oneself on X
X से सलाह लेना	X se salāh lenā	to take advice form X
X से डर लगना	X se ḍar lagnā	to be afraid of X
X से संतुष्ट होना	X se santuṣṭ honā	to be content with X

- **पर + noun + verb**

X पर विश्वास करना	X par viśvās karnā	have faith in X
X पर सन्देह करना	X par sandeh karnā	to suspect X
X पर दया करना	X par dayā karnā	have mercy on X
X पर भरोसा करना	X par bharosā karnā	to trust X

Nominal Verbs

In Hindi sometimes verbs are formed by adding the suffixes 'ना', 'आना', 'इयाना' etc. to nouns, adjectives, pronouns. A list of commonly used verbs of this group made from Sanskrit, Persian, Hindi words is given below.

Nouns/adj./pronoun		Verb	
धिक्कार dhikkār	(m.) reproach	धिक्कारना dhikkārnā	(v.t.) to reproach
त्याग tyāg	(m.) abandoning	त्यागना tyāgnā	(v.t.) to abandon
फटकार phaṭkār	(f.) scolding	फटकारना phaṭkārnā	(v.t.) to scold
चिकना ciknā	(adj.) oily, greasy	चिकनाना ciknānā	(v.t.) to grease, to oil
अपना apnā	(pron/adj) own	अपनाना apnānā	(v.t.) to own

Sound Verbs

Hindi has a rich vocabulary of words based on appearances, sound, feel of things. Usually 'आना' is added to the base word. :

Examples :

भन भन bhan-bhan	(f.)	humming, buzzing sound of insects	भनभनाना bhanbhanānā	(v.t.)	to buzz, to hum (insects)
खट खट khaṭ khaṭ	(f.)	knocking	खटखटाना khaṭkhaṭānā	(v.t.)	to knock
टन टन ṭanṭan	(f.)	ringing	टनटनाना ṭanṭanānā	(v.t. / i)	to ring
छप छप chap chap	(f.)	sound of water splashing	छपछपाना chapchapānā	(v.t.)	to splash water
टप टप ṭap ṭap	(f.)	sound of drops falling	टपटपाना ṭapṭaiānā	(v.i.)	to fall in drops

Sense Verbs

Hindi uses *लगना* lagna for all sense verbs such as to look, to seem, to feel, to taste, to sound.Examples:

महँगा लगना	mahṁgā lagnā	to look expensive
अमीर लगना	amīr lagnā	to seem rich
स्वादिष्ट लगना	svādiṣṭ lagnā	to taste delicious
मधुर लगना	madhur lagna	to sound melodious

Uses of the verb 'लगना' lagnā

के जैसा लगना' ke jaisā lagnā to resemble

पवित्रा अपनी बड़ी बहन जैसी लगती है।
pavitrā apnī baṛī bahan jaisī lagtī hai.
Pavitra resembles her elder sister.

'लगना' lagnā as sense verb given above used with (subject + को ko)

अधिकारी लगना	adhikārī lagnā	to look an officer
व्यापारी लगना	vyāpārī lagnā	to seem a business-man
बीमार लगना	bīmār lagnā	to look sick
उदास लगना	udās lagnā	to seem sad
भूख/प्यास लगना	bhūkh / pyās lagnā	to feel hungry /thirsty
नींद लगना	nīṁd lagnā	to feel sleepy
बुख़ार लगना	bukhār lagnā	to feel feverish
अच्छा लगना	acchā lagnā	to feel good

- छोटे बच्चों को दिन में कई बार भूख लगती है।
  choṭe baccoṁ ko din meṁ kaī bār bhūkh lagtī hai.
  Little children **feel hungry** several times during the day.
- मुझको बुख़ार लग रहा है। I am feeling feverish.
  mujhko bukhār lag rahā hai.

X को ko (v.r.+ ne) meṁ + time clause + लगना' = time taken to do X

- मुझे खाना पकाने में एक घण्टा लगता है।
  mujhe khānā pakāne meṁ ek ghaṇṭā lagtā hai.
  It takes me one hour to cook food.
- आपको हिन्दी सीखने में कितना समय लगा?
  āpko hindī sīkhne meṁ kitnā samay lagā.
  How long did you take to learn Hindi?
- मुझको हिन्दी सीखने में दो साल लगे।
  mujhko hindī sīkhne meṁ do sāl lage.
  It took me two years to to learn Hindi.

film/ exhibition / special market etc लगा होना lagā honā
film to run in a cinema / exhibition etc to be put up

- शनिवार को हमारे इलाके में सब्ज़ी बाज़ार लगता है।
  śanivār ko hamāre ilāqe meṁ sabzī bāzār lagtā hai.
  On Saturday **there is a** vegetable market in our area.
- आज 'रीगल' पर कौन सी फ़िल्म (f.) लगी है?
  āj rīgal par kaun -sī film (f.)lagī hai?
  Which film is on at Regal?
- आजकल दिल्ली में पुस्तक प्रदर्शनी (f.) लगी हुई है।
  ājkal dillī meṁ pustak pradarśanī (f.) lagī huī hai.
  There is a book exhibition in Delhi these days.

(subject + को ko) + disease लगना' lagnā to suffer from.....

(subject + ko)	लू लगना'	to suffer from heat
(subject + ko)	जुकाम लगना'	to catch a cold
(subject + ko)	बुख़ार लगना'	to feel feverish
(subject + ko)	चोट लगना'	to be injured

- राजु को जुकाम लग गया है। Raju has caught a cold.
  rāju ko jukām lag gayā hai.
- मुझे पिछले साल गर्मी में लू लग गई थी।
  mujhe pichle sāl garmī meṁ lū lag gaī thī.
  Last year I had a heat stroke.

X में लगा होना X meṁ lagā honā **be busy doing X**

- वह हमेशा काम में लगी रहती है। She is always working.
vah hameśā kām meṁ lagī rahtī hai.

X का लगना X kā lagnā **be related to X**

- ईशु तुम्हारा कौन लगता है? How is Ishu **related** to you?
īśu tumhārā kaun lagtā hai?
- ईशु मेरा ममेरा भाई* लगता है। Ishu is my cousin*.
īśu merā mamerā bhāī lagtā hai.

X में / पर लगाना X meṁ/ par lagānā **be fix in/at X**

- घड़ी दीवार पर लगाओ। Put up the clock on the wall.
ghari dīvār par lagāo.

Uses of the verb 'मिलना

मिलना' milnā **to be available**

- यहाँ अख़बार कहाँ मिलेगा?
yahāṁ akhbār kahāṁ milegā?
Where could one get a newspaper here?
- इस शहर में हिन्दुस्तानी मसाले नहीं मिलते।
is śahar meṁ hindustānī masāle nahīṁ milte.
Indian spices are not available in this city.

से मिलना–जुलना milnā-julnā **to socialize**

- मैं अपने पड़ोसियों से ज़्यादा नहीं मिलती जुलती ।
maiṁ apne paṛosiyoṁ se zyādā nahīṁ. miltī-jultī
I don't **socialize** much with my neighbours.

से मिलना–जुलना se milnā-julnā **to be matching/ similar**

- मुझे मेरी कमीज़ से मिलते–जुलते रंग का कपड़ा दिखाइए।
mujhe merī kamīz se milte-julte raṅg kā kapṛā dikhāie.
Show me some material **matching with** the color of my shirt.

* ममेरा भाई mamerā bhāī = son of mother's brother

से मिलता–जुलता **se milnā-julnā**	**resembling**

- उसकी शक्ल (f.) अपने पिता से मिलती–जुलती है।
  uskī śakla.(f.) apne pitā se miltī-jultī hai
  She resembles her father.

subj. को **obj.** मिलना **milnā**	**to find s.th. /s.b.** **to meet s.b. by chance**

- मुझे एक दस रुपए का नोट सड़क पर पड़ा मिला।
  mujhe ek das rupae kā noṭ saṛak par paṛā milā.
  I found a 10 rupee bill lying in the street.
- हमें एक बच्चा मंदिर के सामने पड़ा हुआ मिला।
  hameṁ ek baccā mandir ke sāmne paṛā huā milā.
  We found a baby lying in front of the temple
- वह मुझे डाकघर में मिल गया।
  vah mujhe ḍākghar meṁ mil gayā.
  He met me in the post office.

subj. + obj. से मिलना **se milnā**	**to meet s.b.** **planned meeting**

- मैं कल शाम को उससे मिलने जा रहा हूँ।
  maiṁ kal śām ko usse milne jā rahā hūṁ.
  I am going to meet with him / her tomorrow evening.

X, Y, Z मिलाना' **X, Y, Z milānā**	**to mix together.....**

- मैदा, चीनी, मक्खन और दूध अच्छी तरह मिलाइए।
  maidā, cīnī aur dūdh acchī tarah milāie.
  Mix together well white flour, sugar, butter and milk.

X को **Y** से मिलाना'	**to introduce X to Y**
X ko Y se milānā	

- तेजु ने मुझे अपने मंगेतर से मिलाया।
  teju ne mujhe apne maṅgetar se milāyā.
  Teju introduced me to her fiance.

Uses of the verb 'पड़ना' paṛnā

use of **'पड़ना' paṛnā** to talk of weather

- आजकल कड़ाके की गर्मी पड़ रही है।
  ājkal kaṛāke kī garmī paṛ rahī hai.
  It is very hot these days.
- कल रात भर बहुत ओस पड़ी।
  kal rāt bhar bahut os paṛī.
  There was much dew last night.
- पिछले साल हमारे गाँव में अकाल / सूखा पड़ा।
  pichle sāl hamāre gāṁv meṁ akāl/sūkhā paṛā.
  Last year there was famine/ drought in our village.

Similarly:

• ओले पड़ना	ole paṛnā	to hail
• बारिश पड़ना	bāriś paṛnā	to rain
• बर्फ़ पड़ना	barf paṛnā	snowfall

use of infinitive + **'पड़ना' paṛnā** as compulsion compound Ref. pg. 175

- आज रात को मुझे देर तक काम करना पड़ेगा।
  āj rāt ko mujhe der tak kām karnā paṛegā.
  I will have to work late tonight.

use of **'पड़ा, पड़े, पड़ी' paṛā/paṛe/paṛī + होना honā**= to be lying

• कपड़े अलमारी में पड़े हैं। kpaṛe almārī meṁ paṛe haiṁ.	The clothes are lying in the cupboard.
• शब्दकोश मेज़ पर पड़ा है। śabdkoś mez par paṛā hai.	The dictionary is lying on the table.

use of v.r. + **पड़ना paṛnā** compound verb with nuance of rashness, suddenness etc Ref. pg. 200

• गिर पड़ना	gir paṛnā	to fall
• रो पड़ना	ro paṛnā	to bburst out crying
• हँस पड़ना	hams paṛnā	to burst out laughing

Uses of the verb 'निकलना' nikalnā, 'निकालना' nikālnā, 'निकलवाना' nikalvānā.

- आजकल सूर्य कितने बजे निकलता है।
  ājkal sūryă kitne baje nikaltā hai?
  What time does the sun rise these days?
- कुछ औरतें सिनेमाघर से निकल रही हैं।
  kuch aurteṁ 'sinemāghar' se nikal rahī haiṁ.
  Some women are coming out of the cinema hall.
- बागीचे में बहुत सुन्दर, रंगबिरंगे फूल निकले हुए हैं।
  BāGice meṁ bahut sundar, raṅgbiraṅge phūl nikle hue haiṁ
  Beautiful, multicolored flowers are blossoming in the garden.
- मेरे बेटे को खसरा निकला हुआ है।
  mere beṭe ko khasrā niklā huā hai.
  My son has got measles.
- उन्हों ने मुझे नौकरी से निकाल दिया है।
  unjoṁne mujhe naukrī se nikāl diyā hai.
  They have dismissed me from the job.
- कपड़े बाल्टी में से निकाल का अलगनी पर सुखाने को डाल दो।
  kapṛe bālṭī meṁ se nikālkar alganī par sukhāne ko ḍāl do.
  Take the clothes out of the bucket and put them on the rope to dry.
- मैंने आज सुबह अपना दाँत निकलवाया।
  maiṁne āj subah apnā dāṁt nikalvāyā.
  I had my tooth extracted this morning.

(subj. + को ko) + obj. + दिखाई देना dikhāī denā नजर आना nazat ānā	to be visible

- मुझको कुछ दिखाई नहीं दे रहा। I can not see any thing.
  mujhko kuch dikhāī nahīṁ de rahā.
- हमें विदेशियों का झुण्ड कुलियों से मोलभाव करता हुआ दिखाई दिया।
  hameṁ videśiyoṁ kā jhuṇḍ kuliyoṁ se molbhāv kartā huā dikhāī diyā.
  We saw a group of foreigners bargaining with the porters.

(subj. + को ko) + obj. + सुनाई देना	sunāī denā	to be audible

- क्या आपको कुछ सुनाई दे रहा है? Can you hear something ?
  kyā āpko kuch sunāī de rahā hai?
- अचानक उसे किसीके पैरों की आहट सुनाई दी।
  acānak use kisīke pairoṁ kī āhaṭ sunāī dī.
  Suddenly he / she heard somebody's footsteps.

याद करना (v.t.)	*yād karnā*	to remember
मुँहज़बानी याद करना (v.t.)	*muṁhzabānī yād karnā*	to memorize
याद होना (v.i.)	*yād honā*	to remember
याद रखना	*yād rakhnā*	to retain in memory
याद आना	*yād ānā*	to recall

- याद रखना ! हमें कल सुबह जल्दी उठना है। Remember. (= Don't forget!) We have to get up early tomorrow.
  yād rakhnā. hameṁ kal subah jaldī uṭhnā hai.
- मुझको याद है। I remember.
  mujhko yād hai.
- मुझको कुछ याद नहीं आ रहा। I don't recall anything.
  mujhko kuch yād nahīṁ ā rahā.
- यह कविता मुँहज़बानी याद करो। Learn this poem by heart.
  yah kavitā muṁhzabānī yād karo.

Appendix 1

Usages

है, होता है, रहता है

hai, hotā hai, rahtā hai

है 'hai' is used as verb of the being , or description of state and condition of an object at agiven time.

1. मेरी बहन समाजसेविका है। — My sister is a social worker.
   merī bahan samājsevikā hai.
2. मेरे पति दफ्तर में हैं। — My husband is at the office.
   mere pati daftar meṁ haiṁ.

होता है 'hotā hai' is used for:

all time truths:

1. गेहूँ सुनहला होता है। — Wheat is golden.
   gehūṁ sunehlā hotā hai.
3. दो और दो चार होते हैं। — two and two is four.
   do aur do cār hote haiṁ.

Events that follow a regular time pattern.

1. मेरा दिन सुबह सात बजे शुरू होता है। — My day starts at 7 o'clock in the morning.
   merā din subah sāṭ baje śurū hotā hai.
2. यहाँ नवम्बर से मार्च तक ठण्ड होती है। — It is cold here from November to March.
   yahāṁ navambar se mārc tak ṭhaṇḍ hotī hai.

Commentaries on activities in progress such as games, processions, rallys, meetings etc.

1. लोग खड़े होते हैं। — People stand up.
   log khaṛe hote haiṁ.
2. अब खेल खत्म होता है। — Now the game finishes.
   ab khel khatm hotā hai.

रहता है 'rahtā hai' is used for extended continuity of a certain state over a span of time:

1.	वह हमेशा निश्चिन्त रहती है। vah hameśā niścint rahtī hai.	She always remains carefree.
2.	यह स्थान सदैव शान्त रहता है। yah sthān sadaiv śānt rahtā hai.	This place always remains peaceful.

कितना kitnā **(m.sg.), कितने** kitne **(m.pl.), कितनी** kitnī **(f.sg./pl.) -------------------- how much, how many.**

Used as adjectives, these agree with the number and gender of the noun they qualify.

1.	कितनी लस्सी (f.)	kitnī lassī	how much buttermilk
2.	कितना पानी (m.)	kitnā pānī	how much water
3.	कितने लड़के (m.pl.)	kitne laṛke	how many boys
4.	कितनी लड़कियाँ (f.pl.)	kitnī laṛkiyāṁ	how many girls

☞ **These are also sometimes used to qualify adjectives to mean the maximum of that quality.**

कितना सुहावना!	kitnā suhāvnā	How pleasant!
कितना बहादुर!	kitna bahādur	How brave!

कौन-सा kaun- sā**(m.sg.) ; कौन-से** kaun- se **(m.pl.);**

कौन-सी kaun-sī **(f.sg/pl.) - which one or which ones.**

Used as adjectives, these accord with the number and gender of the noun they qualify.

1.	कौन–सा भवन (m.sg.)	kaun-sā bhavan	which building
2.	कौन–से छात्र (m.pl.)	kaun-se chātra	which students
3.	कौन–सी इमारत (f.sg.)	kaun-sī imārat	which building
4.	कौन–सी लड़कियाँ (f.pl.)	kaun-sī laṛkiyāṁ	which girls

कैसा kaisā (m.sg.), kaise **कैसे (m.pl.), कैसी** kaisī **(f.sg./ pl.) — these have both adjectival and adverbial use meaning**

(1) How? or (2) What kind of..? They agree with the noun or pronoun they qualify.

1. यह कैसा मकान[m.sg] है? — What kind of a house is this?
   yah kaisā makān hai?
2. आप कैसे/कैसी हैं? — How are you? (formal)
   āp kaise/kaisī haim?
3. तुम कैसे/कैसी हो? — How are you? (informal you)
   tum kaise/ kaisī ho?

इतना / इतने / इतनी + adj. कि
itnā /itne/ itnī ki = so + adj. that

1. घर इतना गन्दा था कि मुझे उसे साफ़ करने में हफ़्तों लगे।
   ghar itnā gandā thā ki mujhe use sāf karne meṁ haftoṁ lage.
   The house was in such a mess that it took me weeks to tidy it.
2. बनारस इतना पुराना शहर है कि कोई नहीं जानता यह कब पहले–पहल बसा।
   banāras itnā purānā śahar hai ki koī nahīṁ jāntā yah kab pahle-pahal basā.
   Benares is so old a city that no one knows when it first came into being.

Glossary:

पुराना purānā old ; जानना jānanā to know
बसना basnā to settle (in some place)

जितना ज़्यादा + ... उतना .... jitnā zyādā ....utnā zyādā
the more . ... the more ..

1. जितना धन व्यक्ति के पास आता है, उतना ज़्यादा वह और पाना चाहता है।
   jitnā zyādā dhan vyakti ke pās ātā hai, utnā zyādā vah aur pānā cāhtā hai.
   The more wealth comes to a person, the more he wants to obtain.

2. जितना हम समुद्र के निकट गए, उतनी ही अधिक उमस हमें लगी।
jitnā ham samudra ke nikaṭ gae, utnī hī adhik umas hameṁ lagī.
The nearer we went to the sea, the more sultry we felt.

- उतना............जितना..........utnā..... jitnā...... **as + adj. + as — E 1**
- उतना नहीं ....जितना......... — **not as + adj. + as** — **E 2**
  utnā nahīṁ ..... jitnā...........
- ठीक उतना ही ....जितना.............ṭhīk utnā hī ..... jitnā... **E 3**
  — exactly the same as —
- X के जितना / जितने / जितनी .... **— the same as— E 4**
  X ke jitnā / jitne / jitnī ...

1. यह घर **लगभग उतना ही बड़ा है** जितना वहवाला।
   yah ghar lagbhag utnā hī baṛā hai jitnā vahvālā.
   This house is **almost as big as** that one.
2. वह **उतनी** होशियार **नहीं है जितनी** उसकी बहन।
   vah utnī hośiyār nahīṁ hai jitnī uskī bahan.
   She is **not as clever as** her sister.
3. वह **ठीक उतना ही** वेतन **पाती है जितना मैं**।
   vah ṭhīk utnā hī vetan pātī hai jitnā maiṁ.
   She gets **exactly the same salary** as I do.
4. उसकी उम्र **मेरे जितनी** है।
   uskī umra mere jitnī hai.
   She is **the same age as** I am.

- ऐसा **aisā** **like this** **E 1**
- वैसा **vaisā** **like that** **E 2**
- X के जैसा, की तरह **(like = similar to X, but not actually X)**
  ke jaisā, kī tarah **E 3**
  ☞ Use of के ke is not obligatory with के जैसा ke jaisā
- X की हैसियत से **X kī haisiyat se** = in the capacity of X / is actually X

1. मैं ऐसा हूँ। maiṁ aisā hūṁ. I am like this.
2. मैं वैसा हूँ।। maiṁ vaisā hūṁ. I am like that.
3. मैं उसके जैसा हूँ। maiṁ uske jaisā hūṁ. I am like him/ her.
4. रॉबर्ट डॉक्टर **की तरह/ के जैसे** बोलता है।

   raubarṭ ḍaukṭar **kī tarah/ ke jaise** boltā hai.

   Robert talks like a doctor. **(is not actually a doctor)**
5. उनका घर संग्रहालय के जैसा है।

   unkā ghar saṅgrahālay ke jaisā hai.

   Their house is **like a museum. (but not actually a museum.)**
6. वह वकील की तरह/ के जैसे बोलता है।

   vah vakīl kī tarah/ ke jaise boltā hai.

   He speaks like an advocate. (=is not actually an advocate)
7. वह उसके वकील की हेसियत से बोला।

   vah uske vakīl kī haisiyat se bolā.

   He spoke in the capacity of his advocate.

   (=is actually his advocate.
8. वह प्रधानाचार्य **की हैसियत से** काम करता है।

   vah pradhānācāryă **kī haisiyat se** kām kartā hai.

   He works as Headmaster. **(is actually a headmaster)**

   (की हैसियत से means he is actually a head master)

Glossary:

संग्रहालय (m.)	sangrahālay	museum
वकील (f..)	vakīl	advocate
फ़र्श (m.)	farś	floor
की हैसियत से (ppn)	kī haisiyat se	as, in the capacity of
प्रधानाचार्य (m.)	pradhānācāryă	Principal
के जैसे (ppn)	ke jaise	like

ऐसे ....जैसे कि **—as if** ☞ use of कि is not obligatory

1. ऐसा लगता है **जैसे कि** वह कुएँ में कूदनेवाला हो।
   aisā lagtā hai jaise ki vah kueṁ meṁ kūdnevālā ho.
   It looks **as if** he is about to jump into the well.
2. आप **ऐसे** लग रहे हैं **जैसे** कि आपने कोई भूत देखा हो।
   āp aise lag rahe haiṁ jaise ki āpne koī bhūt dekhā ho.
   You look **as** if you have seen a ghost.
3. उसने ऐसे खाया जैसे उसने सदियों से कभी कुछ न खाया हो।
   usne aise khāyā jaise usne sadiyoṁ se kabhī kuch na khāyā ho.
   She ate **as though / as if** she had never eaten anything for ages.

Glossary:

भूत (m.)	bhūt	ghost
सदियों से (adv.)	sadiyoṁ se	for ages

Some fixed expressions with जैसा कि corresponding to 'as' : कि is not obligatory.

- जैसा कि आप पहले से जानते हैं........ **As** you already know
  jaisā ki āp pahle se jānte haiṁ......
- जैसी उन्हें उम्मीद थी................ **As** they expected
  jaisī unheṁ ummīd thī............

चाहे जो हो cāhe jo ho — Come what may,
चाहे कुछ भी हो cāhe kuch bhī jo ho

- चाहे जो हो, तुम कुछ मत कहना।
  cāhe jo ho, tum kuch mat kahnā.
  Come what may, you don't say anything.
- चाहे कुछ भी हो, मैं अपने सिद्धान्त नहीं छोड़ सकता/सकती।
  cāhe kuch bhī ho, maiṁ apne siddhānt nahīṁ choṛ saktā/saktī.
  Come what may, I can't give up my principles.

X चाहे न चाहे, X cāhe na cāhe ..Whether X likes it or not.

- तुम चाहो या न चाहो, तुम्हें मेरे साथ आना पड़ेगा।
  tum cāho yā na cāho, tumheṁ mere sāth ānā paṛegā.
  Whether you like it or not, you will have to come with me.
- मैं चाहूँ न चाहूँ, मुझे अगले सप्ताह दफ़्तर में अतिरिक्त समय काम करना पड़ेगा।
  maiṁ cāhūṁ na cāhūṁ, mujhe agle saptāh dafter meṁ atirikt kām karnā paṛegā.
  Whether I like it or not, I will have to work overtime in the office next week.

v.r.+ ने के बजाय	v.r.+ ne ke bajāy	Instead of
v.r.+ ने की जगह	v.r.+ ne kī jagah	
न + v.r. + कर/के	na +v.r. + kar/ke ..	

- घर जाने के बजाय / की जगह मैं फ़िल्म देखने चला गया।
  ghar jāne ke bajāy / kī jagah maiṁ film dekhne calā gayā.

= घर न जाकर मैं फ़िल्म देखने चला गया।
  ghar na jākar maiṁ film dekhne calā gayā
  Instead of going home I went to see a film.

यद्यपि/हालाँकि ----- yadyapi/hālāṁki -----although

- यद्यपि/ हालाँकि वह बहुत योग्य थी, उसे काम नहीं मिला।
  yadyapi /hālāṁki vah bahut yogyă thī, use kām nahīṁ milā.
  Although she was highly qualified, she did not get the job.
- यद्यपि / हालाँकि वह धनी है, तथापि वह बहुत कंजूस है।
  yadyapi /hālāṁki vah dhanī hai, tathāpi vah bahut kañjūs hai.
  Although he is wealthy, he is very miserly.

होने पर भी/होते हुए भी/ के बावजूद Inspite of /despite
hone par bhī/hote hue bhī /ke bāvjūd

- बहुत थकी होने पर भी/होते हुए भी माँ ने हमारे लिए खाना बनाया।
  bahut thakī hone par bhī / hote hue bhī māṁ ne hamāre lie khānā banāyā.
  Inspite of / despite being very tired, mother cooked a meal for us.

- मेरी विनम्र क्षमा याचना के बावजूद उसने मुझे क्षमा नहीं किया।
  merī vinamra kṣamā yācnā ke bāvjūd usne mujhe kṣamā nahīṁ kiyā.
  Despite my humble apologising, he / she did not forgive me.

X को कोई फ़र्क नहीं पडता X ko koī farq nahīṁ paṛtā
X do / doesn't care

- मुझे कोई फ़र्क नहीं पड़ता। तुम जो चाहो पहन सकते हो!
  mujhe koī farq nahīṁ paṛtā. tum jo cāho pahan sakte ho.
  I don't care. You may wear whatever you desire.
- मुझे कोई फ़र्क नहीं पड़ता। तुम जिसे चाहो मिल सकते हो!
  mujhe koī farq nahīṁ paṛtā. tum jise cāho mil sakte ho.
  I don't care. You may meet anybody you want to.

ताकि tā ki (so that): ताकि tā ki (clause is in the subjunctive:

- कृपया धीरे बोलिए ताकि मैं आप को समझ सकूँ।
  kṛpayā dhīre bolie tāki maiṁ āpko samajh sakūṁ.
  Please speak slowly so that I can understand you.
- मैंने 'टैक्सी' ली ताकि मैं दफ़्तर देर से न पहुँचूं।
  maiṁne 'ṭaiksī' lī tāki maiṁ daftar der se na pahūṁcūṁ.
  I took a taxi so that I might not arrive late at the office.

बशर्ते कि baśarte ki provided that
Use of कि ki is not obligatory.

- तुम निश्चित ही परीक्षा में उत्तीर्ण होगे बशर्ते कि तुम परिश्रम करो।
  tum niścit hī parīkṣā meṁ uttīrṇ hoge baśarte ki tum pariśram karo.
  You will certainly pass the exam provided that you work hard.
- सोनाली निश्चित ही विदेश जाएगी बशर्ते कि उसे छात्रवृत्ति मिल जाए।
  sonalī niścit hī videś jāegī baśarte ki use chātravṛtti mil jāe.
  Sonalii is bound to go abroad provided that she gets a scholarship.

जब तक नहीं jab tak nahīṁ unless

- जब तक आप जल्दी नहीं करेंगे, आपकी गाड़ी निश्चित ही छूट जाएगी।
  jab tak āp jaldī nahiṁ kareṁge, āpkī gāṛī niścit hī chūṭ jāe gī.
  You will definitely miss the train unless you hurry.
- जब तक आप अनुदेशों का अनुसरण नहीं करेंगे, यह उपकरण काम नहीं करेगा।
  jab tak ap anudeśoṁ kā anusaraṇ nahīṁ kareṁge, yah upkaraṇ kām nahīṁ karegā.
  This gadget will not work unless you follow the instructions.

अभी–अभी abhī-abhī ....Just, just now

- गाड़ी अभी–अभी आई है। The train has just arrived.
  gāri abhī-abhī āī hai.
- बच्चे अभी–अभी लौटे हैं। The children have just returned.
  bacce abhī-abhī lauṭe haiṁ.

अभी नहीं abhī nahīṁ .... not yet अभी तक नहीं abhī tak nahīṁ .

- पिता जी ने अभी अख़बार (m.) नहीं पढ़ा।
  pitā jī ne abhī akhbar nahīṁ paṛhā.
  Father has not read the newspaper yet.
- वे (m.) अभी तक नहीं पहुँचे।
  ve (m.) abhī tak nahīṁ pahuṁce.
  They have not arrived yet.

अभी भी abhī bhī ....still

- वह (m.)अभी भी विद्यार्थी है। He is still a student?
  vah (m.) abhī bhī vidyārthī hai.
- वे (m./ f.) अभी भी भारत में है। They are still in India.
  ve (m/ f.) abhī bhī bhārat meṁ hai.

Suffix भर bhar .... to convey the completeness, fullness of something.

- वह दिन भर सोई रहती है। She keeps sleeping all day.
  vah din bhar soī rahtī hai.
- मैंने तुम्हें शहर भर में ढूँढा। I looked for you all over the city.
  maiṁne tumheṁ śahar bhar meṁ ḍhūṁḍhā.

X के {v.r. + ने) भर की देर होना X ke (v.r. + ne) bhar kī der honā .... to convey the readiness to fulfil the action absolutely without delay:

- आपके कहने भर की देर है, आपका काम हो जाएगा।
  āpke kahne bhar kī der hai, āpkā kām ho jāegā.
  You just need to say, your work will be done.

X को Y कहना X ko Y kahnā to call 'X' 'Y'

- इसको हिन्दी में क्या कहते हैं? **What is this called in** Hindi?
  isko hindī meṁ kyā kahte haiṁ.
- उसे लोग महाबली कहने लगे। People began to call him Mahabali.
  use log mahābalī kahne lage.

X को Y करने को कहना X ko Y karne ko kahnā to ask X to do Y

- उसने मुझको बैठने को कहा। He asked me to sit.
  usne mujhko baiṭhne ko kahā.
- उन्होंने हमें व्यायामशाला जाने को कहा।
  unhoṁ ne hameṁ vyāyāmśālā jāne ko kahā.
  They asked us to go to the gym.

क्या X ...क्या Y kyā X...kyā Y whether X or Y

- क्या अधिकारी, क्या नेता, सब भ्रष्ट हैं।
  kyā adhikārī kyā netā, sab bhraṣṭ haiṁ.
  Whether the officers or the leaders, all are corrupt.

Use of the interrogative *क्या* kya to convey a negative idea.

- What use is life without literacy? — साक्षरता के बिना जीवन का क्या लाभ है?
  sākṣartā ke binā jīvan kā kyā lābh hai?

= Life is no use without literacy. — साक्षरता के बिना जीवन का कोई लाभ नहीं।
  sākṣartā ke binā jīvan kā koī lābh nahīṁ?

हो–न–हो ho - na - ho certainly

- हो–न–हो, वे हमारा पीछा कर रहे हैं।
  ho-na-ho, ve hamārā pīchā kar rahe haiṁ.
  Certainly they are following us.

थोड़े ही/ थोड़े ही न thoṛe hī / thoṛe hī na
used inconversation to negate a proposition.

- मैं पागल थोड़े ही/ थोड़े ही न हूँ।
  maiṁ pāgal thoṛe hī na hūṁ!
  I certainly am not crazy!
- मैं इतनी गर्मी में थोड़े ही/ थोड़े ही न बाहर जाऊँगा।
  maiṁ itnī garmī meṁ thoṛe hī / thoṛe hī na bāhar jāūṁgā.
  I certainly will not go out in such heat.

जैसे–तैसे कर के jaise-taise kar ke
It is a fixed expression meaning ‘in some or the other way.

- जैसे–तैसे करके उसने यह छोटा–सा घर बनाया है।
  jaise-taise karke usne yah choṭā-sā ghar banāyā hai.
  Somehow he has made this rather small house.
- जैसे–तैसे करके मैं आधी रातको उनके यहाँ पहुँचा।
  jaise-taise karke maiṁ ādhī rāt ko unke yahāṁ pahuṁcā.
  Somehow I arrived at his place at midnight.

दोनों donoṁ both

- दोनों आदमी ईमानदार थे।
  donoṁ ādmī imāndār the.
  Both men were honest.
- ये दोनों व्यापार–प्रस्ताव अच्छे लग रहे हैं।
  ye donoṁ vyāpār prastāv acche lag rahe haiṁ.
  Both of these business proposals sound good.

ईमानदार	(adj.)	imāndār	honest
प्रस्ताव	(m.)	prastāv	proposal

दोनों में से कोई नहीं / एक भी नहीं Neither of **the two**
donoṁ meṁ se koī nahīṁ/ ek bhī nahīṁ

- उसके माता–पिता दोनों में से एक भी जीवित नहीं।
  uske mātā-pitā donoṁ meṁ se ek bhī jīvit nahīṁ.
  Neither of her parents is alive.
- हम दोनों में से किसी को भी उसके घर का रास्ता नहीं आता था।
  ham donoṁ meṁ se kisī ko bhī uske ghar kā rāstā nahīṁ ātā thā.
  Neither of us knew the way to her house.

जीवित	(adj.)	jīvit	alive

' सा , से , सी .. = similar to; somewhat + adjectival quality

- मेरी फूल–सी बच्ची बीमार है। my daughter (delicate) as a flower
  merī phūl-sī baccī bīmar hai. is sick.
- वह पीली–सी पगड़ीवाला आदमी that man with somewhat
  vah pīlī -sī pagṛīvālā ādmī. yellowish turban

noun + से se = adverb

- वह विनम्रता से बोला। He spoke politely.
  vah vinamratā se bolā.
- शान्ति से बैठिए। Sit peacefully.
  śānti se baiṭhie.

adjective + रूप से rūp se = adverb

- वह पूर्ण रूप से स्वस्थ है। vah pūrṇ rūp se svasth hai. — He is comletely healthy.
- वह हमेशा बहुत अनौपचारिक रूप से बात करता है। vah hameśā bahut anaupcārik rūp se bāt kartā hai. — He always talks very informally.

noun + वत् vat = adverb

- वह दिन भर यंत्रवत् काम करता रहता है। vah din-bhar yantravat kām kartā rahtā hai. — He keeps working all day mechanically .
- उसने मित्रवत् सलाह दी। usne mitravat salāh di. — He advised in a friendly manner

Use of the postposition को ko

को ko is used with days and date.

• सोमवार को	somvār ko	on Monday,
मंगलवार को	mangalvār ko	on Tuesday etc.
• दो तारीख़ को	do tārīkh ko	on the second (date two)
• दस जनवरी को	das janvarī ko	on January 10 etc.

को ko is used with direct as well as indirect living object. It is usually dropped with nonliving direct object.

- मैं अनिल को मिला। maiṁ anil ko milā. I met Anil.
- मैंने किताब पढ़ी। maiṁne kitāb paṛhī I read a book.

☞ **But while specifying the nonliving object, को ko is used.**

- मैंने उस किताब को पढ़ा। maiṁne us kitāb ko paṛhā — I read that book.

को ko is not used with verbs of movement such a ' ānā, jānā ' to a place, market, locality, city or country .

मैं बैंक / दिल्ली / भारत जाऊँगा। (there is no translation for 'to')
maiṁ baink/dilli/bhārat jāūṁgā.

- I will go to the bank/ Delhi/ India.

Hindi uses 'न na' or 'है न hai na' at the end of a sentence as question tags

- आप बैंक हो आए हैं न? āp baink ho āe haiṁ na? — You have been to the bank, haven't you?
- वे काश्मीर जाएँगे न? ve kasmir jāeṁge na? — They will go to Kashmir, won't they?
- आप चावल खाते हैं न? — You eat rice, don't you? āp cāval khāte haiṁ na?

X के रहते	**X ke rahte**	**while X is there**
X के चलते	**X ke calte**	**on account of X**

- मेरे रहते तुम्हारा कोई कुछ नहीं बिगाड़ सकता।
  mere rahte tumhārā koī kuch nahīṁ bigāṛ saktā.
  While I am there, no one can do any harm to you.
- आपके चलते मेरा काम भी हो गया।
  āpke calte merā kām bhī ho gayā.
  Because of you my work also got done.

X को लेकर	**X ko lekar**	**concerning X,**
X से होकर	**X se hokar**	**via X**

- अपने बच्चे की बीमारी को लेकर वह बहुत परेशान है।
  apne bacce kī bīmārī ko le kar vah bahut pareśān hai.
  He is very upset concerning his child's illness.
- मैं आगरा से होकर दिल्ली आऊँगा।
  maiṁ āgrā se hokar dillī āūṁgā.
  I will come to Delhi via Agra.

तो to ....emphatic particle meaning indeed.

मैं तो जाऊँगा। **I (indeed) will go.**
maiṁ to jāūṁgā.

तो to ....conditional sentences (187)

आप मुझे बुलाएँगे, तो मैं आऊँगा। If you call me, I will come.
āp mujhe bulāeṁge, to maiṁ āūṁgā.

तो to as sentence starter.........emphatic particle meaning 'so' with a pinch of annoyance.

तो, मैं क्या करूँ? **So, what shall I do?**
to, maiṁ kyā karūṁ?

जब तब jab tab every now and then
आए दिन āe din

- वह जब तब / **आए दिन** मेरे यहाँ उधार माँगने आ जाता है।
vah jab tab / āe din mere yahāṁ udhār māṁgne ā jātā hai..
It seems somewhat less than two kilos.

जब तक jab tak as long as / by the time

- आप **जब तक** चाहें, हमारे यहाँ रह सकते हैं।
āp jab tak cāheṁ, hamāre yahāṁ rah sakte haiṁ.
You can stay with us **as long as** you desire.
- **जब तक** मैं लौटूँ, मेरा काम हो जाना चाहिए।
jab tak maiṁ lauṭūṁ, merā kām ho jānā cāhie.
By the time I come back, my work should be done.
- **जब तक** यह काम पूरा न हो, आप कहीं न जाइएगा।
jab tak yah kām purā na ho, āp kahīṁ na jāiegā.
Don't go anywhere **until** this work is complete.

कभी–न–कभी	**kabhī-na-kabhī**	**some or the other time**
कहीं–न–कहीं	**kahīṁ-na-kahīṁ**	**somewhere or the other**
कोई–न–कोई	**koī-na-koī**	**someone or the other**
कुछ–न–कुछ	**kuch-na-kuch**	**something or the other**

- मेरे जीवन में भी कभी–न–कभी, कहीं–न–कहीं , कोई–न–कोई तो आएगा।
  mere jīvan meṁ bhī kabhī-na-kabhī , kahīṁ-na kahīṁ, koī-na-koī to āegā.
  Some or the other time, somewhere or the other, someone or the other will come in my life too.

- उसने कुछ–न–कुछ तो ज़रूर कहा होगा।
  usne kuch-na-kuch to zarūr kahā hogā.
  He must have certainly said something or the other.
- कोई–न–कोई तो ज़रूर आपकी सहायता करेगा।
  koī-na-koī to zarūr āpkī sahāyatā karegā.
  Someone or the other will certainly help you.

कुछ कम ही kuch kam hī = somewhat less than / very little

- यह दो किलो से कुछ कम ही लगता है।
  yah do kilo se kuch kam hī lagtā hai.
  It seems somewhat less than than two kilos
- वह हिन्दी कुछ कम ही जानता है।
  vah hindī kuch kam hī jāntā hai.
  He knows very little Hindi.
- मुझे उनका रहन सहन कुछ कम ही पसन्द आया।
  mujhe unkā rahan-sahan kuch kam hī pasand āyā.
  I didn't quite like their life style.

पर खरा उतरना	**par khārā utarnā**	**to pass the test**

- वह संस्थान की उम्मीदों पर खरा उतरा।
  vah saṃsthān kī ummīdoṁ par kharā utrā.
  He proved himself upto the hopes of the institute.
- मौजूदा सरकार जनता की अपेक्षाओं पर खरी नहीं उतरी।
  maujūdā sarkār jantā kī apekṣāoṁ par kharī nahīṁ utrī.
  The present government did not prove itseft upto the expectations of the people.
- वह अपने लम्बे कार्यकाल की हर कसौटी पर खरा उतरा।
  vah apne lambe kāryǎkāl kī har kasauṭī par kharā utrā.
  He passed all the tests of his long working period.

X (v.r. + ने)को मन होना X (v.r. + ne) ko man honā
to feel like doing X

- मेरा मिठाई खाने को मन हो रहा है।
  merā miṭhāī khāne ko man ho rahā hai.
  I feel like eating sweets.
- आज हमारा कोई पुरानी हिन्दी फ़िल्म देखने को मन हो रहा है।
  āj hamārā koī purānī hindī film dekhne ko man ho rahā hai.
  Today we feel like watching some old Hindi film.

A conversational phrase.:
- **और नहीं तो क्या aur nahīṁ to kyā**

of course ; If not, what else?

1. आप सोचते हैं कि शादी बीसवें साल में होनी चाहिए।
   āp socte haiṁ ki śādī bīsveṁ sāl meṁ honī cāhie.
   you think that marriage should take place in the 20th year.
   - और नहीं तो क्या? aur nahīṁ to kyā? Of course.

2. तुम मेरे साथ चल रहे हो न? You are coming with me, aren't you?
   tum mere sāth cal rahe ho na?
- और नहीं तो क्या? aur nahīṁ to kyā? Of course.

यूँ ही / यों ही yūṁ/ yoṁ hī **just like that/ unnecessarily**

1. तुम क्यों यूँ ही बहस कर रहे हो? Why are you arguing
   tum kyoṁ yūṁ hī bahas kar rahe ho. unnecessarily?
2. तुम क्यों बाहर जा रहे हो?'' ''यूँ ही''
   "tum kyoṁ bāhar jā rahe ho?". "yūṁ hī"
   "Why are you going out?". "Just like that."

यूँ ही / यों ही yūṁ / yoṁ hī / इसी तरह isī tarah **in this manner**

1. आप यूँ ही प्रयास करती रहीं, तो बहुत जल्दी धाराप्रवाह बोलने लगेंगी।
   āp yūṁ hī prayās kartī rahīṁ, to bahut jaldī dhārāpravāh bolne lageṁgī.
   If you keep trying in this manner, very soon you will begin to speak fluently.
2. यूँ ही / इसी तरह बारिश पड़ती रही, तो आवागमन में बाधा होगी।
   yūṁ hī bāris partī rahī, to āvāgaman meṁ bādhā hogī.
   If rain continued in this manner, there will be obstacle in coming and going.

यूँ तो / यों तो yūṁ / yoṁ to.......... **as such**

यों तो मैं सुबह घर पर ही रहती हूँ, परन्तु कल घर पर नहीं होऊँगी।
yoṁ to maiṁ subah ghar par hī rahtī hūṁ, parantu kal ghar par nahīṁ hoūṁgī.
As such I stay at home in the morning, but tomorrow I won't be home.

भला bhalā ..... **Various uses:**

- भला bhalā (adj) e.g. भला आदमी bhalā ādmī good man
- भला हो उसका bhalā ho uskā (interjection) May he prosper!
- भला (sentence adverb with question word conveys a nagative meaning) after all,....

  भला मैं क्यों उसके यहाँ जाऊँ? bhalā maiṁ kyoṁ uske yahāṁ jāūṁ.!
  Why would I go to his place (= I certainly won't)

यूँ yūṁ =यों yoṁ (adv.)

Manner related relatives- correlatives

- **जैसे......वैसे.........jaise .... vaise ...**
- **जिस तरह.......उसी तरह....jis tarah......usī tarah the manner in which.......in the same manner**

जैसे/जिस तरह मैं कर रही हूँ, वैसे ही/उसी तरह ही आप भी करें।
jaise/jis tarah maiṁ kar rahī hūṁ, vaise hī/usī tarah āp bhī kareṁ.
The way I am doing, you too do the same way

Time related relatives- correlatives

- *जब... तब..* **jab....tab... when..........then.............**
- *जब तक.........तब तक..* **jab tak....tab tak...**
  by the time ....by then; as long as...........till then..............
- **जैसे ही jaise hī...........वैसे ही jaise hī .... as soon as**
- **ज्यों ही jyoṁ hī .....त्यों ही tyoṁ hī .... as soon as**

1. जब आप कहेंगे, तब हम आपके साथ चलेंगे।
   jab āp kaheṁge, tab ham āpke sāth caleṁge.
   When you say, we will come with you.
2. जब तक आप वहाँ पहुँचेंगे, तब तक हम भी वहाँ पहुँच जाएँगे।
   jab tak āp vahāṁ pahuṁceṁge, tab tak ham bhī vahāṁ pahuṁc jāeṁge.
   By the time you arrive there, by that time we will also arrive there.
3. जब तक आप चाहेंगे, तब तक हम वहां रहेंगे।
   jab tak āp caheṁge, tab tak ham vahāṁ raheṁge.
   As long as you would want, till then we will stay there.
4. जब तक निरीक्षक पहुँचें, तब तक सब इन्तज़ाम हो जाना चाहिए।
   jab tak nirīkṣak pahuṁceṁ, tab tak sab intzām ho jānā cāhie.
   By the time the inspector arrives, by then all arrangements should be made.
5. जैसे ही/ज्यों ही हम घर से निकले, वैसे ही/त्यों ही बारिश होने लगी।
   jaise hī / jyoṁ hī ham ghar se nikle, vaise hī / tyoṁ hī bāriś hone lagī. (for more examples see page 156)

Place related relatives- correlatives

- .जहाँ........वहाँ....... **where.......there**
  jahāṁ .... vahāṁ ...
- **जहाँ तक.........वहाँ तक..... as far as ....till there.....**
  jahāṁ tak........vahāṁ tak.....

1. जहाँ मैं पली बड़ी, वहाँ भूस्थल बहुत सुन्दर है।
   jahāṁ maiṁ palī baṛī, vahāṁ bhūsthal bahut sundar hai.
   Where I grew up, (there) the landscape is very beautiful.
2. जहाँ तक आपको दिखाई दे रहा है, वहाँ तक सब खेत मेरे हैं।
   jahāṁ tak āpko dikhāi de rahā hai, vahāṁ tak sab khet mere haiṁ.
   As far as you can see, (till there) all fields are mine.

Direction related relatives- correlatives

- जिधर........उधर...... **where.......there**
  .jidhar.........udhar
- **जिस तरफ़........उस तरफ़.... the direction in which ....in the**
  jis taraf......us taraf............ same directionas

1. जिधर उन्होंने कहा, हम उधर चले गए।
   jidhar unhoṁne kahā, ham udhar cale gae.
   Where they said, over there we went.
2. जिस तरफ वे जा रहे थे, उस तरफ घना जंगल था।
   jis taraf ve jā rahe the, us taraf ghanā jaṅgal thā.
   The direction in which they were going, in that direction was dense forest.

Appendix 2
Vocabulary

- **Professions**

actor	अभिनेता (m.)	*abhinetā*
actress	अभिनेत्री (f.)	*abhinetrī*
advocate	वकील (m.)	*vakīl*
barbar	नाई (m.)	*nāī*
directpor	निदेशक (m.)	*nideśak*
doctor	चिकित्सक (m.)	*cikitsak*
electrician	बिजली मिस्त्री (m.)	*bijlī mistrī*
engineer	अभियन्ता (m.)	*abhiyantā*
fisherman	मछुआरा (m.)	*machuārā*
gardner	माली (m.)	*mālī*
inspector	निरीक्षक (m.)	*nirīkṣak*
journalist	पत्रकार (m.)	*patrakār*
judge	न्यायाधीश (m.	*nyāyādhīś*
mason	राजगीर (m.)	*rājgīr*
officer	अधिकारी (m.)	*adhikārī*
tailor	दर्ज़ी (m.)	*darzī*
teacher	अध्यापक (m.)	*adhyāpak*
teacher	अध्यापिका (f.)	*adhyāpikā*
tourist	पर्यटक (m.)	*paryaṭak*
servant	नौकर (m.)	*naukar*
servant	नौकरानी (f.)	*naukrānī*
shoemaker	मोची (m.)	*mocī*
surveyor	सर्वेक्षक (m.)	*sarvekṣak*
watchmaker	घड़ीसाज़(m.)	*ghaṛīsāz*
worker	कर्मचारी (m.)	karmcarī

- **Animals**

1. bird चिड़िया *ciṛiyā* 2. horse घोड़ा *ghoṛā*

3. cat बिल्ली *billī* | 4. jackal सियार *siyār*
5. cow गाय *gāy* | 6. buffalo भैंस *bhaiṁs*
7. crow कौवा *kauvā* | 8. lion शेर *śer*
9. dog कुत्ता *.kuttā* | 10. mouse चूहा *cūhā*
11. donkey गधा *gadhā* | 12. pig सूअर *sūar*
13. duck बत्तख़ *battakh* | 14. snake सांप *sāṁp*
15. elephant हाथी *hāthī* | 16. frog मेंढक *meṁdhak*
17. sheep भेड़ *bheṛ* | 18. goat बकरी *bakrī*

Sounds of animals

1. chirp चहचहाना *cahcahānā* | 2. neigh हिनहिनाना *hinhinānā*
3. miao मिंआना *miṁānā* | 4. howl हुआना *huānā*
5. moo रंभाना *rambhānā* | 6. caw कांव–कांव करना. *kāṁv-kāṁv karnā*
7. roar दहाड़ना *dahāṛnā* | 8. bark भौंकना *bhauṁknā*
11. grunt घुरघुराना *ghurghurānā* | 12. quack कां–कां करना *kāṁ-kāṁ karnā*
13. hiss फुफकारना *phuphkārnā* | 14. trumpet चिंघाड़ना *cinghāṛnā*
15. croak टर्र–टराना *ṭar-ṭarānā* | 16. bleat मिमिआना *mimiyānā*

- **Shapes**

1. round गोल *gol* | 2. square चकोर *cakor*
3. trianle त्रिकोण *trikoṇ* | 4. cylindrical अण्डाकार *aṇḍākār*
5. cube घनाकार *ghanākār* | 6. spiral सर्पिल *sarpil*
7. rectangular आयताकार *āyatakar* | 8. hexagon षडभुज *ṣaḍbhuj*
9. octagon अष्टभुज *aṣṭbhuj* | 10. long लम्बा *lambā*
11. wide चौड़ा *cauṛā* | 12. shape आकार *ākār*

- **Spices**

1. asafoetida हींग *hīng* | 2. bay leaf तेज पत्ता *tej pattā*
3. black pepper कालीमिर्च *kālī* mirc | 4. carom seed आजवायन *ājvāyan*
5. cinnamon दारचीनी *dārcīnī* | 6. cloves लौंग *laung*
7. coriander धनिया *dhaniā* | 8. cumin seed जीरा *jīrā*
9. fennel सौंफ़ *sauṁf* | 10. fenugreek मेथीदाना *methīdānā*

11. garlic लहसुन *lahsun*
12. mace जावित्री. *jāvitrī*
13. mint पोदीना *podīnā*
14. mustard seed राई *rāī*
15. nutmeg जायफल *jāyphal*
16. poppy seed खस *khas*
17. red pepper लालमिर्च *lāl mirc*
18. saffron केसर *kesar*
19. salt नमक *namak*
20. sesame seed तिल *til* .
21. tamarind इमली *imlī*
22. turmeric हल्दि *haldī*

- **Fruits**

1. apple सेब *seb*
2. orange संतरा *santarā*
3. apricot खुमानी *khumānī*
4. papaya पपीता *papītā*
5. banana केला *kelā*
6. peach आडू *āṛū*
7. custard apple शरीफ़ा *śarīfā*
8. pear नाशपाती *nāśpatī*
9. grapes अंगूर *aṅgūr*
10. pineapple अनानास *anānās*
11. guava अमरूद *amrūd*
12. pomegranate अनार *anār*
13. lemon नींबू. *nīmbū*
14. raspberry रसभरी *rasbharī*
15. litchi लीची *līcī*
16. sapodilla चीकू *cīkū*
18. mango आम *ām*
19. strawberry स्ट्राबेरी *sṭraubeṛī*
20. musk melon खरबूजा *kharbūzā*
21. water melon तरबूज़ *tarbūz*

- **Vegetables**

1. beans फलियां *phaliyāṁ*
2. beet root चुकन्दर *cukandar*
3. bitter gourd करेला *karelā*
4. bottle gourd लौकी *laukī*
5. cabbage पत्ता गोभी *pattā gobhī*
6. capsicum शिमला मिर्च *śimlā mirc*
7. carrot गाजर *gājar*
8. cauliflower फूलगोभी *phūlgobhī*
9. cucumber खीरा *khīrā*
10. egg plant बैंगन *baiṅgan*
11. ginger अदरक *adrak*
12. jackfruit कटहल *kaṭhal*
13. knol khol गाँठ गोभी *gāṁṭh gobhī*
14. lotus root कमल ककड़ी *kamal kakṛī*
15. ochra भिण्डी *bhiṇḍī*
16. peas मटर *maṭar*
17. potato आलू *ālū*
18. radish मूली *mūlī*
19. snake gourd चचिण्डा *caciṇḍā*
20. spinach पालक *pālak*
21. sweet potato शकरकन्दी *śakarkandī*
22. taro अरबी *arbī*

23. tomato टमाटर *ṭamāṭar*
24. turnip शलजम *śaljam*

• Grains

1. barley जौ *jau*
2. bengal grams काले चने *kāle cane*
3. chic peas काबुली चना *kābulī canā*
4. gram flour बेसन *besan*
5. kidney beans राजमाह *rājmāh*
6. lentil दाल मसूर *dāl masūr*
7. maize मक्का *makkā*
8. millets बाजरा *bājrā*
9. rice चावल *cāval*
10. semolina सूजी *sūjī*
11. wheat गेहूँ *gehūṁ*
12. white flour मैदा *maidā*
13. whole wheat flour आटा *ātā*

• Fats

1. butter मक्खन *makkhan*
2. clarified butter घी *ghī*
3. cream मलाई *malāī*
4. coconut oil नारियल का तेल *nāriyal kā tel*
5. mustard oil सरसों का तेल *sarsoṁ kā tel*
6. sesame oil तिल का तेल *til kā tel*

• Cooking

1. beat फेंटना. *pheṁṭnā*
2. boil उबालना *ubālnā*
3. to chop/cut काटना *kāṭnā*
4. to cover ढकना *ḍhaknā*
5. crush कुचलना *kucalnā*
6. deep fry अधिक तेल में तलना *adhik tel meṁ talnā*
7. garnish भोजन को सजाना *bhojan ko sājānā*
8. grate रेतना *retnā*
9. grind पीसना *pīsnā*
10. ingredients सामग्री *sāmagri*
11. knead गूंधना *gūṁdhnā* to
12. to melt पिघलाना *pighlānā*
13. peel/skin छीलना *chīlnā*
14. pound कूटना *kūṭnā*
15. recipe विधि *vidhi*
16. rinse खुले पानी में धोना *khule pānī meṁ dhonā*
17. roast भूनना *bhūnanā*
18. to roll बेलना *belnā*
19. scrape खुरचना *khurcanā*
20. season मसाला मिलाना *masālā milānā*

21. serve परोसना *prosnā*
22. shallow fry कम तेल में तलना *kam tel meṁ talnā*
23. simmer कम आँच पर पकाना *kam āṁc par pakānā*
24. to soak भिगोना *bhigonā*
25. to steam भाप देना *bhāp denā*
26 . strain /sift छानना *chānanā*(चाय *cāy*, आटा *āṭā etc)*

- **Astrology: *jyotiṣ* śāstra**

1. astrology ज्योतिष शास्त्र *jyotiṣ śāstra*
2. astrologer ज्योतिषी *jyotiṣī śāstra*
3. numerology अंक शास्त्र *aṅk śāstra*
4. numerologist अंकविद *aṅk vid*
5. pamistry हस्तरेखा शास्त्र *hastrekhā śāstra*
6. palmist हस्तरेखा शास्त्री *hastrekhā śāstrī*

- **Planets ग्रह** graha

1. jupiter बृहस्पति *bṛhaspati*
2. केतु *ketu*
3. mars मंगल *maṅgal*
4. mercury बुध budh
5. moon चाँद *cāmd*
6. राहु rāhu
7. saturn शनि *śani*
8. sun सूर्य suryă
9. venus शुक्र *śukra*

राहु rāhu , केतु ketu are planets in Hindu astrology.

Zodiac राशी–चक्र rāśi cakra

Signs of the zodiac राशियाँ rāśiyāṁ

1. Aries मेष . *meṣ*
2. Aquarius कुंभ *kumbh*
3. Cancer कर्क *kark*
4. Capricorn मकर *makar*
5. Gemini मिथुन. *mithun*
6. Leo सिंह *siṃh*
7. Libra तुला *tulā*
8. Pisces मीन *mīn*
9. Sagittarius धनु . *dhanu*
10. Scorpio वृश्चिक *vṛṣcik*
11. Taurus वृषभ *vṛsabh*
12. Virgo कन्या *kanyā*

- **Body parts:**

1. ankle टखना *ṭakhnā*
2. artery धमनी *dhamnī*
3. bone हड्डी / अस्थि *haḍḍī/asthi*
4. brain दिमाग *dimāG*

5. cartilage उपस्थि *upasthi* 6. chest छाती *chātī*
7. ear कान *kān* 8. throat गला *galā*
9. chest छाती *chātī* 10. eye आँख *āṁkh*
11. finger उंगली *uṅglī* 12. foot पैर *pair*
13. forehead माथा *māthā* 14. hand हाथ *hāth*
15. head सिर *sir* 16. heart दिल *dil*
17. intestine आँतड़ी *āṁtṛī* 18. kidney गुर्दा *gurdā*
19. knee घुटना *ghuṭnā* 20. leg टाँग *ṭāṁg*
21. liver जिगर *jigar* 22. lung फेफड़ा *phephṛā*
31. muscle मांसपेशी *māṁspeśī* 23. nail(s) नाखून *nākhūn*
24. nerve नस *nas* 25. oesophagus भोजन की नली *bhojan kī nalī*
26. rib पसली *paslī* 27. spleen तिल्ली *tillī*
28. stomach पेट *peṭ* 29. teeth दाँत *dāṁt*
30. temple कनपटी *kanpaṭī* 31. throat गला *galā*
32. thumb अंगूठा *aṅgūṭhā* 33. tongue जीभ *jībh*
34. trachea श्वास की नली *śvās kī nalī*

- **Diseases:**

1. acidity खट्टी डकार *khaṭṭī ḍakār* 2. asthma दमा *damā*
3. bleeding खून बहना *khūn bahnā* 4. blister छाला *chālā*
5. blood pressure रक्तचाप *raktcāp* 6. boil फोड़ा *phoṛā*
7. constipation कब्ज़ *kabz* 8. cramps मरोड़ *maroṛ*
9. diabetes मधुमेह *madhumeh* 10. diarrhoea/loose motion पतली टट्टी *patlī ṭaṭṭī*
11. dizziness/giddiness चक्कर आना *cakkar ānā* 12. eczema खुजली *khujli*
13. epilepsy मिरगी *mirgī*
14. indigestion बदहज़्मी *bad-hazmī* 15. injury चोट *coṭ*
16. leprosy कोढ़ *koṛh* 17. numbness सुन्नत *sunnat*

18. paralysis लकवा *lakvā* 19. piles बवासीर *bavāsir*
20. pimples मुंहासे *muṁhā se* 21. plague ताउन *tāun*
22. rheumatism बाय *bāy* 23. ringworm दाद *dād*
24. skin disease चर्मरोग *carmrog* 25.sore throat गला ख़राब होना श *galā kharāb honā*
26. stye आंख की पलक पर फुंसी *āṁkh kī palak par phunsī* 27. swelling सूजन *sūjan*
28. bruise खरोच *kharoc* 29. vomiting कै होना *kai honā*
30. weakness/debility कमज़ोरी *kamzorī* 31. wound जख़्म *jakhm*

- **Airport:**

1. arrival आगमन *āgman*
2. baggage tag सामान नत्थी *sāmān nathī*
3. boarding card विमान प्रवेश पत्र *vimān praveś patra*
4. crew जहाज़ श्रमिक *jahāz śramik*
5. customs सीमा शुल्क *sīmā śulk*
6. departure प्रस्थान *prasthān*
7. distance from departure प्रस्थान स्थान से दूरी। *prasthān sthān se dūrī*
8. domestic services राष्ट्रीय सेवाएँ. *rāṣṭrīyă sevāeṁ*
9. Expected time of arrival at गन्तव्य पर पहुंचने का अनुमानित समय।.. *gantavyă par pahuṁcne ka anumānit samay*
10. Fasten the seat belts. कुर्सी की पेटी बांधें। *kursī kī peṭī bāṁdheṁ.*
11. flight उड़ान *uṛān*
12. gate द्वार *dvār*
13. hand luggage हाथ का सामान *hāth kā sāmān*
14. international flight अंतर्राष्ट्रीय उड़ान *antarrāṣṭrīyă uṛān*
15. lavatory प्रसाधन कक्ष *prasādhan kakṣ*
16. Life jacket is under the seat रक्षा जाकेट कुर्सी के नीचे है। *rakṣā jākeṭ kursī ke nīce hai.*
17. Local time at destination. गन्तव्य का स्थानीय समय। *gantavyă kā sthānīyă samay*
18. lounge विश्रान्ति कक्ष *viśrānti*
19. luggage trolly सामान ढोने की गाड़ी. *sāmān ḍhone kī gāṛī*

20. no smoking zone धूम्रपान निषेध क्षेत्र *dhūmrapān niṣedh kṣetra*
21. notice सूचना *sūcnā*
22. occupied खाली नहीं *khālī nahīṁ*
23. overhead bin सीट के उपर हाथ का सामान रखने का कक्ष *sīṭ ke ūpar hāth kā sāmān rakhne kā kakṣ*
24. pilot . विमान चालक *vimān cālak*
25. Smoking in lavatories prohibited. शौचालय में धूम्रपान न करें। *śaucālay meṁ dhūmrapān na kareṁ.*
26. speed गति *gati*
27. stewar परिचारक. *paricārak*
28. stewardess. परिचारिका *paricārikā*
29. transit passenger पारगमन यात्री *pārgaman yātrī*
30 Wishing you a pleasant flight आपकी यात्रा सुखद हो। *apkī yātrā sukhad ho.*

- **Banks**

1. bank अधिकोश *adhikoś*
2. cash payments नकद भुगतान *nakad bhugtān*
3. currency मुद्रा *mudrā*
4. current account चालू खाता cālū khātā
5. deposit money पैसा जमा करना *paisā jamā karnā*
6. encash check चैक भुनाना caik bhunānā
7. fixed deposit सावधि जमा *sāvdhi jamā*
8. interest rate ब्याज दर *byāj dar*
9. passbook entry खाता पुस्तिका प्रविष्टि *khātā pustikā praviṣṭi*
10. rate of exchange विनिमय दर *vinimay dar*
11 . recurring deposit आवर्ती जमा *āvarti jamā*
12. saving account बचत खाता *bacat khātā*
13. short-term deposit अल्पावधि जमा *alpāvdki jamā*
14. transfer अन्तरण *antaraṇ*
15. traveler's cheque यात्री चैक *yātrī caik*
16. withdraw money पैसा निकालना *paisā nikālnā*

KINSHIP

- **Aunts**

wife of younger brother of father	*cācī*	चाची
wife of older brother of father	*tāī*	ताई
wife of mother's brother	*māmī*	मामी
mother's sister	*mausī*	मौसी
father's sister	*phūphī, buā*	फूफी, बुआ

- **Siblings:**

brother	*bhāī*	भाई
brother's wife	*bhābhī*	भाभी
sister	*bahan*	बहन
sister's husband	*jījā*	जीजा

- **Cousins**

son of mother's sister	*mauserā bhāī*	मौसेरा भाई
daughter of mother's sister	*mauserī bahan*	मौसेरी बहन
mother's brother's son	*mamerā bhāī*	ममेरा भाई
mother's brother's daughter	*mamerī bahan*	ममेरी बहन
son of father's brother	*cacerā bhāī*	चचेरा भाई
daughter of father's brother	*cacerī bahan*	चचेरी बहन
son of father's sister	*phupherā bhāī*	फुफेरा भाई
daughter of father's sister	*phupherī bahan*	फुफेरी बहन

Grandparents

father's father	*dādā*	दादा
mother's father	*nānā*	नाना

father's mother	*dādī*	दादी
mother's mother	*nānī*	नानी

Parents

father	*pitā jī*	पिता जी
mother	*mātā jī*	माता जी

Uncles

younger brother of father	*cācā*	चाचा
older brother of father	tāyā	ताया
brother of mother	*māmā*	मामा
husband of mother's sister	*mausā*	मौसा
husband of father's sister	*phūphā*	फूफा

- **Cardinals**

0	*śūnya*	शून्य	1	*ek*	एक
2	*do*	दो	3	*tīn*	तीन
4	*cār*	चार	5	*pāṁc*	पाँच
6	*chah*	छः	7	*sāt*	सात
8	*āṭh*	आठ	9	*nau*	नौ
10	*das*	दस	11	gyārah	ग्यारह
12	*bārah*	बारह	13	*terah*	तेरह
14	*caudah*	चौदह	15	*pandrah*	पन्द्रह
16	*solah*	सोलह	17	*sattrah*	सत्राह
18	*aṭhārah*	अट्ठारह	19	*unnīs*	उन्नीस
20	*bīs*	बीस	21	*ikkīs*	इक्कीस
22	*bāīs*	बाईस	23	*teīs*	तेईस
24	*caubīs*	चौबीस	25	*paccīs*	पच्चीस
26	*chabbīs*	छब्बीस	27	*sattāīs*	सत्ताईस
28	*aṭhāīs*	अठाईस	29	*untīs*	उनतीस
30	*tīs*	तीस	31	*iktīs*	इकतीस
32	*battīs*	बत्तीस			
33	*taiṁtīs*	तैंतीस	34	*cauṁtīs*	चौंतीस

35	*paiṁtīs*	पैंतीस	36	*chattīs*	छत्तीस
37	*saiṁtīs*	सैंतीस	38	*aṛtīs*	अड़तीस
39	*untālīs*	उन्तालीस	40	*cālīs*	चालीस
41	*iktālīs*	इकतालीस	42	bayālīs	बयालीस
43	*taiṁtālīs*	तैंतालीस	44	*cauvālīs*	चौवालीस
45	*paiṁtālīs*	पैंतालीस	46	*chiyālīs*	छियालीस
47	*saiṁtālīs*	सैंतालीस	48	*aṛtālīs*	अडतालीस
49	*uncās*	उन्चास	50	*pacās*	पचास
51	*ikyāvan*	इक्यावन	52	*bāvan*	बावन
53	*trepan*	तिरपन	54	*cauvan*	चौवन
55	*pacpan*	पचपन	56	chappan	छप्पन
57	*sattāvan*	सत्तावन	58	*aṭṭhāvan*	अट्ठावन
59	*unsaṭh*	उनसठ	60	*sāṭh*	साठ
61	*iksaṭh*	इकसठ	62	bāsaṭh	बासठ
63t	*irsaṭh*	तिरसठ	64	*causaṭh*	चौसठ
65	*paiṁsaṭh*	पैसठ	66	*chiyāsaṭh*	छियासठ
67	*saṛsaṭh*	सड़सठ	68	*aṛsaṭh*	अड़सठ
69	*unhattar*	उनहत्तर	70	*sattar*	सत्तर
71	*ik'hattar*	इकहत्तर	72	*bahattar*	बहत्तर
73	*tihattar*	तिहत्तर	74	*cauhattar*	चौहत्तर
75	*pac'hattar*	पचहत्तर	76	*chi'hattar*	छिहत्तर
77	*satattar*	सतत्तर	78	*aṭh'hattar*	अठहत्तर
79	*unnāsī*	उन्नासी	80	*assī*	अस्सी
81	*ikyāsī*	इक्यासी	82	*bayāsī*	बयासी
83	*tirāsī*	तिरासी	84	*caurāsī*	चौरासी
85	*pacāsī*	पचासी	86	*chiyāsī*	छयासी
87	*sattāsī*	सत्तासी	88	*aṭṭhāsī*	अट्ठासी
89	*navāsī*	नवासी	90	*navve*	नव्वे
91	*ikānve*	इकानवे	92	*bānve*	बानबे
93	*tirānve*	तिरानवे	94	caurānve	चौरानवे
95	*pacānve*	पचानवे	96	*chiyānve*	छियानवे
97	*sattānve*	सत्तानवे	98	*aṭhānve*	अट्ठानवे
99	*ninyānve*	निन्यानवे	100	*sau*	सौ
1000	*hazār*	हज़ार	100,000	*lākh*	लाख
10,000,000	*karoṛ*	करोड़			

• Ordinals

first	*pahlā*	पहला	second	*dūsrā*	दूसरा
third	*tīsrā*	तीसरा	fourth	*cauthā*	चौथा
fifth	*pāṁcvāṁ*	पाँचवा	sixth	*chaṭā /chaṭhā*	छटा / छठा
seventh	sātvāṁ	सातवाँ	eighth	*āṭhvāṁ*	आठवाँ
ninth	*nauvāṁ*	नौवाँ	tenth	*dasvāṁ*	दसवाँ
eleventh	*gyārahvāṁ*	ग्यारहवाँ	twelfth	*bārahvāṁ*	बारहवाँ
twentieth	*bīsvāṁ*	बीसवाँ	thirtieth	*tīsvāṁ*	तीसवाँ
fiftieth	*pacāsvāṁ*	पचासवाँ	hundredth	*sauvāṁ*	सौवाँ
hundred and first		*ek sau ekvāṁ*		एक सौ एकवाँ	
thousandth		*hazārvāṁ* हज़ारवाँ			

• Aggregates

both	दोनों	*donoṁ*	all three	तीनों	*tīnoṁ*
all four	चारों	*cāroṁ*	all five	पाँचों	*pāṁcoṁ*
scores of	बीसों	*bīsoṁ*	thousands of	हज़ारों	*hazāroṁ*
hundreds of thousands of		(literally) vast numbers		लाखों	*lākhoṁ*
millions of / vast numbers	करोड़ों	*karoṛoṁ*			

• Multiplicatives

double	*dugunā*	दुगुना
thrice	*tigunā*	तिगुना
four times	*caugunā*	चौगुना
five times	*pañcgunā*	पंचगुना
six times	*chahgunā*	छहगुना / छगुना
seven times	*satgunā*	सतगुना
eight times	*aṭhgunā*	अठगुना
nine times	*naugunā*	नौगुना
ten times	*dasgunā*	दसगुना
a hundred times	*saugunā*	सौगुना
a thousand time	*hazārgunā*	हज़ारगुना
a million times	*lākhgunā*	लाखगुना

- **Fract ions**

a quarter	*ek- cauthāī*	एक चौथाई
half	*ādhā*	आधा
three fourth	*paun*	पौन
one and three fourth	*paune do*	पौने दो
one-onefourth	*savā*	सवा
one and a half	*ḍeṛh*	डेढ़
two and a half	*ḍhāī*	ढाई
three and a half	*sāṛhe tīn*	साढे तीन

- **calendar पंचांग pancāṅg**

year	*sāl/varṣ*	साल / वर्ष
month	*mahīnā / māh*	महीना / माह
week	*saptāh /haftā*	सप्ताह / हफ़्ता
day	*din*	दिन
hour	*ghaṇṭā*	घण्टा
weekend	*saptāhānt*	सप्ताहान्त
date	*dinānk / tithi*	दिनांक / तिथि

- **Calculation गणणा gaṇaṇā**

math	*gaṇit*	गणित
statistics	*āṁkṛe*	आँकड़े
plus	*dhan / jamā*	ऋण / जमा
minus	*ṛṇ / nafi*	ऋण / नफ़ी
multiplication	*guṇ ā*	गुणा
division	*bhāg*	भाग

INDEX–ENGLISH

INDEX–HINDI